Chris Long was born in 1991 and grew up two days' hike from the nearest road, at Gorge River on the wild West Coast of New Zealand. After seventeen years living with his family in remote isolation, he left home to attend school in Wanaka. On completing his education, he set off to explore as much of the world as possible, travelling to sixty countries on six continents and taking a variety of jobs, including teaching extreme survival skills in Antarctica, working as a dog musher with huskies in arctic Norway, and crewing on a small yacht sailing through the Northwest Passage. Chris's father, Robert 'Beansprout' Long, and mother, Catherine Stewart, each published bestselling memoirs, *A Life on Gorge River* (2010) and *A Wife on Gorge River* (2012). This is Chris's first book.

The Boy from Gorge River

From New Zealand's remotest
family to the world beyond

CHRIS LONG

HarperCollins*Publishers*

HarperCollins*Publishers*
Australia • Brazil • Canada • France • Germany • Holland • Hungary
India • Italy • Japan • Mexico • New Zealand • Poland • Spain • Sweden
Switzerland • United Kingdom • United States of America

First published in 2022
by HarperCollins*Publishers* (New Zealand) Limited
Unit D1, 63 Apollo Drive, Rosedale, Auckland 0632, New Zealand
harpercollins.co.nz

A catalogue record for this book is available from the National Library of New Zealand

ISBN 978 1 7755 4177 6 (pbk)
ISBN 978 1 7754 9208 5 (ebook)

Cover design by Luke Causby, Blue Cork
Front cover image by Helene Enoksen
All other images courtesy of Chris Long
Typeset in Minion Pro by Kirby Jones
Printed and bound in Australia by McPherson's Printing Group

To Grandad, who was the first to suggest I write a book.

*And in memory of Lochie, whose adventurous spirit
will live on with us forever.*

CONTENTS

Prologue

The engine revs and the propellers of Hank Sproull's Cessna 185 bite into the air. The acceleration pushes my sister Robin and me into the backs of our seats. We are racing down the Queenstown runway at the base of the iconic Remarkables mountain range and soon we say goodbye to the ground, rising up and over the deep blue water of Lake Wakatipu. After a banking right-hand turn we fly northwest through Skippers Saddle, and Queenstown with its roads, supermarkets and crowded streets fades into the distance behind us. Hank is using his vast experience of flying in Fiordland to steer us skilfully through the tussock-covered mountains of the Skippers Range, past the last township of Glenorchy and on into the heart of the mighty Southern Alps. We have to find a way through these tall, cloud-covered peaks to reach our home at Gorge River, next to the ocean on the other side.

Although I have flown through these mountains more than 50 times over the years, it is never boring. As we enter the Rockburn

Valley the strong southwesterly winds that are ripping in from the Southern Ocean, piercing every river valley in the Southern Alps, begin to buffet us. Above us a layer of cloud is thickening, clinging like cotton wool to the jagged peaks rising on each side of the valley we are flying through. We are heading towards Park Pass, the lowest point in the mountains in front, and everything hinges on the cloud layer being high enough above the pass to let us through. Robin and I glance at each other and in that instant of time no words need to be spoken. We have been through this process of going home so many times that we almost call this exhilarating experience normal. Almost …

I am actually en route from a deserted tropical island in Tonga to Antarctica. After receiving a last-minute contract for my dream job as a field trainer at Scott Base, I hitchhiked off the island on a luxury catamaran yacht. This will be my one chance to see my family at Gorge River before disappearing to the land of snow, ice and penguins for the next five months.

Getting home is always complicated, and Dad has spent the last week trying to organise this flight through our satellite broadband internet connection. First he contacted our regular pilot and family friend Roger Monk, but his plane is currently undergoing a routine maintenance check in Wānaka. Then he tried Hugh, but he was away in Australia and couldn't fly us either. While at Suva Airport in Fiji I received an email from Dad informing me Hank had agreed to do the flight. Hank usually flies to Milford Sound with tourists each day and a flight to Gorge River is a nice change from the usual milk run for him. He told me there would be a fine six-hour gap in the weather between two storms that would align with my afternoon in Queenstown. Robin was in Wānaka, had also just

2

arrived from overseas and was ready to join me on the flight. It had been 18 months since I had been home and my family would all be together again, albeit for just a couple of hours.

Eventually, after a cancelled flight and a rough landing on the Air New Zealand Airbus A320, I met Robin at Queenstown Airport mid-morning. After a quick hello we drove around to the New World supermarket at Frankton in her car and searched the aisles for the items on Mum's shopping list. Eggs, flour, sugar, sausages, fresh fruit … etc. Robin already had the mail from Roger and his partner, Debbie, and in 30 minutes we bought two huge shopping trolleys full of food – enough to stock Mum and Dad's cupboards for six weeks or more.

Hoping we hadn't forgotten anything, we headed over to Hank's hangar at Queenstown Airport. Hank's large hand enveloped mine as we shook hands in greeting. 'The passes are still closed to the West Coast,' he informed us. 'The front has gone through but there's still some remaining cloud. It's windy up there, so it could open up at any time. I'll call you in an hour or two with an update.'

Robin and I sat on the grass nearby and chatted about our recent adventures. She had just returned from her first trip in Europe, where she had hiked through the Pyrenees mountains. Since we'd last seen each other, I had travelled through South East Asia exploring the streets of some of the world's largest cities, taught outdoor education in China, and backpacked right across Eastern Europe, Egypt and Israel. It had been an insane trip through twenty-two non-English-speaking countries, mostly in the developing world, and along the way I had experienced eighteen different languages, eight major religions and sixteen different currencies while staying in over a hundred different hostels, hotels and Airbnbs and on friends' couches, all over the course of fifteen months.

Time ticked by. Would the weather clear in time to make it home today? I knew Mum and Dad would be desperate to see us – a visit from their children is always a highlight for them since we both left home and made lives away from Gorge River. Finally, at 1 pm we received a phone call from Hank. 'The weather is clearing, let's go!'

I emailed Dad: 'Taking off in 15 minutes.'

Robin and I know the routine. After loading the boxes of groceries into the rear of the plane we climb into the back seats. Then it's fasten seat belts, earmuffs on, a deep breath and hope for a safe flight. Hank jumps into the pilot's seat and his son Anthony is the co-pilot. Half a dozen planes have gone missing without a trace in the Southern Alps and every time we take off our fate is in the hands of these incredibly skilled bush pilots, the plane and the unpredictable weather. The engine turns over and Hank taxis towards the runway. Even in my exhausted state, I watch and absorb his every move. A crackling reply comes over the radio from the Queenstown control tower: 'Echo, November, Whiskey, you are clear for take-off.'

Now we enter a kind of time warp where nothing else in the world matters besides the engine, the pilot's decision-making, and the power of nature and the clouded mountains. With not only my emotions on the line, but also those of Robin, Mum and Dad, Hank calmly flies the plane up the huge U-shaped valley of the Rockburn towards Park Pass. Everything has led up to this moment and it is up to him to either guide us safely through the Southern Alps to Gorge River, or to make the heartbreaking decision to turn back to Queenstown. Having flown through these mountains thousands of times, Hank is one of the most experienced pilots in the area and he has our full trust.

We are flying along under the thick cloud layer and the bushy valley floor below has given way to tussock and a small rocky mountain stream flowing past a few scattered thickets of beech trees. The little plane is shaken up and down and from side to side as we hit lumps and bumps of turbulence and Robin and I hold on tight to our seats. The steep sides of the Rockburn Valley slide past and as we approach the pass I can see Hank edging the plane closer to the hillside on the right-hand side, preparing for a sharp 180-degree turn back towards Queenstown.

The valley bends slightly and suddenly we can see Park Pass, sitting in front of us like a gigantic U-shaped door in the wall of mountains, and through it we can see the other side. The pass is clear and we aim straight for it. On top of the pass there are two extra-large bumps and with a sharp, banking left turn the cliffs drop away into the abyss below, making me feel giddy for a second, and we slide through to the wild West Coast.

We are now in the remotest corner of New Zealand. The northern border of this area is Haast. To the west is the mighty Southern Ocean, to the east are the Southern Alps, and Puysegur Point is 250 kilometres to the south. The landscape here has been carved by glaciers over thousands of years, leaving behind steep mountains, deep fiords and lakes, and large rivers. The valleys are covered in thick podocarp forest rising to tussock-covered tops that give way to steep basalt slopes and snow-covered granite mountaintops. The average yearly rainfall is between five and ten metres and the frequently flooded rivers combined with the thick forest, the exposed rocky coastline, crashing Southern Ocean swells and clouds of pesky sandflies make this area quite inhospitable and thus almost completely untouched by humans. Over the years, many people have tried to call this land home, but few have succeeded. An abandoned settlement at Martins Bay is all that is left behind, and besides three isolated seasonal whitebaiting communities and a small tourist village in Milford Sound, only a few hardy souls have adapted to survive against the forces of nature in this area.

I see a ray of sunlight breaking through the cloud somewhere around the snowy tops of Mt Madeline and it lights up the confluence between the meandering Pyke and Hollyford rivers. The Hollyford then flows into Lake McKerrow and down to Martins Bay in the distance, where I get my first glimpse of the shimmering Tasman Sea.

Hank turns to the right up the Pyke Valley and Lake Alabaster and Lake Wilmot pass below, connected by the clear-flowing river snaking through the forest under tall rimu trees that lean out over the log-jammed rapids. Big Bay, with its long sandy beach and tall headlands, is far off to our left-hand side and we follow a dip in the hills formed by the Alpine Fault that leads us into the head of the Gorge River.

The river is quite steep and runs over boulder-strewn rapids most of the way until, just before it meets the ocean, the hills close in, forming the tight gorge that gives the river its name. The river is usually a deep green colour. However, today, because of the recent storms, it is a dark shade of tannin-stained brown. Every week or two a new storm rolls in from the west, bringing heavy rains, and the river turns a light chocolate brown, swollen bank to bank and flowing like an angry dragon out to sea, tearing at the forest on each side and carrying with it uprooted trees that succumb to the incredible force of the water. After a few days the storms give way to blue skies and sunshine that dries out the land and unveils the sheer, untouched beauty that first attracted my dad to Gorge River 40 years ago.

We follow this river, losing altitude as we go, and suddenly we pass over the last ridge of rainforest. In front of us is a clear horizon of ocean with waves whipped up by the strong southwesterly winds. Hank tips the plane sharply to one side and directly below us, nestled into the forest where the dark brown river meets the milky blue sea, is my family's home. There are three buildings. The largest is our house, next is a public Department of Conservation (DOC) hut used by hikers and fishermen, and then there's an old freezer shed. Between them and the ocean is a narrow, 380-metre-long grass airstrip lined by tall flax bushes that runs parallel to the bouldery beach. Five hundred metres out to sea in front of the river mouth the waves crash onto the Gorge Islands, a tall limestone rock formation jutting up from the ocean. From our house to the closest road is a 42-kilometre hike along the coastline to the north and the closest permanent neighbours are about 50 kilometres away at Jackson Bay. We are about 80 kilometres southwest of Haast and 100 kilometres northwest of Queenstown.

I can make out someone standing on the doorstep of the house, scanning the sky for our plane, waving. That will be Dad. Hank circles in a wide, arcing left-hand turn to drop our altitude before passing low over the airstrip to feel the strength and direction of the wind. There is a strong southwest wind blowing and the conditions for landing are going to be very challenging. As we circle back around to start our final approach, I can see the *Southern Legend*, owned by Denis Nyhon, working away at his crayfish pots around the Gorge Islands, the crew seemingly unfazed by the choppy conditions. We turn in towards the airstrip and as I stare north towards Cascade Point and Barn Bay, I think about the times I leapt from boulder to boulder around the rugged shoreline as a child.

Hank pulls on full flaps as we settle into a long final approach from the north. Over the intercom I remind Hank and Anthony about a strong downdraught that occurs in these conditions over the river mouth just 50 metres before touchdown. This downdraught pulling you towards the river, combined with the turbulence caused by the tall flax bushes, makes it very tricky to get the wheels safely on the ground in the airstrip's wheel ruts. With one to two metres of space either side of the wheels, there is no room for error and Hank must get everything right to land safely. I have never seen a serious accident on this airstrip but I have seen a couple of close calls.

Now there's just one kilometre to go and we pass Kelp Rock … 500 metres … 200 metres … 50 metres. Hank gives the engine an extra burst of power and the river passes 40 metres below us. He is moving the controls aggressively from side to side, adeptly counteracting the wind gusts. The house, with Mum and Dad standing outside, passes in a blur. Adrenaline is high and it all comes down to this moment. We are below the level of the flax bushes now and suddenly our wheels meet the bumpy grass and we bounce. Soon the plane is on the ground, right in the wheel ruts. The strong headwind slows us quickly and we roll to a stop in about 200 metres. After days of organising for Dad, three days of travelling for me, the weather delays of that morning and Hank's incredible flying skills, we have finally made it to Gorge River. Relief floods through me and I congratulate Hank on the safe landing.

As we taxi back to the north end of the airstrip, Mum and Dad are standing in their usual place waiting for us outside the deer fence that protects our all-important garden. The wind is blowing their hair into their eyes and the energy of the wilderness around Gorge River is reflected in their weathered faces. Dad has his ear muffs on to protect him from the noise of the plane. He is wearing Red Band gumboots, an old pair of fleece pants, a black down jacket decorated with spots of paint from his artwork, and a possum-fur hat. Mum is in bare feet with clean pants and a maroon shirt. As soon as the propeller stops turning, Mum opens the doors of the plane and Robin and I jump out. It's been a few months since we have seen our parents and we hug each other for a really long time.

Although this particular visit will be a short one it's still magical nonetheless. We all help to carry the groceries inside the shelter of the house, leaving the gusty wind outside. My nose is tickled by the familiar smell of wood smoke mixed with the aromas of fresh baking, newly cut firewood and possum skins. Growing up in such a wild and rugged place has shaped my life and made me who I am today. I hear Mum ask Hank and Anthony, 'Would you like a cup of tea?', and my mind flashes back to the early days of growing up in this house surrounded as far as one can see by the forest, the river and the ocean.

PART ONE

Growing Up at Gorge River

CHAPTER 1

The Early Years

Everything started for me on the 26th of September 1991 on a small farm near Arrowtown, New Zealand. Mum and Dad had chosen to have a home birth but decided that Gorge River was too isolated for it. So they'd taken up an offer to look after the farm while some friends were away whitebaiting. The local midwife, Denise Black, was present and in the early hours of the morning I came into this world a fit and healthy spring baby, surrounded by daffodils, lambs and asparagus. When I was four weeks old, we flew over the Southern Alps to Gorge River and there began my childhood out on the wild West Coast.

Before my arrival, Dad, complete with long, wild, dark hair, long beard and bare feet, had already lived at Gorge River for 11 years, most of which he'd spent alone. He had found the house there in 1980, aged 25, as he hiked along the coastline in search of a place to live. He stayed a couple of nights and after meeting local fishermen at Barn Bay learned that the house had been abandoned by another fisherman a few years earlier. They suggested he move in and become the caretaker of Gorge River.

The original part of the house had been built by the Nickel Spoon Mining Company in 1968 and the fisherman, Eion Wiley, had built onto it to use it as a base for crayfishing and hunting. At six metres by ten metres it was a comfortable size and even had a flush toilet and running water from rain catchment tanks. Dad was finally able to live his dream of self-sufficiency by expanding the vegetable garden and collecting food from the surrounding rainforest. When he needed money, he could crew for the fishermen at Barn Bay and Big Bay. He would often be seen hiking along the coastline of South Westland in his bare feet and green Swanndri, carrying a homemade backpack. Dad was vegetarian at this stage and he used to grow a range of different sprouts, some of which he would keep in his hat to eat on his journey. Soon he became known to the Haast locals as 'Beansprout', a nickname that has stuck to this day.

One day Dad was in Queenstown staying with a friend when he met two girls who were planning a hike through the Pyke Valley to Big Bay and up the coast to Haast. He was meant to go to Nelson the next day but decided to take a detour and join them, as he knew the area well and the Pyke track can be hard to follow. One thing led to the next, and a couple of years later Mum, who had been working as an immunologist in Dunedin, moved to Gorge River. Both my parents shared a vision of raising a family away from the modern world of TVs, phones, electricity and all the other mod cons that people seemed to be relying on more and more in the 1980s and '90s. This sort of idea was very unusual at the time and most people thought they were crazy. But Gorge River was far enough away that they could choose their own lifestyle and live out their dream relatively undistracted by what other people thought of them. It wasn't long before I came on the scene.

Although we already had the airstrip, my parents didn't have enough money to charter aircraft. Therefore, when they wanted to leave Gorge River they would walk and I would ride in their backpacks. Mum and Dad carefully stitched leg holes into their packs and I would sit on top of their sleeping bags. The 42-kilometre hike to the nearest road takes two days and the route follows the coastline north to Barn Bay and inland to the Cascade Road end. To the south, reaching the nearest road takes five to eight long days' walking, the route eventually joining the Hollyford Track, which leads to Gunn's Camp at the Hollyford Road end. One time when I was about one year old my parents did this hike from the Hollyford. They had so much food that their backpacks were too full to fit me inside and I rode in a front pack. They had to stop for a day at Lake Alabaster to eat some of the food so that I could fit in the back again for the rest of the ten-day hike.

The landscape in South Westland is rugged, and moving around in this type of environment, with its rough ocean waves and flooded rivers, is constantly challenging. When I was a baby, Dad was still working on crayfishing boats for income and sometimes to save walking we would hitch a ride on board one of the boats going back and forth to Barn Bay or Big Bay. There is one such hitchhiking story Mum and Dad often tell from this time.

Dad had been working with Dale Hunter at the south end of Big Bay and it was time to head back to Gorge River. To save four hours' walking, Dad persuaded Dale to drop the three of us at Crayfish Rock on the last day of fishing. To get me ashore, Mum passed me from the fishing boat, which was being tossed in the waves, to Dad, who was standing in his bare feet on a large boulder in the waves. He then waded in to shore. Afterwards they realised how stupid that had been and obviously they got a big fright because they still talk about it 30 years later. For years Dad had been taking these sorts of risks alone in the wilderness but now with a wife and baby he had to learn to be more careful. And Mum had to learn when to speak up and say no if she thought something was going to be too dangerous, rather than just following Dad's lead.

Their next fright occurred on a walk out to Haast. After hiking up the coast with me, still a baby, from Gorge River, they arrived at the mighty Cascade River to find it partially flooded after some recent rain. It was too full to wade across, but that didn't matter because there was a Canadian canoe they could use that was hidden in the bushes on the south side of the river. They managed to paddle the canoe safely across, but with only a few inches of freeboard above the water it probably wasn't the smartest thing to do. Afterwards they realised they had once again pushed the safety limit too far and that had to change.

Eventually they took a really cautious approach and accepted that with a young family it wasn't wise to take these extra risks. They learned to say no to things like free helicopter or boat rides even if it meant a few extra days' hiking. One time when I was nine we were walking home and to break up the journey we stayed in the abandoned house at Barn Bay for a couple of days. One of the local venison hunters, Barry Guise, saw smoke rising from the chimney and landed in his R22 helicopter to say hi. He had been hunting deer that morning further down the coast and had a few loads to fly from south of Gorge River out to the Cascade Road end. He would be flying back south empty each time and offered us a free ride home on these return flights, which would take about ten minutes and save us two days' tramping. No doubt they would have loved to accept his offer, but helicopter venison hunters have a poor safety record. So they politely refused and we continued our hike to Gorge River. Two years later, while hunting deer north of Haast, Barry and his shooter Gutty were killed when their overloaded helicopter crashed into a mountainside. Each of them left behind a young child.

Almost all the food we ate in the early years came from the wilderness around Gorge River. This was not only because we wanted to be self-sufficient but also because with an income of just $2000 a year we couldn't afford to fly food in from the supermarket by plane. Mum worked tirelessly year-round in the vegetable garden in front of our house to grow food for the family. Over time, as a result of burying fish frames, seaweed and homemade lime from burnt mussel shells, the soil became more and more productive and we were able to grow a wider variety of vegetables. In springtime Mum would start the seedlings off in 'pots' made from plastic milk bottles lying on one side in the warm sun on the windowsill. The seedlings would then be planted out in the main garden and would grow over the summer.

The tomatoes couldn't handle the rain and wind of South Westland, so Dad built a greenhouse out of plastic and driftwood and attached it to the front of our house. Then we could grow tomatoes and eventually lettuce. Outside the greenhouse we grew potatoes, parsnips, Jerusalem artichokes, silver beet, yams, leeks, broad beans and peas, and a few leafy greens like watercress and turnips grew wild. During the autumn Mum would bottle some of the beetroot, leeks and zucchinis, but since we rarely got frosts things like carrots and silver beet would stay alive in the garden all winter.

While Mum did most of the gardening, Dad would do the fishing (with me always by his side). Whenever the weather allowed, he would set a gill net in the river mouth at low tide, and he would retrieve it the next morning. A net is more efficient than a fishing rod at Gorge River and in summer he would usually return with a few yellow-eyed mullet or a big kahawai in the bucket. During the winter months it's harder to catch fish in the river and he would often have to go to the south end of the airstrip to catch 'kelpies' (blue-striped wrasse) on a hand line in the rock pools on the incoming tide. Some days he would stand down there surrounded by crashing waves for hours through the middle of a cold southerly storm just to catch us enough fish for dinner. He would never give up. Usually Mum would fillet the fish and fry them in oil in a heavy cast-iron frying pan on top of the stove. However, if we only had one or two fish, she would keep them whole so as not to waste any food. The fish stocks in the area are pretty good but often the biggest challenge is the weather. If the sea is too rough and the river flooded, there is simply no way to catch fish. At those times, Dad would try to snare a rabbit on the airstrip to eat instead.

One of my earliest memories is of helping Mum and Dad collect sedge-grass seed to make flour. Sedge grass grows along the sides of the airstrip and on each spiky stalk is a marble-sized seed that looks a bit like a light brown, fluffy ball. We would dry the seeds in a metal camping pot behind the chimney of our wood fire. Once they were dry, Mum would grind them into flour. If we had wheat, she would also dry and grind that to make heavy wholegrain flour and I would watch intently as she mixed some of it together with the sedge-grass flour, yeast, salt and water in her stainless-steel bowl to make a thick brown dough. Mum would leave the dough to rise for an hour while she stoked the fire with dry wood and placed a large aluminium camp oven on top of the firebox to preheat. Then she'd bake the bread for two hours in a round enamel baking pan, turning it over just before it was done to finish cooking the top. The bread from that camp oven smelled so good and tasted delicious with its thick, crunchy crust. We didn't always have much to put on the bread when I was young, but we might have some butter or jam or canola oil and that was extra exciting. We always had Vegemite because hunters would leave it in the hut next door.

One of the more interesting foods we ate was bull kelp, which grows in some places along the coastline, its long tentacles waving backwards and forwards in the surging waves. The huge ten-metre swells that come straight from the Southern Ocean regularly tear clumps from the rocks and after a big storm we would always search the beaches for freshly washed-up kelp. My favourite way to eat it was to dry 30-centimetre lengths (again behind the fire) for a few days until it was crunchy. I loved the salty flavour that tasted like the sea. Mum would also grind it up to make kelp powder, which I see is now very expensive in some shops. Dad liked to make a pudding out of fresh kelp tentacles chopped into three-centimetre lengths that floated in a milky broth. However, that, along with smoked kahawai stew, was one of my least favourite foods as a kid. Luckily, we didn't have either of them too often and generally I loved all the food that we ate at Gorge River and was never a picky eater. I especially enjoyed eating any fish that I'd helped catch or vegetables that I'd helped grow.

We couldn't keep any type of livestock for meat or milk, so any food that Mum and Dad could not catch or grow at Gorge River – for example, wheat, rice, oil and milk – had to be carried in from Haast in their backpacks. Occasionally we might get a box of food dropped off by a fishing boat or passing helicopter, but in the early days this didn't happen very often. When I was a baby, we would go out to town three or four times a year and on our return Mum and Dad would carry home as much food as they could fit in their backpacks. When something ran out, like cooking oil or butter, we would have to go without for a month or three until we had the opportunity to get to the shop again. I learned as a kid to appreciate what food we had and not to miss the food we didn't have.

For my birthday I would always get a cake, but its ingredients would be quite simple. It wouldn't usually have sugar, but if it included some butter or cooking oil then I felt like the luckiest child alive! After tasting sugar for the first time when I was three, I exclaimed to Mum in my baby voice, 'Sugar's really nice!' I didn't taste chocolate until I was four years old.

From as early as I can remember, I was absolutely crazy about fishing. There are pictures of me on Dad's back while he checked his whitebait net, and as soon as I could walk I would follow him everywhere. When I was three years old, Dad made me a fishing rod out of a long, thin piece of wood and I found a blue, wedge-shaped fishing lure left in the DOC hut next door. Dad was concerned I could accidentally get a hook stuck in my skin or, worse, in my eye, and wouldn't allow me to use an actual sharp hook on my lure. And he had his reasons for being concerned. Our only contact with the world was an emergency locator beacon given to us by a local fisherman, Geoff Robson. This device when activated will send a distress signal to the rescue coordination centre via a passing jet plane or satellite. In a best-case scenario with good weather, one of the local rescue helicopters could get us to a hospital within about five hours. In a worst-case scenario with bad weather, it could be days. Therefore, my parents were very cautious about what we were and weren't allowed to do and what tools and equipment we could use.

Not having a hook didn't bother me in the slightest and I spent many hours fishing in the river mouth with that blue lure. I was always in search of 'Fishy Bear', a large mythical fish that had taken the hooks of two possum hunters who stayed in the DOC hut. Sometimes I would throw my lure out in the river near Dad's net and would return to find a fish on the line. I was always over the moon and wouldn't stop talking about my catch for days. Little did I know, Dad would go down early and take a fish from his net to attach to my line before putting it back in the water for me to find later.

During the spring months a small amount of whitebait comes up the Gorge River. Dad would set his whitebait net at the bottom of 'the bluff', a large limestone cliff, originally carved by a glacier and now covered in rātā trees, which lies about 200 metres upstream from the river mouth and forms the gorge that gives Gorge River its name. When I was two or three, Dad hand-stitched me a small whitebait net out of lace curtain material, and after that I would always have my net set in front of his. Again, unbeknown to me, Dad would go down first and put a couple of whitebait in my net. We never caught many, and on a good day there might be 20 or 30 bait in my net and a couple of hundred in his. To me that was an amazing catch. If there were more whitebait in the Gorge River, there would have been lots of whitebaiters' huts to go with them. We were quite happy to have the river to ourselves and were content with just catching a feed here and there. Mum would mix the small, translucent, five-centimetre-long fish with egg (if we had any) and fry them in the pan.

We often caught eels in the whitebait net, especially when the water was still dark brown after a flood. One day we caught a particularly fat eel and, since we had nothing else to eat, Dad decided we would smoke it for dinner. As he gutted the slimy black eel, he discovered its belly was full of whitebait and they were only a little bit digested. So he squeezed them all out and we carried them home to Mum. She made two whitebait patties out of that 'catch' to go with the freshly smoked eel for dinner.

One day when I was about three, I went with Dad to check the fish net. As he pulled it in, there was an eel partly tangled in the netting and he managed to grab it just as it came out of the water. I needed a pee and since Dad was busy with the eel I walked up into the driftwood and pulled down my pants. Dad was wrestling the eel on the riverbank with his hands covered in slime, trying to cut off its head, when suddenly he heard a scream. I couldn't get my pants back on and bawled my eyes out as I waited for Dad to come and save me from the huge cloud of sandflies that had descended on my bare buttocks. It's moments like that in South Westland that make you really tough. Sandflies must have been a nightmare for me as a baby; I don't really remember, but it did help me to be immune to them once I was a bit older. Don't get me wrong – they still bite and it feels like a needle is puncturing your skin, but when you are used to them it goes away in a few seconds and there is no further reaction.

When I was four, I would always talk about catching an eel myself. I talked about it so much that eventually Mum and Dad stopped listening to me when I started up about eels. One afternoon I told them, 'I'm off to set the eel line down at the bluff.' 'Yeah, yeah,' came their unbelieving reply, this being probably the tenth or eleventh time I had said this already. A little while later I returned and started talking about how I had set the eel line. 'Yeah, yeah,' came the reply again, and they still didn't take much notice. About two hours later, I came running up the garden path, screaming in excitement. I was dragging a huge, squirming eel that was longer than I was tall! This was the first fish I had ever caught completely by myself and, from that day on, no one could ever stop me talking about fishing again. I was hooked!

Even today, all of the heating and cooking at Gorge River is done by our wood fire. Dad built the firebox from a rusty old fuel drum lying on its side, with a door where the bottom of the drum would be and a chimney constructed from corrugated iron that he stamped flat and then rolled into a tube held closed with crayfish-pot wire. On top is a cast-iron plate with a removable circle that allows the flames to lick directly onto the bottom of the kettle or pots, making cooking very efficient. Hidden away inside the firebox is a wetback that's connected to a hot-water cylinder concealed in a warm cupboard next to the fireplace. This cupboard is the driest place in the house and Mum hangs our washing in there on ropes strung under the roof. Below the hot-water cupboard we keep our firewood in a blue fish case that we found washed up on the beach. The fire is like the beating heart of our house and keeping the wood box full is almost a full-time job. As a baby, I spent many hours riding in a small backpack on Mum's or Dad's back as they collected bag after bag of driftwood.

Trees get washed down the river during floods and the combined power of the river and the ocean splinters them into nice long 20- to 30-centimetre pieces. Consequently, we rarely need to use a saw to cut wood and have never had to use a chainsaw or an axe. We try to collect the wood off the beach after a few days of sunny weather, when it's at its driest. By then a light, warm northerly breeze will signal an approaching storm and the sandflies will be out enjoying the humidity. We gather it up in coal bags and carry it inside the workshop to keep it dry for burning. Every few years the salt from the driftwood rusts away the stove drum and Dad has to build a replacement.

We didn't have a normal bath when I was really small, so Mum would bathe me in the kitchen sink or a 20-litre bucket on the floor. I loved my hot bucket bath so much and I have pictures of me watching the world from its safety. As I got older, I would join Dad as he bathed in an extra-tall white fish case, also from the beach, that he had turned into a bath by blocking the drainage holes in the bottom with wooden plugs and Silastic glue. The fish case would sit on the living-room floor in front of the fire and we would fill it with a hose connected to the hot-water tap. How we both fitted in there I don't know, but I remember it being very warm and cosy.

When I was a baby, all of our water was collected from the roof when it rained and stored in 44-gallon drums at the back of the house. Luckily it rains a lot on the West Coast, but still there were times when the tanks ran out. Then Mum would have to collect water in buckets from the river 100 metres away. When not in flood, the Gorge River has a beautiful deep green colour and the water is some of the cleanest you will ever drink. However, it's also very heavy to cart that distance and I'm guessing the novelty would have worn off for Mum after the first bucket.

When I was one, we had two hunters stay with us. The DOC hut next door was already full and in exchange for the accommodation they helped with some jobs around the house. It was March and it hadn't rained for weeks, and after helping Mum carry buckets and buckets of water from the river one of them said, 'You can do better than that – I have ten kilometres of water pipe on my farm!' He owned a dairy farm in the North Island and next time he returned for hunting he brought with him 600 metres of brand-new half-inch water pipe. Since then we've had unlimited fresh water from a spring that runs off the hill about 600 metres behind the house. It flows all year round and only needs to be fixed every now and then when a big flood blocks up the intake filter with leaves or washes it completely away.

Up to the age of three, I was an only child and had no other kids to play with at Gorge River. The only time I saw other children was when we went to town – in other words, not very often. I guess my parents thought I needed a playmate and on the 22nd of

November 1994 my sister, Robin Grace, was born into this world on a farm in the Waikaia Valley, Central Southland. Again, Mum and Dad had wanted a home birth with a midwife, and a local pilot, Peter Bowmar, had invited them to have the baby on his farm. In exchange Dad worked on the farm for a few weeks and we lived in a nice cottage there. Nana (Dad's mother Ngaire) came over from Australia and helped look after me while Mum wasn't able to. When Robin was four weeks old, Peter flew us back home to Gorge River in his blue Cessna 185.

Having a second child meant a few changes for us all. I was super excited to have a baby sister but now it meant that when we walked out to town my parents could no longer carry me. So, from the age of three and a half, I had to walk every step of the 42-kilometre hike to the Cascade Road end. The only time Dad would carry me was when crossing the Spoon, Hope and Cascade rivers. Robin's arrival also meant Mum and Dad could no longer bring enough food in to feed the family and would now have to rely on air deliveries.

By this point Dad had given up crayfishing. Crayfish numbers had declined through the 1980s, and just before I was born he had worked for two months with Dale Hunter, living in Dale's house at Big Bay, but had caught very few crayfish. To top it off, they had very nearly been capsized by large waves while crossing the Hollyford River bar. Fishing was too dangerous and there was little money to be made. Shortly after finishing the fishing season Dad sold 12 of his greenstone carvings to Murray Gunn at Gunn's Camp and made as much money from that one sale as from the entire fishing season. From that day on, he decided his oil-on-canvas paintings and jade carvings would be his sole source of income. With practice his artwork was getting better and was becoming more popular. By the time Robin was born he was making $4000 a year, so we were able to plan supply drops of food by plane.

At least one third of the time, it's raining in South Westland, and on wet days you have to be prepared to spend lots of time inside. Our average annual rainfall at Gorge River is about five metres and I remember huge storms lasting for days that might bring 30 centimetres of rain in 24 hours. During breaks in the deluge I would stare in awe at the river. The water we rowed our dinghy across would become a swollen torrent the colour of chocolate milk, stretching from the tall rātā on one side to the limestone bluff on the other and flowing at a speed of about 30 kilometres per hour towards the ocean like a gigantic dragon. The landscape here is used to these heavy rainfalls and the mountains shed the water in a day. Within three days of a storm Dad would already have his net back out to catch our next feed of yellow-eyed mullet. Our house sits high above the floodwater level and due to the large limestone bluff deflecting the main flow of water to the north we have never had issues with flooding.

The house is cosy but every bit of space is used and after a few rainy days it can get quite cramped. Robin and I would be bouncing off the walls with our pent-up energy. If we were naughty, for punishment Mum or Dad would make us sit in the workshop for a few minutes, depending on the severity of our crime. I hated being punished and would therefore make out I wanted to be in the workshop by pretending to rub some jade with a piece of sandstone or cut some wood with my hand saw. Eventually I would ask, 'Can I come in now?'

Dad used these wet days to paint and set up his driftwood easel (his original easel made from planks of wood was used to fix the house) in the middle of the living room in front of his favourite seat. Doing his artwork inside allowed him to make a living at Gorge River, come rain, hail or shine, where no one else had managed to before him. Mum would often sit in bed knitting jerseys or hat-and-bootie sets to sell in a shop in Queenstown with Robin next to her. I would be flying my wooden plane around the house, landing it on the floorboards, and when I was bored with that I would set up my easel next to Dad and start painting my own picture, all the while talking non-stop about fishing.

When I was older, I braved the weather for a bit of adventure. At a safe distance from the flooded river, a large pond forms from a small creek behind the house, and when the rain stopped I would jump on my styrofoam 'surfboard' and paddle it up and down the 30-metre-long pond, dodging floating logs. Once I even built a small sail for my surfboard out of some straight sticks and an old sheet so I could get a bit of extra speed.

As soon as I was able to walk I would follow Dad wherever he went. Every two weeks with the full and new moons we would have spring low tides, when the tide would drop lower than normal, making it possible to find pāua. I would follow Dad up the beach to find these camouflaged shellfish that cling to the undersides of seaweed-covered boulders right where the crashing waves meet the shore. Dad taught me how to pry the pāua off the rocks with a pocket knife. First you have to decide what pāua to go for. It's best if you can see a space between the shell and the rock to place the blade. The pāua also needs to be over the takeable size of 125 millimetres. If you are too slow, the pāua will suck itself tightly onto the rock, so with one swift movement you slide the blade under its black foot and flick it off. Usually the waves were too big for me to go out as far as Dad and I would play around in the rock pools closer to shore.

I was too young to have a knife at first, so if I did find a pāua in a rock pool I would try to pull it off with my little hands, which didn't work so well. When I was three years old, Dad made me a blunt, square-ended pocket knife. On one really calm day I followed him right out to the edge of the splashing waves. I saw a huge pāua under a large rock and carefully pried it off with my little knife. I was so happy that evening that Mum took a photo of me on our camera with my first pāua!

After collecting a few pāua Dad would come back to the beach and I would help him smash open a spiky kina (sea urchin) with a rock. We would eat the milky roe that we'd peel off the inside of the shell. The more yellow and juicy-looking roe would always have the most disappointing flavour. My favourite was the older-looking brown roe that had the creamiest taste.

Other times we would collect mussels at the south end of the airstrip. Again, I would fossick around in the rock pools and find a few older mussels encrusted with barnacles to put in my little sack, but I was never allowed to go out as far into the waves as Dad. He had a special rock further out that he would go to and the mussels collected from there had a smooth green shell and were juicier than mine. One day when the ocean was really calm and there was an especially low spring tide he took me out to that rock. It was about five metres long by two metres wide and at first glance looked like a standard rock covered in short, pinky-coloured seaweed the shape of iceberg lettuce. However, as I looked closer, I noticed that the seaweed was actually growing on top of mussels and the whole rock was smothered in a layer of perfect-sized mussels. I helped Dad collect 20 or 30 of them to take home for dinner.

Usually Mum would send me down to the ocean to get some sea water and she would boil the mussels in it for a couple of minutes. This would give them extra flavour and we would pry open the shells at the kitchen table looking for the juiciest mussels. The leftovers would be marinated in vinegar and salt for the next day.

Because we always rely on the food from nature around Gorge River, we only ever collect what we need. If we see only five pāua then we know we can only take one or two. And if the rock has fifty mussels, we can take just ten. This relationship with nature is critical if you want to live sustainably off the land. Upsetting the balance by overfishing is the largest crime you can commit. Despite my family collecting food at Gorge River for the last 40 years, the fish stocks have not decreased. Sadly, there are very few such places left in the world. Natural food supplies are the first to pay the price for overpopulation and poor resource management. The fact is that most of the world's fish species have already been decimated beyond repair and humans are directly to blame. Looking back on the way that I was raised, and on our relationship with the land, I feel lucky to have learned first-hand about the delicate balance of living sustainably in nature.

CHAPTER 2

A Typical Day

Because Gorge River is on the west side of the Southern Alps, the mornings there are the coldest part of the day. The sun takes a long time to rise and in winter there is a bitterly cold katabatic wind that blows down the river, which is intensified by the narrow gorge upstream from the river mouth.

As kids, Robin and I would start the day by getting cosy, tucked up in the safety of Mum and Dad's bed. They would take turns lighting the fire and if it was Mum's turn in bed we would sit next to her and knit a scarf with tiger stripes while she read us an exciting story. If it was Dad's turn, we would plan the day ahead and talk about what fish we would catch and things around the house that needed to be built or fixed. Once the fire was going and the kettle was boiling, we would be brought a cup of hot mint tea. Ideally the mint would be picked fresh from the garden and steeped in our yellow enamel teapot, though in winter we'd use the mint we'd helped Mum pick and dry over the fire for two weeks in the autumn before putting it into resealable, airtight tin cans. To make the cup more like an early breakfast, we would add a spoonful of milk powder and some oats and sultanas. Then we would sit back and enjoy our 'cuppie tea' as we waited for the wood fire to warm the house. Dad would add some black tea to his cup as well.

For my second breakfast I would have a bowl of muesli. I would choose rolled oats, sultanas, milk powder and a spoonful of raw sugar from the jars on a shelf above the kitchen sink. I would always leave a little mess on the bench and Mum would yell at me to clean it up as I ran out the front door. Often I'd be going after Dad, having seen him, wearing his dark green Swanndri jacket and tall gumboots, heading down the back track towards the river. That meant it was time to check the net! I would run past him and down the hill through the forest to the river as fast as I could and then Dad would catch me up. Our fish net was attached to the end of a long rope in the estuary. Dad would pull it in, hand over hand, while I stared excitedly into the emerald-green water, trying to catch a glimpse of the shiny silver fish. We usually caught yellow-eyed mullet that would come into the estuary at night and sometimes there would be an extra-large shimmering in the bottom of the net and that meant there was a kahawai.

We would take the fish out of the netting carefully and place them on the river stones for scaling. Dad had replaced the handle on an old kitchen knife with a fresh piece of deer antler and I would scale the little fish with this knife as Dad scaled the big ones. The net would be left untangled to be set at low tide, and if we had caught more than eight mullet or two kahawai we would have enough food for a couple of days and wouldn't need to set it again that day. When there was heavy rain forecast overnight it wasn't safe to set the net and we would stash it out of the sun under a rātā where it couldn't wash away. Finally, we would carry the fish back to the house in a bucket for Mum to fillet at the kitchen sink. Afterwards Mum would ask me to bury the fish frames in the garden.

When we caught a big kahawai, Dad would fillet the fish and place each fillet on a rack made out of recycled stainless wire from a craypot and sprinkle on lots of salt. Then we would go down to the beach and start a fire in our fish smoker. The rack would hang in the top of an old 44-gallon fuel drum that acted as the smokehouse. At the bottom, off to one side under a separate piece of corrugated iron, we would make a fire and place large rātā logs from the beach on top of the embers to smoulder away for the day. The smoked fish would taste amazing and it was a fantastic way to cook fish for a different flavour. Alongside Dad's fish smoker was a smaller one made out of a flattened sheet of corrugated iron and this was mine. Here I would copy Dad's every move and smoke some smaller yellow-eyed mullet.

After dealing with the fish, it would be time to go for a walk down the airstrip. On the hill behind the house there is a slip where the trees have fallen away. Deer sometimes come out in the morning to eat the grass on the slip or at the side of the airstrip, and I would keep a sharp lookout for any sign of them. I would also disappear into the bush a few times to check on Dad's rabbit snares, and if there was a rabbit in one of them, I would tell him when I got back.

The waves from the Southern Ocean would be crashing along the rocky shoreline, and if the sea was rough, the spray would reach halfway up the sides of the jagged Gorge Islands sitting half a kilometre offshore. Staring at the power of nature each morning would energise me, and the larger the waves and the stronger the wind, the more alive I would feel. Sometimes I'd spot Jimbo, a local fisherman, on his boat, *Albacore*, pulling up craypots around the Gorge Islands, and I would watch for a little while, dreaming of the day when I would be out on a fishing boat too. If the boat wasn't there, I would imagine when I would be old enough to row a boat, or perhaps a kayak, out through the two-metre breaking waves to fish there myself. I knew it would be dangerous, so I would spend a few minutes studying the never-ending line of heavy, crashing surf and the tangled mass of waves and currents around the river mouth, working out the safest way to navigate through to the open ocean beyond.

Afterwards, I would head back along the beach and practise running on the boulders, skipping from rock to rock almost as fast as I could run on flat grass. Some days I would study the rocks around the river mouth at a slower speed, hoping to find a nice piece of jade. Once every couple of years I would find one and excitedly carry it home to show Dad.

After my walk it would be time to start my home-school work. I would sit at the kitchen table and ask, 'Mum, what's my schoolwork today?' Mum would select a workbook off the shelf near my bed and as she handed it to me would say, 'Do you know where you're up to?' My main subjects were maths, social studies, science, English and spelling, but often they would be incorporated into a project. One time when I was ten, I designed the front page of a newspaper called *The Gorge Weekender* and wrote the headings with a black Vivid pen. The breaking news was 'Trampers Arrive at Gorge River' together with some smaller articles about 'Cricket', 'Deer Spotted' and 'Yacht Sighted'. Each article was handwritten in columns in my neatest writing and instead of using photos all the pictures were hand-drawn. In another project about countries of the world, each day I would write a one-page summary about a specific country, using our encyclopaedias to research and draw a map and a picture of its flag with coloured pencils. Eventually I bound 16 pages together to present my project in a workbook, with a map of the world carefully drawn on the cover. Thinking back on this now, it's incredible to think that I have since visited 12 of the 16 countries that I researched.

One of the most amazing things about my education was that Mum and Dad showed me how things worked and then we studied why they happened that way. I was fascinated by numbers, statistics and trends in the world around me. When I was four, the Correspondence School sent a packet of sunflower seeds to grow. We planted them in a freshly dug patch of the garden in front of Dad's workshop. I watched them develop with fascination and each day would measure the height of each plant. When they were fully grown, I plotted their heights and the widths of their flowers on a graph and a distinct trend was obvious. The next year we had a rainy summer and the sunflower seeds we planted didn't grow. Instead, I used Dad's callipers to measure three pumpkins that were growing in the garden, carefully plotting the measurements on graph paper under the headings 'Pumpkin One', 'Pumpkin Two' and 'Pumpkin Three'.

I would finish the day's schoolwork by drawing a picture of a plover or a tūī to send to the Kiwi Conservation Club magazine. I would start by sketching the outline of the bird and the background behind it with a normal lead pencil, before using my coloured pencils to bring it to life. My drawings were often published, and a few months later when the mail arrived, I would proudly show off my picture in the magazine to Mum and Dad.

When I'd finished my schoolwork I might hear Dad cutting some jade with his diamond saw powered by two solar panels on the roof. I would watch for a few minutes before pulling out a rough piece of jade that I had found on the beach. Then I would sit patiently polishing it with some sandpaper and water, stopping every now and then to see if it was becoming shiny. When Dad walked past, I would exclaim, 'It's going to take me a while!' I was hoping he would let me use his machine.

Mum would usually have done the washing in the morning and after soaking the dirty clothes in buckets for an hour or two it would be time to take them down to the river to rinse them in the clean fresh water. 'Christan, can you please come down in 15 minutes and carry the washing buckets?' she would ask from the bathroom. 'Yes, okay,' I would grumpily agree. Afterwards, if it was summer, I would convince Robin to go for a swim in the river and I would ask Mum, 'Can you please watch us while we go swimming?' 'Yes, okay,' she would always say. 'I will collect firewood.'

We learned to swim while visiting Nana and Grandad in Queensland, and after that I was always keen to jump in the river. Mum and Dad bought me a wetsuit to help with the ten- to twelve-degree water. I would put on my flippers and mask and spend hours swimming up and down the estuary. I practised diving to the bottom to collect rocks, chasing yellow-eyed mullet back and forth in the shallows, and sometimes Robin and I would have races on our homemade styrofoam body boards. Being older, I would always win, and she would usually lose interest. And fair enough too – most of the games we played were invented by me and were specifically designed for me to win. I was an older brother after all and could be quite mean to my little sister in a normal brother–sister way.

After swimming, Mum would often remind me about the bags of firewood on the beach that needed to be brought back to the house. I would run down and carefully count the bags, making sure that Robin carried exactly half of them. One bag would be full of long pieces of driftwood and Mum would ask me to cut them into shorter lengths to fit inside our fireplace. If the bags were down at the airstrip, we would use our little four-wheeled trolley, built by Dad out of a baby pram and a fish case off the beach. The trolley would comfortably fit two bags and was an easier way to move firewood along the airstrip. I would fill the trolley with as many bags as possible because I thought I was super strong. Dad would then tell me off for overloading it because he knew he would have to fix it if it broke.

Mum and Dad never gave us money, but instead gave us opportunities to earn it. We would get 50 cents per bag of firewood collected and 25 cents for each bag if we just did the carrying part. The garden constantly needed fertiliser too, and if there was seaweed washed up on the beach we would bag it up and carry it back to put on the garden. Sometimes Mum would have a slug problem in the garden and would pay me five cents for each dead slug. That was my least favourite chore and I always bargained for a better price.

In the evening just before dark I would carefully select my best fishing lure out of a jar of random hooks and sinkers and would run down to the river to try to catch a fish. I would happily fish every evening when it wasn't raining and stand there casting my lures out into the water. A huge swarm of sandflies would follow me and I found that if I wore a hat with a wide brim then at least they couldn't buzz in my face. I always wore a long-sleeved shirt and pants. There is just no point wearing a T-shirt and shorts in South Westland because the sandflies will eat you alive. My hands would be covered in bites by the end of the evening but it never bothered me that much. Sandflies could never put me off fishing! By the time I would get home the sun would have sunk beneath the western horizon and it would be getting quite dark.

Mum would have lit some candles to light up the house and she would be preparing dinner on the wood fire, smoke rising from the chimney before swirling down into the garden in the chilly wind that usually starts blowing through the river valley at sunset. Until I was six, in 1999, we had no form of electricity and used candles and a Tilley lantern for lighting. Eventually we bought our first solar panel, and above the kitchen table went two fluorescent lights connected to a 12-volt deep-cycle battery bank. If the sun had been shining during the day, then we would have light all night, but if it had been raining the charge would be low and we would still need to use candles.

Just before dinner, Mum would ask Robin or me to pick a fresh salad. She had a stainless-steel bowl that she would want filled and we would carefully pick broad beans, carrots, peas, parsley and tomatoes. Some green salad leaves such as mizuna, watercress and lettuce would be made into a salad with any other edible leaves we could find growing wild in the garden. Sometimes in the autumn we could pick a handful of mushrooms along the airstrip. Mum would always grate the carrots and distribute the pile of juicy, bright orange shreds evenly on our four dinner plates. I have never eaten tastier carrots or tomatoes than the ones Mum grows at Gorge River.

We would always eat dinner as a family. The table was made from two bedheads nailed together and four driftwood legs. I would sit to Dad's left on the same bench seat and Mum sat to his right nearer the fire on her homemade driftwood stool. Robin would sit across the table from me on another stool. The stools had been made by Mum – out of three straight pieces of driftwood, crosspieces that fitted into each other, and a padded piece of plywood on top – when we started home schooling. On the wall behind where I sat hung two of Dad's half-finished paintings and on other parts of the walls Robin and I had stuck our favourite stickers.

Mum would always cook dinner and usually it would be yellow-eyed mullet fillets rolled in egg and breadcrumbs and fried until crispy golden brown. On the side would be potato chips and steamed silver beet and broad beans and the leafy green salad – all from the garden. Sometimes Mum would fry up the fish roe and they looked just like little sausages. Quite often she would sit down at the table and announce proudly, 'Tonight, all this food is from Gorge River!' I was growing fast and would eat anything she put in front of me. Yellow-eyed mullet was my favourite and I could easily devour five or six fillets in one meal. I liked my fish with tomato sauce or salt and vinegar, with some extra to go on the homemade chips.

Poor Robin wasn't quite so lucky. She absolutely hated fish but didn't have much choice. Fish is what we had and she had to eat at least one fillet each day. She would sit there sometimes for half an hour, slowly chewing her way through her piece of fish. I could never understand because to me this would just prolong the agony. One of her favourite foods was yams, which Mum grew and harvested each autumn.

After dinner we would carefully put any leftover food in the mouse-proof cupboard under the sink. If we had a pot of venison from some hunters it would go on the floor in the bathroom, which is the coolest part of the house. As long as we boiled the pot each day, we could keep food there for a couple of weeks. We never wasted any food and would only throw away vegetable scraps, which would rot down in the garden, fertilising the soil. It almost makes me cry to see how much good food is wasted by people in the developed world. So many resources go into creating a meal, just for someone to throw it away because it's a day overdue or has some flavour someone doesn't like. And most is not even composted properly! If we wasted food at Gorge River, then later we would have to go without.

After tea we would often play a game or do a puzzle. Our favourite board game was 'Holiday'. Mum had made this game for us after being inspired by a board game in Lou Brown's old house at Barn Bay. In the game there is a family going on a holiday around a board visiting different places and encountering different obstacles along the way. Our holiday would take us on a walk out to town and then a bus or hitchhike to Queenstown, from where we could fly home with Roger. Some of the obstacles we encountered were things like flooded rivers or seals blocking the way. If you were lucky, you could pull a 'Helicopter' card that gave you a free ride and jump forward a few spaces.

If we weren't playing games, then either Mum or Dad would read us a library book, or I might flick through my *Amazing Facts of the World* or *The Guinness Book of Records*. I would stop and read out my favourites. 'Hey! Did you know the record for the longest spaghetti shot from the nose is three metres! And this guy has the world's longest fingernails!' I was fascinated that someone would think of setting such records and was inspired to break a record myself. So I set out to break the finger-knitting world record and each evening I would knit a few metres to roll onto an ever-expanding ball. After showing everyone my finger knitting, Mum suggested, 'Perhaps you can get the record for the fastest person to tear the knees out of a pair of pants.'

Some evenings Dad would play a song on his guitar, and when I was very young I might strum along on an older guitar at the same time, much to his annoyance. Dad loved to collect stamps and therefore I did as well, and together we would carefully remove the stamps from our last mail delivery and place them into my stamp album that Nana and Grandad had sent me for Christmas. My favourite stamps had images of the Ross Dependency in Antarctica and the best one had an emperor penguin. Inside the front cover of the album were two banknotes, one from Thailand and another from Singapore, that Grandad had included with the gift. I would stare at them, trying to imagine their far-off countries of origin.

Soon it would be time to brush our teeth and go to bed. Mum and Dad have a large bed in the front corner of the house, with windows that look out to the ocean. When we were very young, Robin and I would sleep there too, but once we were a little older Robin moved to a bed in the back corner of the house and I slept in a bed against the wall in between Mum and Dad's bed and Robin's. We didn't have walls forming bedrooms. Instead we had curtains that could be pulled back during the daytime, creating an open-plan living area and allowing us to make better use of our limited space. Mum would always stay up late reading after Dad, Robin and I had gone to bed. Finally, with a click, Mum would turn off the light and the house would be plunged into darkness. On a moonlit night a shaft of light would shine through a window above my bed and onto my face. I would drift off to sleep to the sound of the waves crashing on the shoreline. If there was a storm outside, the rain would make a heavy pitter-patter on the corrugated-iron roof and the rātā outside my window would creak and groan in the howling wind.

CHAPTER 3

Planes, Choppers and Boats

The Gorge River airstrip had been cut out of the bush by bulldozers at the same time as the mining company had built the first part of our house. At 380 metres it had plenty of length, but a plane's wheels had to be in exactly the right place, and the wings hung out over the flax bushes on each side of the strip. Only the most skilled bush pilots dared to land on it and they had to get everything just right. From early on, Dad knew that eventually his family would be landing on the airstrip themselves, so it had to be widened. He spent many days of hard work digging out the flax bushes on each side until eventually he had widened the whole airstrip by a few metres. There were no longer flax bushes under the wings of the aircraft and there was now some room for error.

After Robin was born we started to have regular supply drops flown in from Arrowtown by our friend Roger Monk. He had been flying in the area for many years and owned a Cessna 180 that was perfect for landing on the Gorge River airstrip. We used his address in Lake Hayes for our mail and he soon became our main lifeline to the outside world. Over the years, we have had many incredible flights through the Southern Alps with Roger, through all sorts of weather. There is no one I feel safer flying with than him. Words can't describe how much it meant to us as a family to have him visit, and it always felt like Christmas whenever he arrived. We could recognise the sound of his plane even before we could see the registration letters. Since we had no way to contact him directly, each time he visited us we would give him a shopping list and ask him to return in 'about six weeks'. We wouldn't actually know what day he would be back and as the sixth week approached we would be listening to the five-day weather forecast on National Radio, trying to guess when he might come.

Each day, we would wait in anticipation and sometimes there would be a long spell of beautiful weather that would go by with no sign of Roger. Finally, the wind would turn to the north and the waves on the ocean would start to show little whitecaps warning of an approaching storm that could last for days. Late in the afternoon, Dad would stand out on the end of the airstrip, staring at the sky to the north and studying the rising wind and lenticular cloud formations. Eventually he would turn back to the house and shake his head. 'Surely it's too late for Roger today.'

However, Roger always seemed to arrive after everyone had given up on him and, sure enough, about 30 minutes later, we would hear the low-pitched rumble of a plane approaching from the south. It would get louder and louder and with a final *rrrrrRrROOOmmm* a white plane with rainbow stripes would fly low over the house.

'It's Roger!' we would yell in excitement as we ran outside. After checking the airstrip, he would do a steep banking turn before lining up for his final approach. I would watch in fascination as the plane, buffeted by the unpredictable winds, would land perfectly in the airstrip's wheel ruts. I've watched him land there a hundred times and never seen him make a mistake. One particular day there was a blustery 25-knot southwesterly blowing and he touched down in exactly the same wheel marks twice in one day.

Roger would taxi up in front of the house and, with a final burst of power, turn the plane using the brake on one wheel and leave it facing back down the airstrip ready for take-off. The propeller would come to a stop, the doors would open and we would be greeted with 'G'day' from a smiling Roger. Often his partner, Debbie, would be in the co-pilot's seat, or perhaps Warrick Mitchell from Big Bay or Ian Todd from Arrowtown. 'Do you want a cup of tea?' Dad would ask. 'Yeah, we have time,' would come the reply.

Before the cup of tea, Roger would unload the plane and we would carry everything inside. There would always be a big bag containing six weeks of mail, four or five banana boxes of groceries, some wood or hardware supplies for building, and any other odds and ends that he thought we might need. The mail bag was the most exciting part and if it was the right time of year there would be some Christmas or birthday presents from family and some letters from our friends in town. Over the years, the mail bag grew bigger with the arrival of library books and eventually it brought all the Correspondence School lessons for Robin and me. The grocery boxes would contain staple foods like milk powder, cooking oil, eggs, brown sugar, flour, sultanas, peanuts and rice. Luxury items would be apples, oranges and bananas and perhaps a fresh bottle of milk – and if we were very lucky a block of chocolate or a packet of biscuits. All of this would last us for another six or so weeks. Each day we would get two squares of chocolate each or one piece of fruit until they ran out.

Eventually Roger would get up and look out the window at the weather. 'Well, I guess we had better go,' he would announce. We never wanted him to leave. Dad would hand him a long shopping list. 'See ya in six weeks.' We would take this opportunity to send out a bag of mail with all the replies to the letters we had received on the previous mail drop six weeks before. The plane would usually be empty on the flight out, so Roger would also take our rubbish and any of Dad's finished artwork or my possum skins, which we would pick up from his hangar near Arrowtown when we were next in town. After Roger gave us a big smile and a wave, the engine would roar into life and with a burst of throttle the plane would start bouncing down the airstrip, quickly gathering speed. With a gust of wind, the plane would lift up into the sky and within a couple of minutes disappear out of sight behind Longridge Point.

One time we were expecting Roger around a certain date in April 1999 and were waiting eagerly for his arrival. The days went by with sunshine and settled weather but there was still no sign of him. A couple of weeks passed and we were getting a little worried that something had happened. Then one day a Cessna 206 nose-wheel plane that we didn't recognise started circling overhead and after two practice runs landed smoothly on the airstrip from the south. An elderly guy jumped out and introduced himself as Dave Bunn,

Debbie's father. He informed us that Roger had bent the wheel of his plane in a hole while taxiing. It wasn't badly damaged but it could still take six months to be repaired. Dave had our standard load of groceries but suddenly we didn't know how we would get the next order. Shortly after, we walked out to town and spent a month around Haast, Wānaka and Queenstown. We left a planeload of food in Roger's hangar and asked him to bring it in when his plane was fixed. Then we returned to Haast and flew home with Morgan Saxton, son of pilot Dave Saxton, in his Hughes 500C helicopter.

The months went by and still there was no sign of Roger. Our food supplies were getting low and since it was winter Dad spent most of his time fishing just to make sure we had enough food on the dinner table each night. He was trying to relieve the pressure on our dwindling food supplies, and every day, come rain, hail or shine, he would catch five or six kelpies at the end of the airstrip – in winter there aren't so many fish in the river. Every two weeks, if the sea was calm on the spring low tide, he would collect pāua in the rock pools and smash open a kina so we could eat the roe. I helped him with the fishing as best I could, but I was still quite young so he had to do most of it himself. Sometimes the weather was too cold or the waves were too big for me to safely fish from the rocks.

Each day we listened to the transistor radio, intrigued to hear that the rest of the world was so worried about the impact of Y2K and the change of millennium. One day Dad caught a possum (which were still in very low numbers at that time). We were ready for a change of diet after eating fish for months, so decided to eat it. Dad skinned the possum and cut it up into pieces for Mum to cook. The dish tasted pretty good, so we nicknamed it 'millennium stew'. We decided that if the world was to fall apart as a result of the so-called Y2K bug and we never received another food drop, then we could eat 'millennium stew' for the next few years.

By July the oats had long since been finished, so for breakfast Robin and I started eating rice pudding with milk, sultanas and sugar. Then the sultanas and sugar ran out. It is possible to live off the land completely at Gorge River, eating only fish and vegetables from the garden, but it is very challenging, especially in winter. When there are only fish and a few vegetables to eat for lunch and dinner, it's really nice to have some oil to cook them with.

Eventually, by the end of August, our food supplies had almost gone. We were down to just six days of rice left in a bag. Dad decided he had to do something. He called Darren King-Turner, a passing crayfisherman, on our VHF radio and asked if he could phone Roger on his return to Milford. We needed to know when the plane would be repaired. If Roger wasn't coming back any time soon then Dad would have to leave us and walk out to the shop in Haast. The next day we saw *Saracen*, Darren's fishing boat, just a couple of hundred metres outside the river bar. Obviously he had a message for us and Dad turned on the VHF. 'Roger's plane is ready in four days and he will come and see you then,' came Darren's update across the radio waves.

This was welcome news and, sure enough, four days later we heard the familiar sound of Roger's Cessna 180 as it zoomed low over the house. His newly painted, shiny yellow and white plane touched down on the airstrip. We were very relieved to see him and as we unloaded the groceries we marvelled at the paint job, in which the rainbow had been replaced by sunflower-yellow stripes along each side of the fuselage and wingtips. It was now the start of the whitebait season and Roger told us we had been invited by our neighbours

Graeme and Anne Mitchell to join them for a week of whitebaiting at Big Bay, 30 kilometres south. He could fly us down that afternoon. We packed our bags, climbed aboard and off we went.

During the whitebait season Big Bay is a buzzing little community, with six whitebaiters' huts and between ten and twenty people at any one time. Each hut has a couple of whitebait stands and some of the families have been coming back for generations. All access is by air and the planes use the long, hard-sand beach as a runway at low tide.

The first thing Dad noticed at Big Bay was the food everywhere. The Mitchells had sausages, venison, bacon, bread, milk and most other things you'd have in a normal house, and Dad felt mixed emotions. For months we had been living on the edge. Each day he'd had to find food in the wilderness for his family to eat. And now there was food everywhere. Yet in some ways he actually preferred what we'd just experienced. There is a kind of beauty and a feeling of satisfaction you gain from hunting and gathering your own food that you don't get when you eat food from the supermarket.

Roger's food drops were without a doubt one of the most critical parts of our life at Gorge River, and unloading his plane is still one of my favourite childhood memories. Whenever I see a Cessna 180 anywhere in the world, I instantly think of him and his trusty yellow and white plane.

When I was very young most of the air traffic that passed Gorge River consisted of small, two-seater Robinson R22 helicopters used for hunting deer. Most mornings we would see two to four 'Robbies' flying south at first light, hunting all the slips and beach edges between Haast and Martins Bay for red deer. Then around 9 am they would all fly back, with a few carcasses hanging beneath them, to the Cascade Road end and the waiting meat trucks. About two hours before dark they would head south again, and then just on dark they would all head back north. Therefore, as a young child, helicopters were a big feature of my life. I would look up at the choppers flying past and dream of the day when I would be the one in the pilot's seat.

The idea of receiving loads of expensive presents on my birthday or at Christmas never entered my mind. Instead, I was given toys made by Mum or Dad that were usually handcrafted from wood or other natural materials sourced from around Gorge River. When I was three years old, Dad built Robin and me a life-size R22, skilfully fashioned out of different-shaped pieces of driftwood from the beach. The main rotor blade was a long, straight plank of milled wood that had washed up and the tail rotor was a piece of driftwood roughly 80 centimetres long that naturally turned in the wind. On a windy day the tail rotor would spin so fast that Dad had to tie it up for fear it would hit one of us in the head.

I would be the pilot and with Robin as 'shooter' we would fly all around the imaginary hills of South Westland hunting deer. The deer were brightly coloured crayfishing buoys that we had found on the beach and we would scatter them around the flax bushes in front of the house. Most importantly, our helicopter had a number-8-wire 'hook' beneath it for carrying heavy loads of 'deer' back to Gorge River. Robin would jump out and collect the deer and I would yell, 'Hook on!' or 'Hook off!' as I moved the driftwood controls backwards and forwards to manoeuvre the helicopter. Every now and then one of the skids holding up the helicopter would break and we would have a 'crash'. The helicopter would end up lying on its side with us still in the seats, laughing so hard we cried. Robin was less enthusiastic about the hunting games but she went along with them and we had endless hours of fun.

My other toys included a small wooden plane with a 30-centimetre wingspan. I would run up and down the airstrip with my little plane flying through the sedge grass and I even had my own set of 'bush airstrips' that I could land on. I copied every move that I had seen my pilot heroes make when they landed at Gorge River. The people I looked up to were flying legends like Roger Monk, Dave and Morgan Saxton, Harvey Hutton and Ken Hutchins. On rainy days I would fly my wooden helicopter round and round the house, picking up driftwood deer.

If he was flying in the area, Haast pilot Dave Saxton would often land in his dark green Hughes 500C. He would always have with him some bags of groceries from the Haast shop. There would be so many luxury items, such as a fresh bottle of milk, sausages, shop bread, oranges, apples and a few bags of lollies. He was one of the most generous people I have ever met and he never expected anything in return. If Dad knew he was coming he would collect some pāua and keep them in a holding pot to give to 'Sax' to say thank you, like a form of 'bush payment'. That's how things work in South Westland. On one particular day when Dave was picking up a party of deer hunters he brought us a big load of groceries. When he unloaded the bags from the helicopter, one of them started to break and as he carried them over to us he left behind a trail of pineapple lumps. After he left, we scoured through the long grass and were still finding those pineapple lumps hours later.

A few years later Sax crashed that same helicopter at the mouth of the Spoon River, about seven kilometres north of Gorge River, with four people on board. No one was hurt in the accident and they decided to turn off the emergency locator beacon to avoid creating a panic back in Haast. They had no other form of communication, so decided to walk down to Gorge River to see if we could get a message out to Haast. Dad recognised Sax from across the river. Helicopter pilots never hike and he guessed immediately that something must have gone wrong. 'What's for dinner?' asked Sax, as Dad rowed them across in our aluminium dinghy.

We had only a handheld VHF radio at that time and were unable to talk with anyone who wasn't in line of sight, so all we could do was wait. We just happened to have some bacon, so Mum cooked them bacon and eggs and we gave them blankets and sleeping bags to use in the DOC hut. Early the next morning Dad talked to a fishing boat off Barn Bay and they relayed the message to Haast. By that time there was a full-scale search on for the missing helicopter and it wasn't long before Harvey Hutton and Dave Baldwin landed to pick up Sax and his mates. A few weeks later, Sax and Geoff Robson landed with a single-sideband radio for us. With this we could now talk to Bluff Fisherman's Radio if we needed to get a message out.

The pilots and fishermen have always liked us being at Gorge River, because when something goes wrong in the area it's a long way to reach help and the more people around the better.

From the age of 17, Morgan Saxton was already following in his father's footsteps by flying out hunters in a Hughes 300. He was another regular visitor to Gorge River and Dad watched him grow up from a child. The first two helicopter flights that I remember were with Morgan and he was certainly one of my childhood pilot heroes. He always had a huge smile on his face and within a few years had become a highly skilled pilot.

One warm, sunny day in September 2008, Morgan stopped for a cup of tea in his blue R22 with his shooter Phil Wright. They were heading home from hunting and had three deer hanging on the cargo hook. He was much more relaxed than normal and we talked and told stories for a couple of hours.

One month later I was standing on the riverbank at Big Bay staring intently at the fast-flowing water for any sign of the elusive whitebait. There was a rumour going around the whitebaiters' village that morning about a missing helicopter near Wānaka. I saw Warrick Mitchell driving down the shell bank towards me on his quad bike and as he began to speak I noticed he looked a bit shaken up. 'You know that helicopter that's missing – it's Morgan,' he said.

For days they searched the shores of Lake Wānaka for Morgan and slowly bits of news made it through to us at Big Bay. First they found some helicopter debris washed up on an island and then some oil floating on the surface of the lake. Eventually, with the use of a remote-controlled submarine, Navy divers managed to recover his body and the wreckage of that little blue R22 from 90 metres below the spot where the oil slick had been seen. A few days later, we attended his funeral at Wānaka Airport. It was the second funeral I had been to and it was attended by over 2000 people from all over New Zealand. Morgan was a huge part of the South Westland community and was sorely missed.

Sadly, Morgan's death wasn't the only aircraft fatality close to home for my family. Another time I was at Big Bay whitebaiting with Warrick, and although Mum and Dad had satellite internet by then, I had not been in contact for a few days. They were listening to National Radio one evening when they heard the news we dreaded hearing. 'One person is dead after a fixed-wing plane crash on a private airstrip near Arrowtown.' To put this in context, Roger owns the main airstrip near Arrowtown and 95 per cent of the landings there involve either himself or Debbie. And to make matters worse, I was at Big Bay and for all they knew I could have jumped in Roger's plane and flown out to Queenstown for some reason.

Dad went straight to the computer and turned on the internet. A message popped up immediately from our friend Sue Todd: 'There has been an accident on Roger's airstrip but it was not Roger's plane.' I'm guessing that was one of the biggest frights Mum and Dad have had when Robin or I have been out of contact – and if it had been Roger or Debbie killed, that would have been devastating for my family also. As it was, we didn't know the pilot but he was a friend of Roger's. He had aborted a landing and tried to take off again but crashed 200 metres off the end of the runway into the Arrowtown golf course and was killed. His two passengers survived.

While I have always dreamed of becoming a pilot, accidents like these have put me off. One day I will learn to fly, but not until I have done everything I'd like to do in life.

Besides planes and helicopters, the other thing that fascinated me as a child was fishing boats. I would watch the local crayfish boats from Jackson Bay and Milford Sound as they motored past each day, collecting their craypots. If there was a storm, they would disappear in huge clouds of spray as they crashed their way directly into the rough, stormy seas. When I was very young, Dad used to fly a flag made from an old sheet on a long piece of driftwood to show the fishermen we were home. Naturally enough, I had my own flag flying on a short stick under Dad's. I wanted the fishing boats to know I was home too!

One day when I was very small, I watched as Dad rowed his four-metre aluminium dinghy (we never had an outboard motor) out over the Gorge River bar to visit a local fisherman known as 'Swag'. For the West Coast it was a beautiful calm day with only one- to two-metre waves crashing on the shoreline. Dad had salvaged a washed-up craypot and attached it to the back of the dinghy with ropes. He had organised a rendezvous with Swag's boat *Sharcaree* on our handheld VHF radio and Swag was very happy to get his craypot back and gave Dad a bag of crayfish and some 'lollies and fruit cake for the kids'. We ate very little sugar, so Swag's lollies were a huge treat. The crayfish were a welcome change of flavour too, although we would only eat a couple of them. The rest we would keep alive in a holding pot at the end of the airstrip to give to passing trampers or pilots when they called in for a cup of tea. There's a saying in South Westland: 'A crayfish eaten is gone, a crayfish given away is there forever.' It was a good way to say thank you to the people who helped us.

Mum bought me a toy radio and I spent many hours trying to call the local fishermen like 'Elmo', 'Swag' and 'Jimbo'. It never fazed me that they didn't reply. I even had my own boat made from a banana box. A plank of wood and a piece of drainpipe served as oars. Robin was just a baby and she would come along as my 'passenger' as I attempted to 'row' the cardboard box across the living-room floor on a rainy day. Both Robin and I had fantastic imaginations and could make up games out of the simplest materials around us. I think it helped that we didn't have a TV, because the kids we met in town who watched TV were never as creative.

Sometimes I'm a bit surprised I didn't end up working on fishing boats full-time later in life. Although I have spent quite a bit of time at sea over the years, so far the only fishing boat I have worked on was a salmon-fishing boat in Alaska. However, I still have that avid fascination with the ocean and have lived out some of those childhood dreams by going on sailing expeditions and working on ships in Antarctica.

CHAPTER 4

Visitors

Some people live in the wilderness because they don't like other people, but for my family that was not the case. We are all very sociable and one of the biggest challenges of living at Gorge River was the lack of other people to talk to. For Robin and me, growing up without other kids to play with shaped the early part of our lives and we were affected by social awkwardness at the beginning of our adult life in the outside world. Therefore, when we did receive visitors, we would drop everything to welcome them into our home.

Most of our visitors arrived by air and whenever I heard the sound of a helicopter or plane, I would run out the front door as fast as I could to see it. We could usually tell instantly from the registration and colour of the aircraft who it was and whether they were likely to stop. If a plane flew low over the airstrip there was a good chance the pilot was checking it out for a safe landing. After it had passed, I would watch intently for it to make a sharp turn out to sea, which would signal the pilot was considering landing. 'They're going around!' I would yell, jumping up and down excitedly. If the plane was a nose-wheel like a Cessna 172 or 206 it was unlikely to land, but if it was a yellow Piper Cub then it would be Blair Holt from Haast or Max Wendon and Lisa Holliday from Makarora and they almost always landed.

Sometimes an unknown plane would circle once or even twice over the airstrip before flying away, and that was always disappointing. If it was a helicopter, then we would hear the distinct *chop-chop-chop* made by the rotor blade punching through the air from a few kilometres away. As the helicopter neared Gorge River we would listen for the change in pitch to the *thump-thump-thump* noise the rotors make as a helicopter begins to slow in preparation for landing. A blue Hughes 500 might well be Dick Deaker or Harvey Hutton and they would usually stop for a visit.

I would watch intently as the aircraft prepared for landing, Dad would be searching for his earmuffs in the workshop, and Mum would be tidying the kitchen table and putting the kettle on. Helicopters would always land on the end of the airstrip in front of the house and the planes would park there as well once they had landed. Regardless of whether we knew the aircraft or not, we would always go out and say hi. West Coast hospitality is important and it is never fun standing and chatting in a cloud of sandflies, so after a quick introduction Mum or Dad would always ask, 'Do you want a cup of tea?' Most people would accept and we would head inside for a cup of tea or coffee and a slice of Mum's freshly baked cake.

Among our favourite visitors were the Marchants, Cliff and Diane, who flew a blue and white Cessna 185. They lived at Port Gore at the very north of the Marlborough Sounds and would fly down to South Westland from time to time for some whitebaiting. Their home was quite isolated and the main access was by plane. Cliff would fly across Cook Strait to Wellington Airport in his 185, where he would change into an Air New Zealand uniform and pilot Boeing 777s around the world. With lots in common, we enjoyed sharing numerous cups of tea and discussing many different aspects of isolated living. Dad would talk with Cliff about boats or solar power supplies while Mum and Diane would discuss gardening and what the children were doing. The Marchants had five kids of their own and sometimes the youngest son, Mike, would be with them. He was a year older than me and I would take him for a walk along the riverbank as we talked about hunting possums, fishing and flying.

Once when we were in Picton we had the opportunity to visit the Marchants' home by helicopter. Located in a beautifully sheltered bay, their house sits next to a sandy beach. The long grass airstrip nearby makes it look quite similar to Gorge River. Randomly I bumped into Cliff later in life, at Los Angeles Airport on one of my overseas trips. We were both headed for New Zealand – me in economy class and him in the pilot's seat.

Generally, pilots are not all that relaxed and most visitors who come by air won't stay more than an hour or two. Trampers, however, have walked at least two days to get to Gorge River and are much more laidback.

Late one evening we were about to go to bed when we heard a loud yell that sounded like it came from out in the garden. It turned out to be two trampers on the north side of the river – we could see them waving their torches. The river is not usually crossable on foot, especially in the dark, and the two guys were very relieved when Dad ferried them across the icy-cold waters in his dinghy. They had missed the track that goes over Sandrock Bluff halfway between Gorge River and Barn Bay and decided to wait for the tide to go out so they could pass around. As a result, they had arrived late at Gorge River. We made sure they were dry and warm and Dad showed them across to the DOC hut. They were very relieved to have a roof over their heads and Dad invited them to come over for a cup of tea in the morning.

Robin and I were taught to respect the river and as children we were never allowed near it alone. Later we could fish or row the boat by ourselves, but when swimming we had to have someone keeping an eye on us. And there was a good reason for that. Mum and Dad often told us of a tragedy that had occurred when they were away in Arrowtown awaiting my birth.

Two guys had walked down the coast from Barn Bay and arrived on the north side of the Gorge River just ahead of an approaching storm. The tide was in and there was no way to walk across the river. They could see our aluminium dinghy on the south side but neither of them could swim. It was starting to rain and they didn't want to sleep under a flax bush for the night, so one of them decided to attempt the crossing. He managed to flounder his way over to the southern riverbank. However, when he tried to pull himself out of the water the loose gravel gave way under his weight and he slid back into the water. He struggled to find a way out and began to lose energy. Meanwhile his friend watched helplessly, unable to do anything. Before long the cold took over and the guy slid out of view beneath the surface. The only thing his friend could do was return to Barn Bay, where Lou Brown raised the alarm over the radio. That night it rained and the tramper's body was later found at Ryans Creek, eight kilometres to the south. Since then, we have always left some sort of boat or canoe on each side of the river when we are away.

When we are at home it goes without saying that Dad will row people across the river at any time of night or day. Sometimes, however, trampers would take matters into their own hands. One cold winter's afternoon Gerry McSweeney, the director of Forest and Bird, turned up in his underwear on our doorstep, dripping wet. He was shivering with cold and had obviously just swum across the river. 'Can I borrow your boat to row my two friends across?' he asked. 'Yeah, sure,' replied Dad with a smile as he grabbed him a warm jacket and some pants. 'It's on the other side!'

Other times, trampers would arrive from the south and we would receive a knock at our front door. That was always a big surprise and we would invite them in for a cup of tea and cake. We really liked it when people would stay an extra day because then we could really get to know them. Sometimes the weather would hold people up for a couple of days and we would invite them over for a dinner of freshly caught yellow-eyed mullet, pāua or crayfish.

It was quite common for us to go for a couple of weeks at a time without having visitors and a few times we were six or seven weeks without even seeing a fishing boat or passing aircraft. That type of isolation gets really hard and it's amazing to finally have someone new to talk to. Then, often after a long spell of no visitors, everyone can arrive at once …

One fine sunny day in January we heard a yell from across the river. Dad disappeared for half an hour and returned with our friends Ron and Doreen. They were keen trampers and had done the walk to Gorge River at least five times, but they were now in their sixties and more exhausted than normal. They explained that there were six trampers behind them and they had had to walk extra fast to claim a bed in the DOC hut before the others arrived.

Sure enough, a couple of hours later we saw the second group of trampers a few hundred metres up the beach, making their way towards the river mouth. By now the tide was very low and the sea was unusually calm so Dad suggested we leave them to find their own way across. There was a beautiful curving river bar and the water was only knee-deep. We heard some of them screaming as they jumped into the freezing-cold water to wash off after a long, sweaty day among the sandflies.

Soon we could hear quite a few voices over in the DOC hut, but we decided to give the trampers some space and say hi after they had all settled in. It seemed to be very busy and people kept walking back and forth to the river for swimming and there were now four tents set up on the airstrip. We were puzzled – there are six beds in the hut and there were only eight trampers, so why four tents? Eventually, two of them came over to say hello and we got talking about the good weather. 'How was the Cascade River crossing?' Dad asked. 'The Cascade? No, we haven't got there yet. There's eight of us and we came up from Big Bay today.' Unbeknown to us, while we were watching the six trampers arrive from the north, another party of eight had arrived from the south. After weeks of not seeing anyone, we had 16 trampers all at once!

Another time we hadn't seen a single sign of an aircraft or boat for about three weeks. Finally, one sunny afternoon, a Cessna 172 circled over the airstrip before lining up an approach in a light southerly breeze. After a safe landing, an older couple jumped out of the nose-wheel plane and we all introduced ourselves. They were from the North Island and it was their first time landing on our airstrip. We were hanging out to talk to someone so we invited them in for a cup of tea, which they eagerly accepted. They were just cruising along the coast and had plenty of time.

We were chatting away when all of a sudden we heard the heavy *thump-thump-thump* of an approaching Squirrel helicopter to the north. It was obviously lining up for landing and the rotor wash was soon tearing at the flaxes as the helicopter settled its skids on the grass about 50 metres down the airstrip in front of the 172. The pilots jumped out and we recognised them as locals Simon and Peter. As they introduced their passengers, we noticed another person appear from the flaxes at the south end of the airstrip. Then another and another, and before we knew it, five trampers were introducing themselves to everyone as we all stood on the airstrip chatting. They had just walked up from Big Bay that day and headed off to make themselves comfortable in the DOC hut. 'Come over later for a cup of tea,' Dad told them as he led Simon, Peter and their friends towards our house.

Inside they joined the other couple for tea and luckily Mum still had some cake left. We talked about how quiet it had been and laughed about everyone arriving all at once. The conversation moved on to painting, carving, possum hunting and the recent wet weather, and Simon's friends ordered a jade dolphin from Dad. Eventually the older couple became restless and were keen to continue their flight north. However, there was now a large helicopter blocking the runway so Peter agreed they would continue on their way as well. We shook hands with everyone and wished them a safe flight back to civilisation. Simon, Peter and their passengers piled back into the helicopter and the couple climbed into their plane and started the engine. We always watch the aircraft take off to make sure everything goes smoothly and we waited for the helicopter to start up. But nothing happened.

Eventually Simon and Peter climbed back out of the helicopter and went around the right side of the bubble to open one of the side compartments. 'The battery has no charge,' Peter told us as we approached. 'It's not going to start. We'll have to get Geoff to fly down from Neils Beach.' He gestured with concern behind the helicopter to the plane, whose engine was still running. 'We have plenty of time but these other guys want to take off.' Dad suggested using some of our 12-volt batteries but Peter shook his head and pulled out his satellite phone. A quick phone call confirmed that Geoff Robson was on his way with a helicopter jump-starter kit and we walked over to inform the pilots of the Cessna. By now they had really itchy feet because they would soon be overdue on their logged flight plan north and people would start wondering where they were. Peter offered them the sat phone to use but first the pilot wanted to try something.

As I've mentioned, our grass airstrip is about the width of a Cessna's wingspan with a thick tangle of flax bushes running down each side. The helicopter was parked right in the middle of the runway and so at a glance there was no way for the plane to taxi around it. But what if we could push the flax bushes down just enough for a wing to pass over them?

By now the trampers had registered the kerfuffle and come over to see what was happening. With their help, we carefully pushed the plane along the airstrip up to the back of the helicopter. Then the trampers, Simon and his friends, and Mum, Dad and I all lay down on the thick flax bushes and managed to hold them just lower than the plane wing. Peter and the couple pushed the plane to the left, making sure there was a sizable gap between the right wingtip and the body of the helicopter. The rotor blades were well above the plane wing so that part was easy and the left wingtip slid smoothly above the bent-over flax bushes. The plane was back in the middle of the airstrip, now in front of the helicopter, with just enough runway left for a safe take-off. The couple started their engine, proceeded to take off and before long, with a wave of their wingtips, were headed north towards Haast.

Not much later, Geoff Robson's green and white R44 appeared out of the river valley and landed in front of our house. Geoff and his son Mike unloaded a starter battery and they dragged it over. After plugging it into the appropriate socket, the helicopter's turbine began turning over and with a *click-click-click* roared into life. Everyone piled back into their respective aircraft and with a loud whirring of blades we watched the two choppers take off. They turned in different directions, Geoff and Mike heading back to Neils Beach and Simon and Peter turning up the river valley towards Wānaka.

After so long not seeing anyone, a day like that can be quite overwhelming, and it's much nicer when our visitors are more spaced out. But still, we have to make the most of every opportunity to socialise because sometimes they are few and far between. As the helicopters disappeared out of sight, we turned to the five trampers who were standing in front of the DOC hut, enjoying the evening sun. 'Are you ready for that cup of tea now?'

One time when I was about 11, three trampers arrived – Pascal, Julia and Sam, all in their early twenties. We invited them over for a cup of tea and cake. They had been hiking for a few days along the Hollyford Track and decided to take a rest day at Gorge River. They asked if we had any games to play, so Robin and I took our Monopoly set over and had a fun afternoon hanging out with our new friends. The next day the weather forecast for crossing the Spoon, Hope and Cascade rivers was not good and they stayed another day. This time we took over a pack of cards and played for most of the afternoon. They must have hit a really bad spell of weather because this routine continued for seven days. We played so many games of Monopoly that we learned who was good with finances, who was a bad loser and who would cheat at all costs.

After a few days the trampers were running very low on food, so we invited them over for meals of fish and vegetables from our garden each night. This way they could save their own food for the last two days of their hike. Before they left, Mum made sure they had enough pasta, rice, oats and sultanas to make it to the Cascade Road end and we gave them instructions on how to find our emergency food stashes if they got stuck. They had almost become a part of the family and it was very sad to see them go. Dad rowed them across the Gorge River on day seven and we waved them a final goodbye as they turned and hiked away into the distance along the coastline to the north.

Pascal and his friends were not the first trampers to run out of food in South Westland. If we are away and someone needs food, it is important they can get into our house to take what they need, so we never lock it – there isn't even a lock on the door. People have done this in the past and no one has ever stolen anything from us. Normally we never notice the missing food on our return until a big box of groceries arrives with Roger or Sax, with a thank-you card from some hungry trampers attached.

We have received some incredible generosity ourselves from other people over the years, both at Gorge River and away in the outside world. We always do our best to repay this with crayfish, pāua, fresh yellow-eyed mullet fillets or a feed of whitebait. Isolation pulls people closer together and it still amazes me when I see people in cities walk past each other without even an acknowledgement, or when someone is in need of help and they are left to fend for themselves. At Gorge River that is unimaginable. Usually within a minute of us meeting someone they have already been invited into our house. We have met many of our family friends this way and when we are out in town we take time to repay the visit in Wānaka, Dunedin or maybe even the North Island on our way to Auckland to see family.

For Christmas 2004, our cousins Elena and Kevin came from Dunedin with my Auntie Alison (Mum's sister) for a visit. Elena is one year older than me and Kevin one year younger. On Boxing Day we heard the terrible news about a devastating tsunami in Indonesia and Thailand that had killed hundreds of thousands of people.

The next day was beautiful and sunny with relatively calm seas – perfect conditions for snorkelling. We decided to take everybody to our secret crayfish pool where we can catch crayfish in one to two metres of water. We had enough masks, snorkels and flippers for everyone to have a set each, so off we all went to our secret place.

When we arrived, we were quite surprised to see that the water was much lower than it was meant to be. It was out about as far as the lowest spring tide would go. 'That's perfect,' we said and walked out to see if we could spot the crayfish from the rocks. Sure enough, we could see some feelers sticking out from within the seaweed. As we were searching, the tide started coming in quite fast. Not fast enough to notice at first, but within ten minutes we were almost waist-deep in water. It became quite hard to walk around and there were hundreds of kina under the swirling water. Dad found some pāua while Kevin and I put on our wetsuits and caught four crayfish. Every half-hour or so the whole level of the ocean was changing, up and down about a metre, as if the sea was gently breathing. 'How very strange,' we all thought.

How it didn't occur to us what was happening I don't know, but finally that evening we worked it out. We were listening to National Radio and one of the news items mentioned that a 60-centimetre tsunami, originating in Asia, had been measured by a tide recorder at Jackson Bay. Now it all made sense. We are more exposed to the west than Jackson Bay and probably had more like 80 centimetres to one metre.

Because our house is just 50 metres from the ocean, tsunamis, along with earthquakes, are one of the biggest threats. That tsunami had travelled for 24 hours and had passed around Australia to get to us. That was lucky, because we had failed to notice the most basic warning signs of an approaching wave. It was a good learning experience for us and, if there is a next time, I'm sure we will be more wary of the advancing and retreating water.

Robin and I loved it when Elena and Kevin visited us and they enjoyed the experience of staying in the wilderness and participating in our unique lifestyle too. Kevin and I would hunt possums and catch fish every day while Robin would make the most of having another girl to play with. With Elena she could do the girly things she wouldn't get to do with me. They wrote a play and called it *Midsummer Night's Scream*. We took pictures with deer skulls and shovels and Mum made the story into a homemade kids' book for our family collection.

Every few years my grandparents would visit. One time when I was young my Grandma Rosamond and Great-grandma Dai, aged 84, came to stay, along with Uncle Andrew and cousin Maddy – all from Mum's side of the family. They flew in from Queenstown with Roger and we had a big family Christmas together, eating crayfish, smoked fish, Mum's camp-oven Christmas cake, and the ham, turkey and a delicious jelly pudding they'd brought with them. Mum said the cake was the best thing she had ever cooked in the camp oven. Dad had cut a Christmas tree from an oak planted by a previous owner of the house and sat it in a bucket. Maddy, Robin and I decorated it using our box of Christmas decorations and everyone placed their presents underneath. On Christmas morning I received a mathematical board game, a wooden model sailing boat, a T-shirt hand-painted with a fish from Maddy, and a handmade kite sent by Grandpa.

The last time I saw Nana, Dad's mum, was during another family Christmas at Gorge River many years later, with her and Grandad and Dad's sisters Annette and Susan. They had all flown over from Australia and despite it being summer the weather was really cold and we joked that we might get a white Christmas. They brought shiny silver and gold Christmas crackers and bright balloons with 'Merry Christmas' written on them.

Over the years, we have had a few especially interesting visitors. We once had two former world tennis number ones, Martina Navratilova and Monica Seles, visit on a helicopter tour. We knew one of the pilots and he always liked to stop at Gorge River with his guests to buy a piece of Dad's artwork. Another time, Colin Tuck landed with Chuck Yeager, the first person to fly faster than the speed of sound. Australian adventurer Dick Smith and his wife, Pip, landed in their bright blue Jet Ranger helicopter one sunny summer's day. They were on a tour of New Zealand and someone had suggested they stop at our place for a cup of tea. We had a plague of bumblebees that summer and they love the colour blue. By the time Dick and Pip went to leave, the helicopter was covered in a few hundred buzzing bees.

When I was very young, we had a visit from *Jurassic Park*'s main actor, Sam Neill, and Kiwi musician Tim Finn, who turned up in a plane from Queenstown. Sam was looking for ideas for a new movie and later starred in *Perfect Strangers*, a movie set in a small house on the West Coast. Hopefully he drew some inspiration from our unique lifestyle.

People are often different from what you would expect, and famous people are usually quite down to earth when you meet them so far out of their comfort zone. But the wilderness doesn't have that effect on everyone. When I was one year old, a wealthy American businessman turned up in a bright red Squirrel helicopter. He wanted to buy some jade but since it was Christmas Day all the shops on the West Coast were closed. The pilot figured Gorge River wouldn't be shut for Christmas and decided to pay a visit. We were actually at Big Bay but eventually they found Dad and flew him back to Gorge River to show his jade. After pulling out a large wad of American hundred-dollar bills, the businessman offered $US500 for the entire table. Dad explained that almost half the pieces weren't for sale and the rest were worth much more than that. Eventually they settled on a deal for a couple of nice jade rocks, and Dad was commissioned to make a small jade fish necklace and a logo for the businessman to hang in his private jet. He paid a deposit for half the logo and fish necklace and agreed to pay the rest once he received it.

Back then we had no electricity and it took Dad weeks to make the carvings by hand, using sandstone, water and flint. Once the artwork was finished and carefully packaged, he sent it off to a US address. When asked for the payment, the businessman made excuses and insisted he couldn't send money to a bank account without a US ZIP code. Mum's sister Alison lived in Montana at the time and Dad suggested he pay it into her bank account. The excuses continued back and forth for some time until Dad finally gave up. With his millions of dollars of wealth, this man was one of the richest people to commission artwork from us. To this day, he is the only person who owes Dad money.

I have many happy memories of visitors but my earliest helicopter memory is a very sad one. This particular evening was just like any other. The strong southwest day breeze was easing and the sun was hanging near the western horizon in the clear blue sky. I was sitting next to Mum and Dad eating a dinner of fresh yellow-eyed mullet fillets with Mum's potato chips. Halfway through dinner we heard the familiar thumping noise of an R22 approaching from the south. As we did every time an aircraft flew over, we all ran outside and waved. I remember the shooter was hanging half out of the door, wearing a red jumpsuit and holding a semi-automatic rifle. About 500 metres north of the river the helicopter took a sharp turn and swooped in towards a slip on the 45-degree hillside. *Bang! Bang! Bang!*

'There must be some deer there!' I said to Dad excitedly.

The helicopter hovered for a short time above the slip before turning and landing on the beach. I was watching its every move with excitement, dreaming of the day it would be me hunting deer from helicopters.

After five minutes the helicopter lifted back into the air and we could see a strop (rope) dangling beneath it. 'The shooter's on the strop,' said Dad in a really concerned voice. We had heard of keen shooters who would be lowered into tight clearings and slips to retrieve the deer when the helicopters couldn't land. We knew it was an extremely dangerous manoeuvre and had never actually seen someone do it. Cautiously, the pilot lifted the guy off the ground and gradually gained altitude above the beach.

When the shooter was about ten to fifteen metres off the ground the pilot began to move towards the slip. Suddenly the rope disconnected from the helicopter and I vividly recall seeing the shooter fall back to the beach as if in slow motion. I was four years old and Robin was one, and both of us remember that moment to this day. I stared in disbelief, perhaps not quite understanding what had happened. Dad turned and ran straight into the house and a minute later reappeared, pulling on his Swanndri with one hand and clutching our first-aid kit in the other. He disappeared down the back track towards the river and paddled across in our fibreglass canoe.

Mum tried to keep Robin and me inside for the rest of the evening, but I kept slipping out to see what was going on up the beach. I saw the helicopter fly away north to Barn Bay half an hour later and shortly after it returned. Then around two hours later in the last of the evening light a blue rescue helicopter landed about two kilometres up the beach. When I awoke in the morning there was a helicopter parked outside and a strange guy staying in our guest bed. Dad told me he had to fly up to Haast to talk to a police officer and did not return until later that day.

So, what had actually happened? Now I switch over to Dad's story of the events. He arrived at the scene in his bare feet after running up the beach. He found the shooter, whose name was Andy, lying on rocks, clutching his ribs and in a huge amount of pain. Together Dad and the pilot tried to lift him back into the helicopter but he wouldn't cooperate. Eventually, with difficulty, they got him into the passenger's seat and the pilot took off towards Haast. They only travelled about two kilometres before the pilot had to land. Andy kept grabbing at the helicopter's controls and it wasn't safe for the pilot to continue. He left Andy on the beach and came back to pick up Dad. The tall hills behind Gorge River form a radio shadow and there is no VHF reception along our part of the coast. The pilot left Dad to look after Andy on the beach and flew north to Jackson Bay, where he phoned for help. Back on the beach, Andy fell unconscious and lost his pulse and Dad began CPR, despite Andy's broken ribs. An hour later the rescue helicopter piloted by James Scott arrived from Fox Glacier, but it was too late. Andy had already passed away.

James Scott flew Andy's body out to Haast, leaving Dad, the pilot and the 'Robbie' on the beach. Dad suggested to the pilot that he could stay at Gorge River for the night. The flight back down the coast was just a few minutes, but by now it was dark, the pilot's mate had just been killed, and they couldn't see out the front of the helicopter due to oil on the windscreen. They flew sideways along the beach with Dad trying to point out 'the Steeples' – two 30-metre-high rocks that stick up out of the beach one kilometre north of Gorge River. As they were struggling to find their way along the coast, another helicopter passed close above them flying in the opposite direction with a large spotlight that blinded them for a moment, disorienting them further. To this day, Dad remembers that as the worst helicopter flight of his life. The next morning, he and the pilot flew up to Haast together and that was the last time the pilot ever flew a helicopter.

After extensive testing of the cargo hook the accident was blamed on faulty equipment. Andy was another casualty of deer recovery, joining a list of about 70 young men who have died over the years chasing deer from helicopters.

From a very young age I was learning to respect the unforgiving nature of South Westland and Fiordland. There are two types of people in this area – those who can stay and survive, and those who leave or don't make it. I needed to learn to be a survivor.

Each year in March and April, hunters head into the New Zealand bush to chase stags during the roar (rutting season). Gorge River is a popular balloted block because of the DOC hut that the hunters can stay in. For us it was always an exciting time because it meant we would have neighbours for a few weeks and many of the hunters returned year after year.

The distant whine of an approaching helicopter in late March would signal the start of the roar and we would watch in excitement as the helicopter landed and Morgan Saxton jumped out to unload the hunters. The first party would usually be Brent and Paul from near Ōmarama. After hunting at Gorge River for many years, they knew the area very well and over the week they would usually shoot a couple of deer and take some pictures to take home. After that some hunters we didn't know would usually come for a week or two, and then Greg, Simon, Dave and Malcolm from Christchurch would arrive. They were the keenest hunters and each afternoon we would see them returning from up the river with the back ends of deer on top of their backpacks. Every second night we would go over to the DOC hut to find out how their hunting was going and it was from talking to them that I learned much of what I know about hunting deer. We even celebrated Dave's fiftieth birthday all together in the DOC hut one evening.

Usually by the last day they would be tired of hunting and we would all have a game of cricket on the airstrip – one of the highlights of my year. Finally, the helicopter would return and it would usually take at least two trips to fly them out with all their meat. Over the week, we would give them some pāua and crayfish and before they left they would leave us a couple of legs of venison, which in the cooler months of autumn we would hang in our meat safe for several weeks before making into stew. We would wave as the helicopter took off towards the north, knowing our friends would be back again for more hunting next year.

We also had a few TV crews visit us over the years to make documentaries about my family. Most of them arrived with their theme for the story already made up and would focus on small details of our life and exaggerate them. One such programme reported that I would 'hang out with possums' and another stated that 'Robin's only birthday gift was a jade dolphin' while showing a shot of her holding it. Neither of these statements could have been further from the truth, and it was in this way that we learned how manipulative the media can be. One particular presenter from Wānaka spent weeks filming at Gorge River. We opened up to him and helped him make what we thought was going to be a positive, in-depth, one-hour documentary. Without consulting us, he eventually turned the story 180 degrees to make us look like outcasts from society.

After these experiences as a child, I could never understand how people can believe what they see on TV and the internet as much as they do. I have always been very sceptical about any news, documentary and social media articles because I know how much a story can be distorted. It's best to never take something at face value. Do your own research, dig deeper and perhaps you will find a story closer to the truth.

The most genuine documentary about us was produced by a TV crew from Channel 5 in the UK and was presented by adventurer Ben

Fogle. The film crew flew out from London and spent a week with us in 2012. The storyline showed Ben hiking into Gorge River (which he actually did), and meeting my family to learn more about our lifestyle in the wild. He joined in our daily routine of living off the land and helped Dad to collect seafood for the dinner table. The programme was full of laughs and showed many of the hard facts of living in such a wild, isolated environment. Ben also connected with us on a deeper emotional level, which was evident in the documentary. National Geographic and BBC Earth eventually picked up the documentary and it has aired in at least 30 countries around the world, including India, Brazil, the Philippines and the US. It was so successful that the same crew returned in 2019 for a follow-up episode.

We have never contacted media outlets. They have always asked to visit us. Many never actually make it to Gorge River, but the film crews that do arrive make quite fun visitors. It's great to have people around for a few days and to show the world an example of how to live sustainably off the land. We have inspired countless people around the world to become more sustainable and over the years media exposure has steadily increased the value of Dad's artwork.

While I had much less social interaction than most youngsters, the people I did interact with came from all walks of life and from across the globe. This enriched my understanding of the world and helped me better appreciate the social encounters that I did experience.

CHAPTER 5

Walking Out to Town

Although we lived so far out in the wilderness, it didn't mean we couldn't visit the city. 'Going out to town', as we called it, was one of the highlights of the year. Every six months or so, Dad would have finished his latest batch of artwork and we would be ready for a change of scenery and a few more people to talk to. We would pack our bags and set off up the beach towards the Cascade Road end. Our first trip out would be in early May after the last roar hunters had left and Dad could fly his artwork out with Dave Saxton. Our second trip would align with the end of the whitebait season in early November because many of Dad's artwork commissions were from whitebaiters in Haast.

For Robin and me, hiking out to town was always fun but it must have been very hard work for Mum and Dad. The main reason for travelling that way was to avoid having to pay a few hundred dollars for an aircraft. But looking back now, completing this hike every six months also helped define who we were as a family and who I now am as an individual. How many other families hike 42 kilometres to get to the nearest road?

For two weeks before leaving we would prepare for the trip. Dad would be frantically finishing the last of his paintings and carvings before rolling them up and placing them in protective tubes made from drainpipe. He would carefully wrap his jade penguins and dolphins in velvet cloths and place them inside empty baked bean cans and add them to the bag to send out with Sax.

Like Dad, I would be working on carvings and would also wrap them in velvet for the journey ahead before placing them in a shoulder bag with dolphins on the outside that Mum had made me. All of our belongings would go inside large plastic milk-powder bags that we'd turned into pack liners, which in turn would go inside our homemade backpacks. On our twelfth birthdays Robin and I received new hiking backpacks but before that we used homemade rucksacks that Dad fashioned out of white or green canvas. He had the same.

Every day at 12.30 we would gather around the transistor radio and listen intently to the five-day weather forecast. We always needed at least three days of good weather in a row – one day for the rivers to drop after the previous rain, and two days to hike to Barn Bay. Sometimes in South Westland it can rain for weeks on end and we would have to wait for a fine spell. When one was on the way we would frantically finish all the chores that hadn't yet been done. On the final evening Robin and I would tally up the firewood and seaweed bags we had carried in the previous six months and work out how much pocket money we would have for the upcoming trip. If we had been busy, we could have between $50 and $70 to spend. I would make a list of everything I needed to take in my backpack in a small blue notebook and would double-check I had it all, ready for the big day to come.

The next morning, I would lie in bed trembling with excitement. Mum and Dad would finish cleaning the house and I would help Mum to bleach the floor under the kitchen table and nail closed the windows. Mum would boil a dozen eggs to eat along the way, along with boiled potatoes, carrots, beetroot and anything else that we might have in the garden. She would have a full loaf of freshly baked bread and Dad would pick some fresh watercress and turnip leaves from the garden. All this would go in the backpacks and we would usually step out of the door just after midday. That way we could listen to the forecast one last time before setting off.

We would cross the Gorge River in our aluminium dinghy and start hiking along the bouldery coastline to the north. First, we would walk along Hungry Beach, where giant waves crashed against huge piles of rolling rocks, tearing at them as if trying to pull us back into the ocean. We'd pass the Steeples, Bivvy Rock, Cutter Rocks and the sheltered bays of Browns Refuge.

It was a big challenge when Robin was born, and suddenly I had to walk the entire coastline on my own two feet. I was only three and a half but I embraced the challenge with extreme excitement. I would walk along counting flax stalks (some years there are literally millions of them) and invariably lose count and have to start again. Such was my enthusiasm for counting flax stalks or Fiordland crested penguins that I didn't always have time to look at the ground in front of me. Mum would be walking beside me with her huge backpack, guiding my feet in the right direction over the rough terrain. By the time Robin was three and a half she had already seen her big brother walking and she refused to be carried any more.

With his long legs and fast steps, Dad would always end up way ahead. He would choose good resting places to stop, and, as he waited for us, he would hide lollies under pāua shells, behind rocks or up trees. Once we caught up, he would tell us a little story. 'The last tramper said he left some lollies somewhere around here. It could be worth a look.' Sure enough, after a minute or two Robin and I would have found the lollies and we would sit down to enjoy them as well as a boiled egg on Mum's homemade bread and some sultanas and peanuts mixed in an old recycled bread bag. After recovering for 15 minutes or half an hour, we would be ready to continue walking. Dad would tell Robin she could have an ice cream when we got to Haast and she would be pulling at his arm trying to get him up and walking faster. 'Dad – we have to go!' Poor Dad would be carrying 20 to 30 kilograms in his backpack and probably needed the rest. On the sandy sections of Browns Refuge I would copy Mum and Dad and walk barefoot, feeling the cool, soft sand between my toes.

Dad showed us a layer of what looked like black clay in an eroding bank at the top of the beach partway along Browns Refuge. Looking closely, you could see it was actually charcoal, which along with a few broken fire rocks indicated this could have been a small Māori campsite before Europeans came to New Zealand. Unlike the iwi (tribes) in other parts of the country, those in South Westland were peaceful. They would collect jade to make into tools that could be traded with iwi elsewhere. Dad once found a buried cache of Māori adze blanks as he was extending the garden. He has also shown me many midden sites along the coastline and I have even discovered a couple myself. The easiest thing to search for is that distinct layer of charcoal in rock layers that have been eroded by the river or sea.

After about eight kilometres we would arrive at the Spoon River, our home for the night. Provided it hadn't been raining that morning, we could easily cross the Spoon and I would hold on tightly to Dad's hand as we waded through the freezing-cold, knee-deep water tumbling out of the forest over a bed of slippery, ankle-twisting boulders. We would cross very slowly, as we could not afford an accident.

On each side of the river we had a tent and emergency food stash hidden under flax bushes and we would use the last of the evening light to set up camp. Mum would cut more slices of bread and butter it with her Swiss Army knife, and we would peel more boiled eggs. Every sandfly in the area would come for a visit and Dad would apply another layer of his homemade repellent, a mix of Dettol and baby oil. I never used repellent and instead would slap at the sandflies biting my hands until it was time for bed. We would fall asleep to the sound of crashing waves and rustling flax bushes blowing in the light katabatic winds.

One time, when I was five, we woke at the Spoon River to the pitter-patter of rain on the tent fly. One look outside confirmed my parents' worst fears – the rain would make the Hope River at Barn Bay impassable. All our food for the tramp was carefully calculated and we didn't have much to spare. That's why the weather forecast was so important. This time it had been quite wrong and we had no option but to stay an extra night at the Spoon.

Mum was breastfeeding Robin and to conserve energy she lay in bed for most of the day. I was growing fast and needed to eat, so I was given most of the food and Dad ate just a little. In the evening he managed to find some small mussels along the coastline and we cooked them in Mum's large tin cup. Mum was so hungry she even drank the water the mussels were cooked in.

The next morning, we woke to the same pitter-patter on the tent. Mum and Dad were now very concerned. However, as Mum opened the tent door, she realised with relief that we had been fooled. This time the noise was being caused by thousands of sandflies buzzing between the tent and the fly, and the sky was actually completely blue.

From the Spoon River we'd hike for about two hours along football-sized boulders to Sandrock Bluff. This part is quite rough going and the boulders roll under your feet at each step. It's easy to twist your ankle and you have to be really careful not to fall. One time as we hiked this section of coastline, we found the remains of a southern right whale. The bones were washed up along the beach over several kilometres and Dad collected bits of jawbone for carving. Further north we found a section of vertebrae still stuck together with oozing, stinky flesh. It had a diameter of almost a metre – that whale must have been the size of a bus.

It's possible to pass around the bottom of Sandrock Bluff with low tide and a calm sea, but if you get the timing wrong the waves will drag you in. Therefore, we always took the safe route over the top on an old bulldozer track cut in 1970 by a mining company on its way to Big Bay. It's overgrown with supplejack, ponga ferns and fallen tutu trees but Dad has kept the route marked with red-and-white-striped tape for trampers to follow.

There's a sunny clearing at the top of the bluff with lots of fluffy toetoe and this was always the best place for lunch. From here, through a gap in the trees, you can see back down the coast to Awarua Point in the distance. We are the only inhabitants of that 20-kilometre stretch of coastline and it's our home. But as we look north the feeling is different: we are now entering someone else's area, even though the chances of actually seeing anybody are still low. The section of coastline between Sandrock Bluff and Barn Bay is the roughest, with boulders as large as chairs or tables. It's vital to keep a stable footing, as well as a close lookout for fur seals or Fiordland crested penguins.

One of my biggest fears as a kid was seals. Generally, they see you approaching and will bumble their way down to the water before disappearing under a crashing wave. But there have been isolated instances when they have knocked over people caught between them and the ocean. Consequently, I would spend more time looking ahead than at my feet and if I saw a seal I would freeze or stick close to Dad until it was safely swimming in the sea. Eventually, as I grew up, my fear changed to curiosity.

At Little Cascade Bay there are two waterfalls tumbling off the steep limestone cliffs. We would stop at the creek for a drink and rest for a little while. On a rough day along this stretch the ten-metre-high waves thunder into the steep bouldery beach with the sound of an approaching steam train. As they hit the first rocks, towers of spray shoot into the air like projectiles, before being dissipated by the strong southerly wind. I have never seen a totally calm day on this section of coastline – there always seems to be at least a few metres of swell.

As you approach Barn Bay, the Barn Islands come into view. This commanding set of rocks stands a kilometre offshore and their vertical cliffs rise 30 metres up out of the turbulent water. Waves crash against them with the full force of the Southern Ocean and bold crayfishermen set their pots as close as possible to the 'Widow Makers', a set of three smaller islands to the west, in the hope of catching a few extra spiny rock lobsters. One mistake fishing in these waters can be fatal.

When the islands are directly offshore the Barn Bay airstrip is visible across the last obstacle of the day, the Hope River. Here, Dad would wait for the rest of us to catch up and then we would discuss the plan for crossing. 'We can cross here,' he'd say, 'between the large rock and gravel bar, just up from the fast water, staying up where the water is deeper and the current is slower.' He led the way, standing upstream to the current. I would hold on to him tightly and Mum would hold on to me. Robin would be in Dad's backpack, watching from a safe height. Slowly and carefully, we would enter the icy, thigh-deep water, with me cringing as it neared my waist. The Hope is usually not too hard to cross but was still pretty scary for a child.

Tucked away on the edge of the forest and next to a short grass airstrip is Lou Brown's former house. Lou was a lumberjack from

Canada who moved to Barn Bay in the early 1970s to catch crayfish. He built the two-storey house out of chainsaw-milled timber cut from logs in the riverbed after his first house was washed away in a flood in 1983. A few weeks before each trek out, Dad would walk to Barn Bay with some food to leave at the house for our stay. This way, if the weather was unfavourable, we could stay a few extra days there to recuperate before covering the rest of the distance out to the Cascade.

My favourite thing at that house was to sit upstairs under the ten-centimetre-thick matai beams and stare at the ocean beyond the flax bushes. From there I could see the passing Jackson Bay fishing boats as they worked their craypots around the Barn Islands. Further to the north the rolling swells would crash up on the Sugar Loaf, a huge protruding rock that sits just off the reef at the north end of the two-kilometre-long, crescent-shaped beach that forms Barn Bay.

Between 1972 and 1992, Lou and, later, his wife, Elizabeth, lived here with their five children. He operated a small crayfishing boat between Cascade River and Longridge Point each day and Dad sometimes used to crew for him. They were our closest neighbours and sadly they left when I was one. In the cupboards were games and toys the Browns had left behind, and Robin and I would be wild with excitement as we explored the house's nooks and crannies.

Since the Browns left, the house has been occupied off and on over the years, but few people have stayed very long. For six months once, a couple from the North Island, Hobo and Missy, lived there and we stayed with them a couple of times. They had egg-laying chickens that fossicked around in the abandoned garden during the daytime. Hobo, whose nickname was inspired by his long beard and holey clothes, once had an old sheep hanging in the workshop and as he served the mutton chops he asked, 'Does anyone want some moa bones?' Missy showed us a secret cupboard under the stairs that we had never found and we spent many rainy days playing chess, backgammon and cribbage and running around with stuffed toys.

There was a VHF radio in one of the bedrooms and Dad would listen to the marine forecast each day, looking for another good spell of weather to cross the Cascade River. Robin and I would make such a mess of the house that, when it was time to leave, Mum and Dad had to spend hours packing away all the toys and cleaning up. It would be midday by the time we could start off again on the short walk inland along the Hope River to the next hut.

The Hope Hut (or Ken's Hut, as it was called) was built by Ken Landaus as a base for his goldmining exploits in the Hope River. He never found much gold and the hut has been empty for many years. It's surrounded by majestic rimu and kahikatea that stand proud above the tangled jungle of supplejack and kiekie. After six months of living next to the crashing ocean, our first night of dead silence in the Hope Hut was always really strange. The hut is surrounded by swamp and as the evening draws in the local mosquitoes emerge from its dark corners in search of fresh blood.

Mum would cook us a dinner of rice with lentils on the old pot-belly stove in the centre of the hut, or if we were lucky we might have a tin of baked beans. If Robin's portion was larger than mine, I would be quite upset, so Mum would carefully share the beans equally between our bowls. I would lie awake at night in my cosy sleeping bag listening to the whine of mosquitoes while somewhere near the back of the hut a mouse might be chewing its way into a cupboard. A twig cracking in the deafening silence outside had to be a passing deer, I would think to myself before drifting off into a deep sleep.

For a few years in the early 2000s, Lou Brown's house changed ownership and was locked. We didn't have a key, so we would stay a few days in the Hope Hut to break our journey instead. It's a simple hut, so when it was time to leave we could pack and clean in an hour. Mum would walk ahead with Robin and me, while Dad tidied the hut then caught us up further down the trail.

Between Barn Bay and the Cascade the track follows a rough four-wheel-drive track that weaves its way through the forest. Rimu, kahikatea and tōtara tower above a thick carpet of crown ferns on the forest floor. Ponga ferns drape their fronds over the trail like curtains, sending a shower of little water droplets onto anyone walking past. One feels very small traversing this section of wild jungle.

Every few kilometres the track emerges from the forest into beautiful grassy clearings, where we would often spook deer feeding along the bush edge. After an hour and a half walking through many deep, icy mud puddles we would stop in a sunny clearing next to Robinson Creek for a second breakfast. At Dee Creek, another two hours down the track, we would eat the last of Mum's bread for lunch with the last boiled eggs before pushing on towards the Cascade. Finally, we'd emerge from the forest for one last time, onto a cattle farm owned by South Westland legend Maurice Nolan – the first sign of civilisation.

With my parents at the end of the airstrip at Gorge River, in 1992

Taking a bath in a 20-litre bucket, using water heated by the wetback in the wood fire

Mum chopping up mung bean sprouts for me in Haast when I was one year old

Checking my whitebait net in front of Dad's set-up, near the bluff at low tide, when I was three or four

When gold-panning with Dad at the bluff, I would use a piece of crayfish steel to move the limestone rocks aside.

Stopping for lunch in a sunny spot on Sandrock Bluff during a walk out to town, aged four

Fishing in the river mouth with my first fishing rod – and a lure with no hook

Ready for take-off in my driftwood helicopter. Mum is off to collect firewood from the beach with Robin in her backpack.

Robin (in the doorway) and me at left, eating ice creams with our cousins Madeleine, Kevin and Edward, with Uncle Darrell in the background, at Bethells Beach near Auckland, 1996

Robin, Mum, me and Dad standing in front of our house as we say goodbye to a visitor

Emerging from our tent at the Spoon River on a sunny morning, after the first night of the walk north to town, 1996

Robin, Mum, Dad and me at the Mitchells' house at Big Bay, at the start of the walk to the Hollyford Road end, 1998

Robin and me in our vegetable garden, helping Mum with the digging

Celebrating my seventh birthday with a cake baked by Mum in our camp oven

Aged eight, dressed in my favourite pyjamas, which Mum had stitched on her hand-wound sewing machine

In the garden in 1999, with Mum and Robin, holding the biggest crayfish I had ever seen

Proudly showing my latest painting to Sue Todd in Arrowtown

A family portrait taken when I was eight, in our house at Gorge River

The second time we ever saw snow at Gorge River – Robin and me, with our 'snow penguin'

A small kahawai caught in Dad's fishing net in the river estuary

Dressed in my Black Cap uniform and cricket gear on the airstrip

Robin, Fern, Cam, Lochie and me at Browns Refuge, during our friends' first visit to Gorge River, in 2001

Proudly displaying my pumpkin crop for the year, aged 13

Celebrating my fourteenth birthday with Chooky, our bantam hen

Boulder-hopping with Robin near Barn Bay, on our way out to town

Sitting above the river on my driftwood whitebait stand with Robin

Robin helping me to empty about a cupful of whitebait from my net

Building my whitebait net at age 15

Staying warm inside my waders as I check my homemade sock net. Prior to receiving those waders, I would simply roll up my pants and wade out into the freezing-cold river.

Rowing across the river in our aluminium dinghy to pick up some trampers

Celebrating Dave Hill's birthday in the DOC hut with, left to right, Malcolm, Simon, Dave (with cake), unknown (in red cap), Greg, unknown (at back), me, Robin, Dad and Mum

Hanging my possum skins on the deer fence to dry in the sun, in preparation for sending them to the tannery

Finishing off the first batch of possum-fur pillows I sewed by hand, aged 16

Me, Robin (with Chooky), Mum and Dad at home shortly before I left to attend school in Wānaka

Whitebaiting at the Big Bay river mouth with Aussie Bob (centre) and Barry Gollan (right)

We'd make ourselves at home here in a small corrugated-iron musterers' hut that still stands in the middle of the swampy river flats. Mum would cook the last of our rice on the hut's huge stone open fireplace, combining it with fresh watercress from a nearby creek and some alfalfa sprouts we always carried. The Cascade Valley can be wickedly cold in winter and we would often wake to find our boots and socks frozen by the front door. After a quick breakfast we'd finish packing and head back onto the trail that meanders its way across the farmland towards the river. A pair of paradise ducks might quack or a pūkeko squawk as it flew across the top of the long dewy grasses before disappearing out of sight back into a swamp.

In about an hour we'd arrive at the southern bank of the mighty Cascade. This is the largest river in the area and is the obstacle that separates our part of South Westland from civilisation proper. It was this river crossing that kept Dad awake for many a night, planning how he would get his family safely across to the other side. I would stare in awe at the crystal-clear blue water swirling around logs and over swiftly flowing rapids. We would walk up the riverbank in search of a safe place to cross, such as where the river flows over a wide gravel bar just above a tumbling rapid. There the water would be about waist-deep and the current slow enough to fight against. Often the best crossing would be marked by some farm vehicle tracks, but we could never rely on that.

Once Dad had selected a suitable place we would prepare for the crossing. He would put Robin in his backpack and he and Mum would prepare to cross first, leaving me alone on the south side of the river. Before setting off, Mum would give me strict instructions on what to do if the river swept them away. 'You go back to the hut we slept at last night and stay there until someone finds you.' Those words would send a chill down my spine and I would watch intently as they waded cautiously into the icy-cold, swift-flowing water, their feet making a small splash with each step.

Metre by metre, they would fight their way through the current, going deeper and deeper until the bottoms of their backpacks were almost touching the water. In the deepest section they would be pushed hard downstream by the current. Then the water would start to get shallower and shallower until finally they would emerge safely on the far riverbank almost 100 metres away.

Dad would then make a swift return and hoist me onto his back. From there I watched his every move as he negotiated the river for a third time. In the middle it seemed like we were surrounded by a constantly swirling mass of water and looking down I could clearly make out the grey, blue, brown and green stones on the riverbed below Dad's steady feet. We would all breathe a huge sigh of relief once we had safely crossed.

When I turned eight, Mum and Dad decided I was old enough to ford the river on my own and we could all cross together. I would wade while firmly supported between Dad upstream, with Robin in his backpack, and Mum downstream. Quite often, as we got older, we might bump into Maurice and he would give us a ride across the river in his red Toyota Hilux. Mum and Dad would carry a lifejacket for each of us to keep us extra safe on those occasions.

Once we were on the north side of the river, all the stress of weather and rain was forgotten as we followed the last part of the trail across another farmer's paddocks to a farmhouse at the beginning of the Cascade Road. From here, there is still another 20 kilometres of gravel before you get to the sealed road at the

Arawhata River, and there was no transport. We had to hope there would be someone in the Cascade who could give us a ride out to Haast, otherwise we would have one more day to walk. Maurice lived in Haast and if he was in the Cascade he would most likely give us a ride on his return home in the evening. His generosity has been incredible over the years and Dad has repaid the favour with paintings and jade carvings.

When I was a young child, just arriving at the Cascade was quite overwhelming. Once, before I was three, Dad was carrying me through Maurice's farm and I saw cows for the first time. I was very excited and whenever I spotted another one would announce it by exclaiming 'Cow!' Later that day we arrived at the road end and in the distance I saw a car approaching. 'Cow!' I exclaimed excitedly from the top of the backpack.

After reaching Haast we would settle into a friend's whitebaiting bach that we rented in the small township of Ōkuru, just a few kilometres south of the Haast shop and post office. This was empty most of the year and was a convenient base. Robin would be getting very excited and would ask, 'When can we get an ice cream?' After five days' walking she was ready for her reward! The next morning, we would put on our empty backpacks and hitchhike up the road towards the shop. We always got picked up by some of the Haast locals and it was a good way to catch up with people. At the shop, Robin and I would run inside to the ice-cream fridge and debate what flavour we wanted. After selecting our treat, we would leave it in the fridge while we helped Mum and Dad choose some food for our stay.

We'd explore up and down the aisles, picking items from the selection of fresh fruit, packets of biscuits, fluffy white bread, breakfast cereals, tinned sardines and other food items that we hadn't seen for six months. From the freezers we would choose a packet of saveloys, some beef and pork sausages and maybe a packet of mince, with a bottle of tomato sauce to go with them. Mum and Dad never wanted to buy things like Cheezels, chips or Coca-Cola, and we grew up mostly without junk food. I felt like I was missing out, especially when other kids were eating it, but I learned to accept my parents' rule, and now looking back I really appreciate their persistence on the matter.

From the food shop we would run around to the garage next door, which housed the Haast post office. They sold fishing equipment and I would stare at the brand-new whitebait nets hanging on the walls, imagining how much I could catch if they were mine. On one wall was a large selection of fishing lures and I would carefully pick out four or five to buy with my pocket money. My favourite lure was a large silver wedge that was perfect for catching kahawai in the river mouth at home. I would take my choices up to the counter and carefully count out the notes and coins from my home-stitched wallet. Michelle Manera would hand over the mail to Mum and they would have a quick catch-up. The population of Haast is only about 250, so everyone knows everyone. Usually someone at the garage would be driving south and we would catch a ride back to the bach for the night.

My family has a close relationship with the local hapū (subtribe), the Makaawhio, and we often visited local kuia (elder) Helen Rasmussen and her husband, Ian. They lived just down the road from where we stayed in Ōkuru and would always invite us over for dinner. From them I learned that the Māori name for Gorge River is Huruhuru Manu, which translates to 'He who sees from afar' and probably derives from the tall hills behind our house. Sometimes Helen's granddaughter Niki Lee would be there and we would play in the treehouse near their home, where we might be joined by Rob McDonald from next door.

The most exciting part of our stay in Haast was going to the local primary school. Mum knew the teachers and after a couple of phone calls she would organise for Robin and me to join the classes for a few days. We would catch the school bus the next morning and Mum would come along to keep an eye on us since we were visitors at the school. Haast School had two teachers and I would usually be with the older kids while Robin was with the younger ones. I always found it quite overwhelming stepping into the class with a dozen other kids on the first morning. Everyone would be staring at me, the new kid, and the teacher would introduce me and assign me a desk.

The first playtime and lunch hour could be a bit awkward, but usually someone like Ryan McConchie, Nicole Buchanan or Georgia McInroe would invite me to join a dodgeball game or field cricket and I would quickly reconnect with all the friends I had made on my previous visits. It was fun to have lessons from someone other than Mum, and the teacher might be reading an exciting book or showing a movie. In the afternoon we would learn the words to a new song such as 'Six Months in a Leaky Boat' or 'Nature'. Towards the end of primary school much of the kids' chatter would be about what boarding school they would attend for high school. Everyone would ask me and I would awkwardly explain that I would continue to do home schooling. I never understood why everyone in Haast was so excited about going to boarding school. I couldn't think of anything worse than having to leave home when I turned 12 to live somewhere like Dunedin or Ōamaru.

While in Haast, we would visit some of the people who had ordered Dad's artwork. As Dad showed them his paintings and carvings, I would sit alongside and pull out mine. I gave my paintings or carvings away – usually to people who had bought a piece off Dad. One day, when I was four, we were at Sax's place and Dad was showing his artwork to a guy from Hokitika while I was showing his partner my paintings in the next room. She offered to buy one of my Milford paintings and gave me some money for it. I didn't really know exactly what had happened until afterwards when I told Dad about it. He asked what number was on the money and I replied 'a 20'. Dad was curious whether it was a coin or paper and sure enough it was a $20 note! That was a proud moment for me (and my parents) and in the years that followed I sold many pieces of artwork. Eventually my parents opened a Kiwibank account for me in Wānaka to deposit my money into and that was the start of my savings.

After saying goodbye to our friends in Haast we would board a bus and head over the hill to Wānaka. There we would stay with family friends Andy Woods and Mylrea Bell and their two kids, Finlay and Lachlan. Another bus ride would take us to Queenstown to stay with Ian and Sue Todd and their kids, Willy and Casey, on their farm near Arrowtown. They treated us like family and we would help collect the eggs from their hundred chickens and feed the ducks bread at the pond. Each day we would go into Queenstown and search for all the items on our shopping lists.

At Paper Plus we would get paper, pens and pencils and at Whitcoulls Dad would buy oil paints and brushes for his artwork and I would buy my brushes and acrylic paint. At Mitre 10 we bought any hardware items we might need, such as nails, screws, screwdrivers, a shovel and vegetable seeds for our next season of gardening. Finally, we would end up at New World, where we would fill two huge shopping trolleys with staple foods and other items that we wouldn't usually ask Roger to find for us. Into the trolley would go butter, sugar, eggs, flour, sultanas, potatoes, rice, peanuts, beans, lentils, oats, butter and cooking oil, while for treats we'd get custard powder, some apples and bananas, jelly crystals, cocoa and a packet of sausages for our first night at home. Much of this would stay in Roger's hangar to come in on future flights.

After the five-day walk out and three to four weeks in unfamiliar environments, Robin and I would be worn out. We never ever got sick at home but out in town the latest cold and flu would always catch up with us. It would start with a sore throat one evening and turn into a couple of days in bed with a blocked nose and vomiting. It happened every trip out and eventually Mum started giving us multivitamins to boost our immune systems. These helped a little but we just had to get used to spending a few days of every trip under the weather.

Every second or third Christmas it would be time to visit family, and rather than go straight home from Queenstown we would continue on the bus to Dunedin to stay with our cousins Elena and Kevin, Auntie Alison and her husband, Darrell. From there we would board a plane to Auckland to stay with Mum's mother and brother Andrew and his kids, Edward, Maddy and Leo, or to Brisbane to see Dad's parents. Jet planes were so exciting and I remember one flight from Dunedin to Brisbane on Freedom Air flew straight over our house at Gorge River. Peering through the windows, we could see all the way north along the coast to the Cascade and south towards Milford Sound, but we couldn't see our home directly beneath our seats.

Brisbane was quite overwhelming and I never felt comfortable there. Luckily, we would only pass through the city in Nana and Grandad's car on our way from the airport to their home in a canal estate in Mooloolaba on the Sunshine Coast. Nana was always super excited to see her grandchildren and would serve tea for everyone on the screened-in porch overlooking their swimming pool and the estuary beyond. Grandad would tell us stories from their six around-the-world trips and I would listen in awe as he told of their experiences in foreign cities such as Istanbul, Berlin, New York and Tokyo. One of his most interesting stories was of their trip into East Germany via Checkpoint Charlie in the centre of Berlin. One of the guards took a disliking to him because of someone he had been seen talking to in East Germany and punched out his front teeth. 'That's why I have false teeth today,' he would say with a hearty chuckle, showing us a full row of false teeth top and bottom. Afterwards Dad would show me the places Grandad had talked about in a huge atlas. I'd turn the pages in fascination, dreaming about the day when I would travel to these far-off lands myself.

Nana was very family oriented and missed her family very much. Therefore, everyone would come together at Nana and Grandad's house for a few days over Christmas and it was super exciting to see them all. There would be Dad's sisters, Sue and Annette, and my cousins Jamie, Jurjen, Catherine and Jonnie from

Darwin and Cairns, and Guy and Sue Waterman would drive up from Brisbane with Nicholas, James and Fraser (the sons of Dad's other sister, Vivienne, who had died) and extended cousins Eve and Tom. All the cousins were a little bit older than me but I did my best to keep up. We would go with Grandad in the early morning and walk along the sandy yellow beach. The sand squeaked under our bare feet with each step and small waves dropped little sponges and shells on the shoreline with a splash.

Grandad would drive us to the Kawana shopping mall where I'd be mesmerised by huge department stores like Big W and Target, with their endless shelves of products. Then we would stop at Crazy Clark's where everything cost $2 and was complete junk, before getting doughnuts at a small corner stall. The cousins would head away to get McDonald's but Robin and I would stay with Grandad because we never bought fast food. I was allowed to buy lollies with my pocket money if I liked and my favourite type was the soft banana lollies from the shop at the end of Grandad's street. I carefully set aside a few dollars for lollies but knew if I spent too much then I wouldn't have any left to deposit into my savings account at the end of our trip. In the afternoon we would walk down to the video store and rent a movie to watch. My favourite was *Blue Fin*, about a boy on a tuna-fishing boat in South Australia. Eventually it would be time to hug Nana and Grandad goodbye at Brisbane Airport and head home to Gorge River.

At Roger's hangar we would sort through everything we had collected, taking only the most essential items with us on the flight. We were good at going without, and the rest of our gear could wait until the next supply drop in six weeks' time. I would make sure half of my new fishing lures went with us though.

Roger would stuff everything in the back of the plane, filling all available space with our items. 'Heavy things further forward and light things at the back,' he'd say with a grin. Dad would squeeze into the co-pilot's seat and the rest of us would pile into the back. After Roger had checked in with the Queenstown control tower, we would bounce our way down the airstrip, gathering speed before rising up and over Lake Hayes. Our time out in the big city was over and Roger's trusty yellow plane would transport us safely back home. I was never sad to leave – town was very exciting but I loved my life at Gorge River as well.

CHAPTER 6

Making Do

When I was very young my parents' yearly income was just a couple of thousand dollars. For most people with young kids, that's basically nothing. But by being extremely frugal and using the resources around them they were able to not only live on that tiny income but were even able to deposit half of it into a savings account each year for our family's future. Robin and I grew up with that income being normal to us. Compare this to how most children watch their parents spending money in all different directions. Many modern families are heavily in debt, living in a big house and driving a shiny car that are actually owned by the bank. By stepping out of normal society my parents found a way to avoid debt completely.

A lifestyle in the wilderness is now looked upon by many as 'the dream' but when Mum and Dad chose this path they went to somewhere no one else wanted to be. In the 1980s, moving to an abandoned cabin in the middle of the wildest corner of New

Zealand seemed like the most absurd decision one could make. Back then, the thought of living sustainably and having a lower impact on the planet was not on people's minds. 'Why not use resources?' those in the consumer-driven society would ask. 'They are there for everyone and they are unlimited.'

By stepping out of the modern financial system Mum and Dad were able to find their own freedom. Other people would work in a job they didn't like for an hour to earn $20 to buy a fish caught in a foreign country to cook for their family using an expensive oven powered by coal-fired energy. Using his skills learned by trial and error in the wilderness, Dad would simply go and catch the fish and Mum would cook it for dinner on our homemade wood stove. Rather than buy vegetables and fruit that might travel by truck and plane over hundreds or thousands of kilometres, we would just grow the vegetables in the garden and eat them freshly picked. We ate with the seasons and at various times of the year would go without different things. That's how nature works and this approach to food is much more sustainable.

Easy ways to save money include reusing things as many times as possible and fixing things that others have discarded. For example, our home is a house that was abandoned and we have always repaired it with recycled materials. Because Gorge River is such a wet environment we are constantly battling against rot and huhu grubs eating away at the lower half of the walls, and every ten to twenty years most parts have to be replaced. When I was young, we would search the beaches after a storm for planks of wood and store them in a huge old walk-in freezer belonging to the original owner, which we used as a shed. Every few years we would have enough wood to creatively rebuild another section of the house. I started practising hammering nails when I was one year old, and by the time I was two Mum would hold the nails for me as I hammered, trusting that I wouldn't hit her fingers. By the time I was three, Dad would lay the planks of wood down for the new floor and drill holes where he wanted the nails. I would follow along excitedly nailing them down with old straightened-out nails salvaged from the original rotten section of the house.

The roof of the house was constructed from offcuts of iron collected from friends' building projects and the renovation of the DOC hut. When the builders replaced its roof, Dad asked if he could have a look through the old roofing iron and 90 per cent of it was still usable. Dad can fix or build anything. Sometimes he will take three broken electric motors and after a few hours' fiddling and a few swear words here and there he will have reconstructed one working motor. After we bought our first solar panel in 1998, I remember helping Dad remove a 12-volt windscreen-wiper motor from an old car on Ian Todd's farm outside Arrowtown. He mounted it on a block of wood and jerry-built an attachment for a small diamond-saw blade. This was his first electric motor for carving jade. Once, while Dad was fixing his greenstone carving motor, I was reconstructing a smaller motor that I'd salvaged from a broken cassette player. I attached it to a tiny cooling fan using a rubber band as a mini fan belt and it was driven by a solar panel the size of a small plate that I had purchased from Dick Smith's with my pocket money. On a sunny day I would use this little set-up to wear away at a piece of wood on the beach, pretending I was cutting jade just like Dad.

Although I copied Dad the most, I would follow Mum sometimes too, and she was just as clever. With her hand-wound sewing machine, built by bolting a hand winder onto the side of a normal sewing machine, she could make and fix anything. We never bought brand-new clothes from a store – instead Mum would buy wholesale cloth from Spotlight and stitch new clothes for us with the help of a pattern. She also scoured second-hand shops for clothes that still had plenty of life in them. Some looked as if they had barely been worn. She always made sure that we had some presentable clothes for our trip out to town, but while at home none of us cared what we looked like.

Two trampers from Switzerland, Engelbert and Beatrice, who tramped along the coastline many times over the years, loved Dad's artwork and often ordered a painting from him. Once it was finished, he would post it to their Swiss address in a plastic downpipe tube and a few months later the tube would return in the mail refilled with Toblerone chocolate, crystals to hang in our sunny front windows, and a new set of clothes each for Robin and me. Nana and Grandma would also send us gifts of clothes each birthday and Christmas, which Mum would put aside for our next trips out to town. When I tore holes in my clothes, which was very often, she would rummage through her bag of offcuts looking for a similar colour of fabric. I would sit next to her and turn the machine while she adeptly attached the patch. She even made us sleeping bags with recycled feathers from her old puffer jacket. Another time she made me a super-warm jacket with recycled down from a sleeping bag that Sue Todd had found in a second-hand shop. When Mum wasn't using her machine, Robin and I could use it whenever we wanted.

In 2000, we listened to the America's Cup commentary on the radio as Team New Zealand won the regatta in Auckland. Inspired, one rainy day I collected together some scraps of cloth and made them into sails. I nailed together two planks of wood and fashioned the hull of a one-metre-long yacht, copying what I had seen in a newspaper. Robin did the same and we sailed our homemade yachts up and down the river estuary at low tide. I would commentate on the race just as I had heard Peter Montgomery do on the radio.

I had many sketch pads and often in the evening I would sit and draw. Sometimes I would sketch different landscapes from around South Westland but I would also design things I wanted to build or greenstone carvings I wanted to make. Sometimes I could convince Mum to let that count as schoolwork. Dad was my technical drawing teacher and one time I drew plans for a wooden jewellery box. However, we didn't have any flat wood to make it from and the only thing I could find was a large chunk of Oregon wood of about 20 x 20 x 20 centimetres, which was an offcut from the main beam of our house.

After carefully measuring and calculating, I devised a plan and set out to cut the boards off the block of wood. After sawing away with Dad's semi-blunt hand saw for a couple of days, I finally had what I needed to make the box. I continued measuring, cutting, nailing and sanding until it had taken shape. Next time we were in town I searched in the hardware store for some small decorative hinges to attach the lid with. Then I applied several coats of varnish and glued a thin layer of velvet on the inside. I was very proud of my craftsmanship and showed my 'treasure chest' to all passing trampers. It held the jade carvings that Dad gave me for birthdays and trinkets given to me by other people, as well as my pride and joy, a small medical bottle containing a few grams of alluvial gold that I had panned from the Gorge River. I went gold-panning with Dad a couple of times a week when I was very young. After each session we would weigh our specks and nuggets using a length of wire with film canisters suspended from each end. We counted the number of standard beans in a 500-gram packet to use as a counterbalance and to make even finer measurements we measured grains of rice against the weight of the beans.

By becoming more self-sufficient Mum and Dad were able to reduce the amount of time they had to spend making money. And even when they were working for money, they were still around the house, so Robin and I could help them. Dad's paintings were then his main source of income. He would sit and paint in his corner of the living room, with his canvas stretched out on a piece of hardboard pulled from a wall and placed on a driftwood easel. To his right would be his paints and to his left a large assortment of brushes. When in need of inspiration he could stare out the living-room windows at the flaxes blowing in the wind, the ocean's crashing waves and the ever-changing sky above. Many people wonder why he chose to paint inside when surrounded by such beautiful South Westland scenery. The simple answer is 'sandflies': it's much smarter to sit behind the safety of a window! When Dad did paint outside, hundreds of sandflies would get stuck in the paint and add their own unique texture to the artwork.

From when I was very young, whenever Dad would paint, I would do the same. It wasn't long before he built me an artist's easel of my own, where I would place my homemade 'canvases' made by stretching calico onto a driftwood frame. Dad is an incredible artist and after many years of studying and absorbing the power of the wilderness he is able to re-create a perfect snapshot on the canvas. By watching his every move, I quickly picked up similar skills.

When I was 12, we spent seven weeks in Australia at Nana and Grandad's house and I started watching New Zealand and Australia playing cricket on TV. After that I became crazy about cricket and wanted to be a Black Cap when I got older. From then on, a lot of my enthusiasm was redirected to cricket from painting. I loved listening to matches on the radio and I discovered that by bouncing a ball off the side of the freezer shed I could practise batting by myself. Dad was bitterly disappointed that I stopped painting and I think it's the only thing he has never quite forgiven me for.

As mentioned, jade carving was Dad's other main source of income. Jade is found in rocks that occur naturally along the beaches of South Westland. There is a common misconception that it is easy to find there. Yes, there is jade between Jackson Bay and Big Bay, but even if you scour the beaches every day, it still takes years to find anything good. Another misconception is that it looks green when you find it; in reality, green jade is commonly hidden inside a thick, oxidised coating of pink or brown. I followed Dad keenly as he searched the shoreline for jade, stopping to wet each rock we thought looked promising. Sometimes the outside looks exactly the same as the surrounding boulders but a broken corner will give away the deep green colour hidden inside. Every few years, we would find a good-quality rock somewhere along the beach and would lug it home to cut. Often it would turn out to be lower quality than we'd hoped, scattered throughout with lots of black flecks.

One day Dad found an interesting-looking rock along the side of the airstrip, which had been exposed by erosion after a storm. It had a strange pearly white coating with one small window of green where the surface had been chipped away. We used this big, flat rock for a doorstep for many years until we finally got solar power. It was the perfect size to cut with the windscreen wiper motor and after a week of sunny days the diamond-saw blade cut through to the other side. The stone fell open to reveal a beautiful deep green colour that reminded me of the translucent green water of the Gorge River during a fine spell. To this day, that is the best-quality rock we have found. Dad has carved it into many necklaces and three-dimensional dolphins and penguins since.

In the years leading up to 1999 there was a rush to take jade from the last legal claim in South Westland, located at Big Bay. We watched as hundreds of tons of jade boulders were flown out under a Russian Sikorsky helicopter. Five tons at a time would go past, hanging under that helicopter, and sometimes it would fly right over the top of our house, which made Dad furious. One rock that had passed over us fell off the helicopter chain at Dee Creek and crashed into the forest. Eventually the commercial jade recovery stopped, but it didn't worry us. There is a rule that allows anyone to take jade from the beach as long as it can be carried to your mode of transport within 24 hours. We can just carry it home.

Although all the obvious jade boulders have been flown out of South Westland, some of the most disguised rocks remain. Dad has taught me how to identify the coatings of these rocks, and each time I walk the coastline from Gorge River to Big Bay I see quite a few. They range in size from 200 kilograms to several tons, heavily concealed by weathered pink or brown coatings half covered in lichen and moss. There are few people who could identify these boulders as jade, so they will likely stay untouched for many years to come. One piece weighing several hundred kilograms is sitting at the bottom of the Gorge River. I found it one day by accident when the water was very low in a part of the river where people never walk. It is hard to gauge its quality because of the swift-running water and it is often buried in gravel. Perhaps the next ice age will carry it down to the ocean.

One evening while fishing I tripped over a piece of jade weighing about five kilograms that had been polished by nature. Rocks like this are rare in New Zealand these days, so I polished it further with Dad's diamond sandpaper and it looked magnificent sitting in the sun beneath our windowsill: you could see right into the deep apple-green jade. A dairy farmer, Cliff King, who whitebaits at Big Bay and has commissioned more jade carvings from Dad than anyone else, bought that specimen off me for several thousand dollars as a collectors' piece.

Later I made friends with a Chinese girl called Anya when I was working in Guangzhou. Good-quality jade is worth a lot more in China than in New Zealand and is an integral part of society. A Chinese saying states that if you wear a piece of jade and are in an accident, the jade will take the impact and break, saving your life. Anya herself had once been hit by a car and the jade necklace she was wearing broke in half and she walked away unscathed. Everywhere I go, I wear a jade necklace I carved a few years ago. I have never had an accident, but who knows, maybe it will indeed save my life some day.

The garden was our most important source of food and it was crucial that we could grow enough vegetables each summer to keep us going most of the year. We weren't the only ones who liked to eat the vegetables, however, and we were constantly battling not only against the weather but also the other hungry inhabitants of Gorge River. Before I was born, rabbits were the main pest. Even though Dad was vegetarian at the time, he had to hunt the rabbits just so he could eat the vegetables he grew. It was either him or them.

When I was a child the helicopter hunters were shooting so many deer that it was quite rare to see one. After numerous hunter fatalities and a 1080 poison scare in some exported meat, the wild venison industry almost died out. Suddenly, deer numbers started exploding and it became common to see a deer or two out on the airstrip in the evenings. Slowly, the airstrip's long, wavy grass became shorter and shorter and we started to see evidence of chewing here and there in the garden. After one trip to Australia, we returned to find the garden had been almost flattened. Our entire crop of silver beet was gone and all that was left were the potatoes, carrots and beetroot under the ground. Was this going to be another 'them or us' situation, or could we find a compromise with the deer? Dad never wanted to shoot them so we didn't even have a rifle, but what if we could fence the garden?

A couple of kilometres up the beach, an old washed-up trawl net had been sitting for many years. Dad wondered if he could salvage some of the netting. After a few afternoons spent swearing at the sandflies, he managed to untangle enough netting to make a two-metre-high fence (because deer can jump pretty high) which reached two-thirds of the way around the garden. Some two kilometres up the river was a trap used by former resident Eion Wiley to catch deer. After Dad and I untangled a ten-metre section of this metal fence from the supplejack and ponga ferns we finally had enough fencing to go the whole way around the garden. Because there was no gate in the fence, in the daytime we would lift the netting up with wooden poles, then let it back down again at night.

Around the time we were building the fence, there was one young deer that became very friendly and we called her Flopsy, because of her big floppy ears. We would see her out on the airstrip in broad daylight and she wouldn't run away when she saw us. Since we were on conservation land with a penguin colony nearby, we never had a cat or a dog, but sometimes we would make friends with wild animals and those creatures were the closest things we had to real pets. There was a pair of paradise ducks that lived on the airstrip and after a few years we could get within a couple of metres of them.

One day I sneaked up within two metres of Flopsy before she noticed me and ran away. On another morning I opened the back door to find her about to enter the garden in broad daylight. We checked the garden and found the tops of all the potato plants had already been chewed. We had left the fence propped open all night! Dad realised he would have to finish the job and set out to build two solid gates that would close automatically. He cut some strong tōtara posts off logs on the beach with his hand saw and chose some shorter straight pieces for the swinging gate doors. After sawing, hammering and chiselling away for a couple of days, the gates were finished. The only parts that weren't fashioned from driftwood were the metal hinges and the straightened-out four-inch nails recycled from an old door in the house. A string tied to the top ran through a pulley hanging in a tree, and the weight of a small rock tied to the other end of the string pulled the gates shut after opening.

The whole time that Dad was working on the gates, Flopsy was observing from a safe distance. She was obviously trying to work out how she could get back inside the fence to Mum's juicy vegetables. The gates were one of Dad's Christmas presents to us that year and it meant he wouldn't have to find a way to kill Flopsy. From that day, we have lived on New Zealand's largest deer farm – except that on our farm all the deer stay on the outside of the fence, leaving our garden to thrive on the inside!

This worked for a couple of years but eventually another challenge appeared. This time it was in the shape of cute fluffy animals with long black tails. The possums had arrived. There is nothing possums love more than silver beet and the fence that kept the deer out so effectively was nothing more than a convenient jungle gym for the possums. Once again, it was a matter of them or us, and sadly with possums there is no option but to kill them. Dad bought our first dozen leg-hold traps and the war against the possums began. He found that if he set three of the traps on the rātā trees around the house and the others along the river and airstrip, he could keep the possums out of the garden. Each trap would receive a dash of flour and eucalyptus oil as a lure. Once stepped on, the trap catches the possum's foot and holds it until the next morning. Dad hated killing and each time he had to kill a possum it would ruin his day. Life in the wilderness can be like that sometimes, but the garden was critical to our existence.

Although trapping helped the problem, when we went away for a month or two we needed another solution. So, each time before going out to town, Mum would ask for help building cages to protect the most vulnerable crops. This was my least favourite job: I hated nailing the bits of driftwood together with rusty nails to make the frame for the cage. The old broken wire mesh would spike my hands as I tried to mend every possum-sized hole with string.

I was always very relieved once the cages were positioned over the silver beet and carrot beds.

While I helped Mum in the garden here and there, I was never as enthusiastic about it as I was about fishing. To me gardening always felt like a job. I argued that I played my part by carrying the possum carcasses back from our trap lines and digging the holes in which to bury them for fertiliser. And it was true this made a huge difference to the productivity of the garden, although it took us a while to realise just how much difference it made. Sometimes Mum's beetroot would be as large as a grapefruit on one side of the patch and smaller than a golf ball on the other and we were quite perplexed as to why. Then one day Colin Tuck and his wife, Raelene, stopped in their Hughes 500 for a cup of tea and everyone was busy discussing our life at Gorge River, their life in Fox Glacier, and the flight to Milford Sound. Mum had put together some pickled beetroot on crackers with cheese and when Raelene saw the size of Mum's beetroot she exclaimed, 'Wow, there must have been a big possum under this one!' Later we thought back to the previous winter and I remembered burying possums under only half of the patch. That solved the mystery of the huge beetroot and strengthened my argument for not doing the gardening. Every year I caught more and more possums and I think the most I buried in the garden in one year was about 500.

Although I didn't enjoy being told what to do, if it was my own project I would throw 110 per cent at it. Due to the cold, the abundant rainfall and the salt spray from the ocean, most vegetables don't grow at Gorge River, and by the age of ten I was getting tired of always having the same old potatoes, swede, parsnip and silver beet for dinner. I decided to try growing something different and began constructing my own greenhouse. I found some straight logs on the beach and nailed together a wooden frame, one metre by four metres by one metre high. When we next went out to town, I spent some of my pocket money on a five-metre length of plastic and some packets of zucchini, broccoli, cauliflower and cucumber seeds. To give the seeds a head start, I followed Mum's advice and planted them into cut-out plastic bottles filled with dirt and sat them inside the windows in the warmth of the living room.

When the seedlings were about three centimetres tall I planted them out in my new greenhouse and watered them carefully every couple of days. The broccoli and cauliflower grew slowly and in two years I managed to harvest only one nice-looking head that resembled the huge one in the picture on the seed packet. The zucchinis, however, turned out to be a big success and in the middle of summer I could pick three or four perfect-sized ones each day. Eventually we had so many that Mum didn't know what to do with them. She experimented with preserving them in vinegar and found pickled zucchinis made a delicious snack when put on her freshly baked bread or a salad. One that I left to continue growing turned into a one-metre-long marrow. Sadly, the environment at Gorge River proved too harsh for the cucumbers. The vine grew about 30 centimetres but produced just one cucumber the size of a carrot that tasted as bitter as lemon. I quickly gave up on them.

I liked picking vegetables from Mum's garden and my favourite task of all was to pick the peas off the vines. I would watch them grow through November and December and would have my eyes on the largest peapods. So did everyone else, so it was always a race to see who would get to them first. They would grow and grow until it looked like they were going to burst. Finally, one day I would pick one and pull the pod apart to examine the juicy green peas inside. Funnily enough, it was usually the smaller pods, not the fattest, that had the juiciest peas. Some years if it rained too much in the spring the pea flowers wouldn't be germinated by the bees. That summer we would look sadly at the empty vines, hoping for better luck next year.

One of our least reliable but much-loved sources of food was Chooky. A little bantam hen adopted from the Todds' small chicken farm outside Queenstown, Chooky was our first real pet that lived very long. (Previously we'd had two ducklings for a couple of weeks before a stoat killed them.) She did lay eggs every now and then, but that's not why we had her. She was part of the family and thought she was human. When we left to go to town, she would have to come with us, and she actually laid her first egg halfway to Barn Bay on the walk out. I had her sitting in an upside-down hat hanging off the front of my backpack and all of a sudden she jumped out with a big squawk and when I looked down there was a little cream-coloured egg sitting in the bottom of the hat!

When Robin turned 12, Mum bought her a new backpack. It was essential that it should be 'chicken friendly' and they searched quite a few shops before they found one with just the right pocket for Chooky to sit in when we went hiking. One time she joined us for a hike down the Hollyford River valley. This took us eight days from Gorge River to the Hollyford Road end, and along the way she stayed at the DOC huts with us. She met other trampers staying at the Martins Bay Lodge, then owned by Hollyford Valley Guided Walks. We spoke to a guy later who had been a client on that guided walk and apparently the lead guide, Bard, just couldn't stop talking about Chooky and her hike down the Hollyford. She had become a local legend.

When we went to Auckland or Australia, she couldn't join us, so we would send her out to Arrowtown to live at the Todds' house while we were away. Her favourite place to sit was outside on their windowsill and she would spend her six-weeks-or-so 'holiday' trying to find different ways to get inside their house.

Gorge River is a wild place for a chicken and over time she emerged as a true survivor. When she was two weeks old, she was attacked by a rat that chewed off a couple of toes, and when she was five months old she was lifted a metre off the ground by a New Zealand falcon – she managed to escape and spent the next month hiding in her nesting box or sitting under chairs. (My diary entry of 9/03/2004 goes like this: *A falcon dive bombed Chooky yesterday and she came inside and sat under the seat.*) Later in life she had a stoat hanging off her tail and the falcon even came back and had another go at her in the garden right in front of the house. After a long and dangerous existence dodging predators, she died of old age when she was six.

Besides the garden, our most important source of food was our fishing net. Dad used the same float and weight lines on this net for 30 years, but the thin netting didn't last so long. Every now and then it would catch on a boulder on the riverbed, tearing big holes in it. Eventually most of the fish were swimming straight through the holes and our catches were too small to feed us. Dad would try to make the net last as long as possible by tying the broken bits back together, but eventually the time would come for new netting. He would hang the net up between some trees and would set about stripping all of the old netting from the float and weight lines. Once that was done, he would carefully cut out a 15-metre section of brand-new netting and begin attaching it to the ropes using fishing twine and a netting needle.

Catching fish was such a vital part of our lifestyle that I had to be involved in the fun too. Dad made me a set of float and weight lines about four metres long and found an offcut of netting for me to use. He demonstrated how to load the fishing line onto the netting needle – over the top, around the bottom, twist and do the other side, backwards and forwards, faster and faster until the needle has a good length of line loaded. Then he showed me how to attach every third square of netting to the rope lines using a special type of clove hitch with an extra loop. I was pretty young, so he helped me a bit, and he probably did six metres for each one of mine. Eventually they were both finished. After that when Dad set his net in the river mouth, I would do the same. I even caught a few fish sometimes.

As the value of Dad's artwork increased, so did the value of our birthday and Christmas gifts. For Christmas, Robin and I would get things like a new body board for surfing the small waves in the river mouth, or a new mask and snorkel for swimming in the rock pools. Mum would try to find us gifts that could be part of home-school lessons and one year I was given Dick Smith's 'Fun Way into Electronics' kitset. This consisted of a range of electronic components with a plastic circuit board full of screw holes. By following the diagram in the workbook, I could make 20 simple electronic devices including a speaker, a beer-powered battery, a motion-detector light and a transistor radio (although we were far too isolated for it to pick up any stations). After constructing and reconstructing the different devices over and over again, I was able to design and make some others using the same components. This simple gift, combined with helping Dad wire up the 12-volt electrical system in the house, gave me a basic understanding of electricity and learning this way was so much fun that Mum never had to ask me to do it. When I was hands-on building something, I was always learning the most.

Thinking back now, that was probably the nearest I came to receiving an electronic gift from Mum and Dad until I was a teenager. The only other present that came close was a music cassette tape. We would always play tapes in the evening before dinner on our old car radio-cassette powered by solar panels, and our favourites included albums by Neil Young and Van Morrison, Gheorghe Zamfir's *The Lonely Shepherd* and the *Riverdance* soundtrack. The player sat on Dad's windowsill and was connected to some speakers salvaged from a transistor radio Dad had in the eighties. The first store-bought electronic gift I received was my own transistor radio, so I could listen to the cricket when I was a teenager. I was in a world far removed from the modern one, where kids would be getting PlayStations, desktop computers, Xboxes, cell phones, TVs and eventually iPhones.

By following my parents' every move through this part of my upbringing, I absorbed fundamental principles of resourcefulness and sustainability that would form the foundation of my own personal philosophies. These ideas grew within me and I still carry them with me today.

CHAPTER 7

My Teenage Years

Dad always trapped the possums around our garden and I dreamed about the day when I would be allowed to do it. Finally, the time came. Several years earlier we'd met some trampers named Guy and Lucy Bellerby. They had three children – Cam, Lochie and Fern – and later we visited them on their family farm near Lake Manapōuri. The boys were a year each side of me and Fern was the same age as Robin. We loved staying at their farm and would milk goats, herd sheep, talk about hunting and even attend the local primary school with them. When I was about 12, they flew in with Roger to stay in the DOC hut for a week.

Every waking hour, Cam, Lochie and I would be out catching kelpies and kahawai, snorkelling for crayfish and pāua, walking up and down the beach looking for bits of wood to carve, doing schoolwork together and making the most of every moment. At night Mum and Lucy would cook up huge meals of battered fish fillets, pāua patties, boiled crayfish and pots of homegrown vegetables from our garden mixed with Lucy's vegetables from the huge garden on their farm. There were so many tomatoes, cucumbers, green beans and different varieties of peas and pumpkins that they could grow in their more favourable climate. Cam, Lochie and I were all fast-growing boys and they each ate even more than me. By the end of the meal there would be nothing left on the table and everyone would sit back with full bellies of home-produced food.

Cam and Lochie both hunted possums on their farm and after some persuasion Dad agreed we could use his 12 traps. After filling our backpacks with jars of lure, marker tape, hammers, nails and traps we proudly set off into the forest behind the house to set our possum line. We decided to set our traps every 30 or 40 metres and carefully chose trees with scratch marks from the possums' claws and teeth. One of us nailed the chain to the tree while the other carefully set the attached trap. Using our toes or the palms of our hands we carefully placed the trigger into the footplate, all the while keeping our fingers free of the bars in case the trap accidentally went off. We set the trap at least half a metre above the ground, on the sloping tree trunk, to avoid the possibility of catching penguins. Finally, we shook a large dash of lure higher on the tree trunk and tied up a piece of pink marker tape, before continuing through the tangle of ponga, rātā and supplejack.

The next morning, after a breakfast of homemade muesli, we ran into the forest to check our trap line, each carrying a driftwood club. The first three traps were empty and we were a little disappointed, and upon arriving at the fourth we found the trap had vanished. 'There's a possum!' Lochie yelled excitedly and tugged at the chain that disappeared into a mossy hollow under the tree roots. Carefully he pulled the possum backwards out of the hole and gave it three swift blows to the head with his club. Once it was properly dead and its nerves had stopped twitching, the boys showed me how to pluck the fur off it while it was still warm. It came out in big handfuls and felt as light as thistledown. 'Just put it in a bag and when you have a couple of kilograms of the stuff send it out to us and we'll sell it for you. It takes about 12 to 20 possums per kilogram, depending on how big they are,' explained Cam. 'And the price is $65 per kilogram,' added Lochie. 'They mix it with merino to make possum wool.' We continued along the trap line, following the bits of marker tape hanging in the trees. On each of the following days, we checked the possum line after breakfast and together that week we caught a total of eight possums. I was well and truly hooked.

Once we had finished with the possums, we would join Dad and Guy as they checked the fish net. Each afternoon at high tide a huge school of kahawai would come into the river mouth and we would try to catch them on a shiny lure. Kahawai can grow to about 65 centimetres and they fight harder than salmon.

Cam was the first to get a bite and yelled 'Strike!' as he raised his fishing rod to the sky. The hook stuck in the fish and the fight began. Slowly he reeled it in towards the beach and then all of a sudden the fish charged back out into the waves, causing the reel to make a high-pitched *zzzzzzzZZZZZZZ*. This continued for 20 minutes until Cam pulled the fish close enough to shore to be picked up and deposited on the gravel riverbank by a small wave. Lochie and I raced down and grabbed it before the next wave could drag it back into the water. We held it up in excitement and Lucy took some pictures of us with it. We repeated this process until we had all caught a large kahawai. Guy caught one too and we proudly carried them back to the house to show everybody. Smoked kahawai was added to the dinner menu that night.

The entire time the Bellerbys were at Gorge River we were followed by a cloud of sandflies. They were there when we were plucking possums and again when we were filleting fish. When we were fishing for kahawai they swarmed on our fingers and around our necks. And when we were changing into wetsuits on the beach to go snorkelling they descended on us from all directions to bite our bare butts. The Bellerbys had experienced these persistent biting flies before in Fiordland and we shared our worst sandfly stories over the dinner table each night.

On day seven we hugged the Bellerbys goodbye on the airstrip and they flew back out to Queenstown. Every few weeks, before Roger's supply drop, I would write letters to Cam and Lochie, telling them about all the fishing and possum hunting I had been doing. The letters would be sealed in an envelope along with Robin's letter to Fern and Mum and Dad's letters to Guy and Lucy. Eventually these would be placed in the mail bag and we would eagerly expect replies six weeks later. The Bellerbys visited us twice at Gorge River and their visits are among the fondest memories of my childhood.

After the Bellerbys' visit, the job of protecting the garden from possums fell to me and I embraced the responsibility with great enthusiasm. Each morning I would check my traps, and slowly the bag of fur hanging in the workshop grew heavier and heavier. On our next trip to town, I gave the bag to Cam and Lochie and sure enough when the mail returned six weeks later there was a cheque for $120 to deposit in my Kiwibank account. They also knew a place to buy possum traps and I was keen to extend my possum line. I sent them $45 cash in the mail and another six weeks later three shiny new traps arrived in a box in the back of Roger's plane. It wasn't long before I had 40 traps.

Despite the fact that possums were constantly moving in from the south, there were not enough of them around the house to keep me interested. So I would listen to the forecast on the radio and every time the weather was nice I would set my traps somewhere else. Sometimes I would paddle up through the gorge and set them on the tutu and māhoe trees along the riverbanks. Then I set them all the way up to the top of the hill and down the beach past the airstrip. It was a fantastic way to explore new areas I had never visited before and it developed my tracking and bush skills. I could memorise the shape and colour of different trees and could follow my line of 30 or 40 traps through the tangled forest without a single piece of marker tape. Each time I moved them, I memorised the next trail, and so on. The possum numbers were steadily growing and I could sometimes catch five or six in one night if I had my traps set somewhere new. That number was worth about $20, and the money added up over time. But I was desperate to try trapping somewhere that had plague numbers of possums, like Big Bay.

Every year the most exciting day on my calendar was the 1st of September, the first day of the whitebait season. For the next two and a half months I would think of nothing other than catching whitebait. Since we never caught much of this elusive delicacy at Gorge River, I began thinking up more and more creative ways to fish. For years Dad had set his net on the south side of the river beneath the limestone bluff, and sometimes in the early morning we would sit on a tutu tree that hung over the river and peer down, watching the whitebait swim past one or two at a time. The sun would reflect off the crystal-clear green water, creating a shimmering pattern of light on the mossy cliff face and rātā trees behind us, and a grey warbler would sing its whitebait song announcing the start of springtime. The ones and twos would slowly add up in our net and if we were lucky we might get enough for a whitebait patty each for lunch.

This was fun, but I had seen how much whitebait ran up the river at Big Bay when we stayed there with the Mitchells and I was curious as to why there weren't more in the gorge. What if I used a different net or fished in a different place? On our next trip out to town I bought several metres of green shade cloth from the gardening store – I figured it was the cheapest alternative to the expensive metal screen or soft whitebait net material that cost a staggering $80 per metre. Once home, I drew a diagram for my new net and disappeared into the forest with a measuring tape and hand saw to carefully select 30 one-metre lengths of thick, straight supplejack. Supplejack doesn't float, so I figured it would work well as the main frame of the net, which would need to sit under the water. I trimmed, drilled, nailed and screwed until eventually I had a sturdy frame. Then I carefully measured out the shade cloth, double- and triple-checking the measurements before making the cuts. If I made a mistake, I couldn't just go down to the shop to buy some more. Every cut had to be perfect. I stapled the cloth onto the supplejack frame using Dad's staple gun, then stood back to admire my new box net, which resembled a very large fly trap.

The one-cubic-metre box was enclosed with the shade cloth on all sides except the front, where the whitebait could enter and swim towards the V-shaped trap. That would guide them into the net's end compartment, and once they were in this inner part it would be hard for them to find their way out again.

So now I had a net, but that wouldn't make more whitebait come to me – I had to go and find them. What if I could build myself a whitebait stand? We had never tried whitebaiting on the north side of the river, so I loaded up our dinghy with 12 straight poles and three flat pieces of driftwood, along with a bag of rusty nails, a hammer, a saw and some old crayfish-pot rope, and rowed over there.

Removing my gumboots and rolling up my pants, I waded out into the icy-cold water, which came up to my knees. It still felt like winter and I had my Swanndri on under a rain jacket to keep warm. Using a rock, I hammered the sharpened poles into a shallow gravel bar to form the supports. Then I nailed some pieces between the poles and used some angle braces to lock all the poles together. When I placed the driftwood planks on top of the frame it formed a four-metre-long wooden platform, like a small pier, that protruded directly out into the river. Once the planks were lashed on with the crayfish rope, the structure was sturdy enough to walk along.

Whitebait tend to swim along the riverbank, so I constructed three one-metre screens to guide them towards the net, using the last of the shade cloth and more driftwood. The entire structure still complied with all the rules of pot-net whitebaiting; since we didn't actually have a registered whitebait stand on the Gorge River, I didn't want to break any rules. Besides the shade cloth for the net, the entire structure was made from recycled or natural materials I had found on the beach. I paced backwards and forwards along it, admiring my craftsmanship, but there was no time to waste – the incoming tide signalled the potential arrival of a mother lode of whitebait and I needed to set my net!

With my net firmly in place at the end of my stand, the water slowly rose up the poles and a few surges pushed up the river estuary from the ocean. But no matter how hard I stared into the water I couldn't see many whitebait. There was the odd one or two but nothing more than Dad would be catching in our normal place. Then, finally, I saw a little shoal of about ten, but they were about two metres out beyond my net and swam straight past.

Eventually the water was almost at the bottom of my wooden platform and the waves were becoming stronger. I was completely surrounded by water and it felt like I was in a boat. I decided to empty my net before it washed away and hoisted it up. In the bottom corner were about 20 wriggling whitebait. I was pretty disappointed and tipped them into a bucket to take home. At least I could add them to Dad's catch and we would have an extra patty. Pulling out the screens, I splashed ashore to stash them somewhere safe above the high-flood mark until my return. My clothes were drenched by now and, combined with the cool southwesterly wind, made me very cold. Disgruntled, I paddled home back over the river with my 20 whitebait sitting safely in a bucket on the floor of the boat.

Whitebaiting takes a lot of patience and I had all the time in the world and unlimited enthusiasm. So I returned each day at low tide and repeated the process, come rain, hail or shine. If the river was too flooded to cross safely with the dinghy then I would stay home, but the first day after a flood is usually the best whitebaiting, so I would get ahead on my schoolwork while I waited out the storm.

I loved fishing on my very own whitebait stand but eventually the lack of whitebait became frustrating and I had another idea.

After one large flood washed away most of the stand, I decided that rather than rebuild it I would try somewhere else. Early one morning I carried my screens and net further up the river to another gravel bar just below the high-tide mark (whitebaiting is only allowed inside the tidal area of a river). This time I tried something different. I gave up on the idea of a wooden platform and instead hammered a series of thin, 1.5-metre-long wooden stakes into the gravel riverbed. There was a steady current here and my box net sat beautifully in position, two metres out from a large boulder on the riverbank. I weighted a two-metre length of shade cloth on the bottom with rocks, and tied some small fishing floats along the top to make it float. The water was thigh-deep here and the cool morning katabatic wind was blowing. After an hour standing in the river barefoot, I became quite cold and rowed back home to warm up and eat breakfast. The tide was still low and I could safely leave the net for a while.

After breakfast I scrubbed one of our fish buckets and was just about to head back to my net when a plane landed. Having a visitor was too exciting to miss, so I sat back and listened to Mum and Dad discuss recent events with Peter Clark, who had his five-year-old son with him. He stayed for a couple of hours and I was starting to get anxious about my whitebait net. The tide was coming in and I didn't want a wave to wash it away. Eventually Peter started to make moves towards leaving and Mum turned to me and said, 'Hey, you should check your whitebait net – maybe there will be enough to give Peter a feed.'

'Good idea!' I said and yanked on my gumboots.

I sprinted down to the river with my bucket and rowed across to the other side. The tide had risen and as I recovered my breath by the riverbank, I noticed something strange. There were quite a few whitebait flicking backwards and forwards across the back of the net and beneath the water was a deep purple colour. I had seen this before in Mitch's net at Big Bay and knew there had to be quite a few whitebait in there to create that effect.

After almost falling into the river with excitement, I quickly removed my gumboots, pants and socks before wading out. I barely noticed the ten-degree water lapping above my waist as I gently dragged the net back to the bank with one hand, carefully holding my shirt out of the water with the other. I didn't trust the strength of the shade cloth to hold the catch, so I very gently slid the net out of the water onto the rocks, staring in disbelief at the huge shimmering mass wriggling in the bottom corner. I carefully emptied out my catch the same way I'd seen Mitch do it, and the whitebait rose almost halfway up the sides of the ten-litre bucket.

Quickly I stashed my fishing gear under a tree high above the water level and carried my bucket back to the house, taking care not to trip. As Peter prepared to leave, I proudly displayed my catch, exclaiming, 'There must be four kilograms!' Many of the whitebait were dark in colour – the type commercial whitebaiters would throw away – but we knew they all tasted the same and for giving them away it didn't make a difference. Mum grabbed some old plastic bags from the cupboard under the sink and we filled them with whitebait to give to Peter. 'Here you go! I said excitedly. 'We'll catch some more tomorrow.'

Peter couldn't believe his eyes and carefully placed the bag in the back of the plane. There is nothing more satisfying than giving away fish we catch at Gorge River, and it's a great way to repay the favours people do for us. As the wind from the propellers tore at my hair and the sweet smell of burnt avgas tickled my nostrils, a warm feeling of contentment swept over me. I had finally worked out how to catch whitebait at Gorge River.

I worried that my catch had been a fluke, a one-off run for some unknown reason. But after returning with a kilogram or two every day for a week, I was confident I had indeed found a good place. However, we could never eat that much whitebait and had no form of refrigeration. We could keep it for a day in a pot on the bathroom floor or in the meat safe, but that was all. I needed a better way of storing my catch and came up with an idea.

As mentioned, our water supply runs 24 hours a day and provides us with an unlimited amount of fresh spring water. We don't actually use much of it and the majority overflows into a pond in the forest. By placing a mesh cage in a waterproof fish case and using the overflow pipe, I could provide the caged whitebait with a constant flow of fresh water, and that way they could stay alive for weeks. We could eat a few each day as we needed, and if a visitor turned up we could give them a feed of fresh whitebait! One day Sax landed for a cup of tea and we gave him six kilograms I had caught the day before, still fresh and wriggling. If we didn't have a visitor, after a couple of days I would release the whitebait back into the river. That way our fishery would be preserved for the future season and no whitebait was wasted unnecessarily.

Now that we could actually catch some whitebait, I wanted to invest in better equipment. I realised that if I had a freezer, I could store my catch and sell it to visitors. And if I could make money from it, then it would be worth investing in a better net. The whitebait nets hanging in the shop in Haast were about $500, but the actual whitebait mesh to make a net would cost only $240.

Dad's old net, originally given to us by family friend Murray Bowes from Hokitika when I was one, had been patched so many times with mosquito mesh that there wasn't much left of the original. But I could salvage all the metal rings from it to make a new net. On our next trip to town, I purchased the new netting in Haast and some other odds and ends like cloth tape and strong synthetic cotton from Spotlight in Dunedin.

I had everything I needed and set about carefully measuring, cutting, pinning and sewing backwards and forwards along the three-metre length of netting with Mum's sewing machine. Eventually I installed the rings that would hold the net taut and reinforced them with cloth tape on each side to protect them from sharp rocks. Finally, I stapled the net to a square wooden frame. The frame holds the mouth of the net open for the whitebait to enter, and when the tail is held out tight a huge V-shaped sock is formed. Halfway along, the whitebait swim through a narrow trap, also V-shaped, which prevents them from escaping once inside. These nets are extremely hard to make and I was surprised at how well it turned out. There were no sagging parts and from a distance you couldn't tell my net apart from the one in the shop.

I used that net for a few years at Gorge River and caught many kilograms of whitebait with it. Eventually I convinced Dad to buy a small 30-litre freezer to run from the 12-volt solar power. It cost $1200 and I paid for a bit of it with my savings from possum hunting. I would carefully sort out a kilogram or two of whitebait from the dark green bait and after weighing them into 250-gram portions with a pair of balance scales I'd built from wood they would be placed in zip-seal bags to freeze. By then we had four solar panels on the roof and a small windmill, but in springtime this setup still wasn't enough to keep the freezer cold. So I invested $300 in a small petrol generator that would run at night and on cloudy days, and this would keep the bags just cold enough to stay frozen until the sun came back out. In a little hardcover notebook I recorded every bag of whitebait I had in the freezer and every hour that the generator had to run. I managed to sell a few kilograms to different people from time to time, but after paying for the net, part of the freezer, the generator and fuel I didn't really make the profits I had hoped for. However, I was doing exactly what I enjoyed most and had a huge amount of fun in the process.

Every September or October we would fly down to Big Bay for a week to stay with the Mitchells and there I saw how the real whitebaiters fished. Each person had their own whitebait stand stretching ten metres out into the river. Every morning at 6 am they would start fishing and a long line of screens would be set up to guide the whitebait into the large sock net at the end of each stand. Most of the whitebait would enter the river on the incoming tide and everyone would be eagerly awaiting the day's catch. In the evening I would sit on a tall stool in the shed and carefully sort the bait into 250-gram pottles to store in a large walk-in freezer powered by a diesel generator. During these years the whitebait catches on the river were decreasing and there was concern for the health of the fishery. In the late 2000s, however, the catches increased again and they have remained at quite a stable level ever since.

While at Big Bay, we would sometimes take a walk to the south end of the beach, and on the hills above Dale Hunter's house we started to notice some of the trees dying. It took a couple of years to work out what was causing this but eventually we realised it was the possums. Hunters returning from spotlighting would talk about seeing 'hundreds' of eyes around the McKenzie Creek flats. Each year, more and more trees were losing their leaves and turning into gigantic grey skeletons. Now each time we went to Big Bay I would take ten possum traps with me and set them around the whitebait stands. My catch rate was above 50 per cent and I was itching to set my whole trap line at the south end of the bay, where there were even more possums. I suggested to Dad that we should go on a family possum-hunting trip to Big Bay and, after seeing the damage in the forest behind Dale's house, he agreed. We could even make some money from the fur to pay for the trip.

We made plans to do the trip that summer and, one morning at the beginning of February, Roger dropped us all off on the beach at low tide. Outside the whitebait season the huts usually stand empty, and the only souls to be seen are passing trampers or deer hunters. Sand was blowing off the tops of the dunes in the southwest breeze and the rimu behind the beach were swaying from side to side. Down towards the river mouth not a footprint was to be seen and the tracks from the whitebaiters' quad bikes had long since been washed away. Out to sea, waves were crashing on the rugged coastline around the tips of Awarua Point to the north and Long Reef to the south. These two podocarp-forested headlands form the outer corners of the distinctive square-shaped bay. Roger's plane lifted off and after circling low over the beach turned towards the snowy peaks of the Red Mountain and the Olivine Range ice plateau, standing like an impassable rock wall to the east.

We settled into the Big Bay DOC hut, which stands surrounded by flax bushes just above the sand dunes behind the beach. Its large windows catch the sun and it's always warm and cosy and has a large wood fire that can be used on rainy days. I had brought 50 possum traps and hoped I could catch around 30 possums per night. Usually some get away, while other traps won't be found by a possum. Thirty is good but I knew there were thousands out there and perhaps I could use other techniques to catch them. I had done some brainstorming at home and had constructed a hoop of supplejack about one metre in diameter with a loosely tied bit of fish net draped across it and attached around the side. Perhaps if I could throw the hoop over the possum it would become entangled long enough for me to club it on the head.

After making ourselves comfortable we walked three kilometres down the beach to McKenzie Creek. Along a marked hunting track through the forest from the creek to Dale's house we set out traps at 50-metre intervals. Here we finally saw the full extent of the damage. Previously we had only noticed the tall rātā trees from the beach, but inside the forest we discovered many of the smaller māhoe and fuchsia were also dead, their leaves chewed to pieces by the plague of possums. Even some cabbage trees above the beach were chewed and had dead branches. Dad and I found some pāua in front of Dale's house at low tide and as the sun slipped away we cooked them in their shells over a driftwood campfire. In the distance the jagged twin peaks of Red Mountain glowed in the sunset's final rays.

Just before it got dark we saw a black shape moving around on a patch of grass. Big and fluffy with a long bushy tail: there was no mistaking a large male possum. In the light of my 60-lumen headtorch we could see two glowing red eyes staring back at us curiously. The hunting instinct kicked in and I stalked my way up to the big brown possum, staying out of sight behind some coprosma bushes. From about four metres away I could see it was about to run and I launched the hoop into the air. It landed cleanly over the possum but to my dismay the creature turned and threw it off with one paw before disappearing into a wall of thick flax bushes. I would need to do better than this.

I had a look around the grassy patches nearby and could see a few more sets of eyes shining back in the light of my headlamp. One set was sitting higher than the others, on top of a coprosma bush about two metres off the ground. I slowly stalked forward holding my long driftwood club in both hands: three metres … two metres … one metre … swing and … *WHACK!* The possum was partially stunned but still managed to jump into a flax bush. Flax bushes are quite soft and I launched myself in after it, grabbing its tail with one outstretched hand. It turned and tried to bite me as I backed out, dragging it by the tail. With a couple of clean knocks to the head, the possum was dead. The first one of the trip. I raced back to Mum, Dad and Robin, who were still sitting around the campfire, and Dad offered to pluck it for me.

Immediately, I headed off to find another but the next three escaped. 'Damn, this isn't so easy after all,' I said to Mum as we walked back along the beach to the McKenzie airstrip. In the middle of the airstrip, by the light of my little torch, I could see a medium-sized grey possum eating grass near the bush edge. I stalked up towards it but when I was about six metres away it turned and made a run for the bushes. I followed at full speed, weaving around the sedge grass, trying to get in front of it and cut it off from reaching the safety of the māhoe trees. The thick grass slowed it down and I was now only four metres behind. I leapt over rotten logs, dodging around random tree branches and flax bushes. Now there was just two metres between us … and then just one. Almost at the bush edge, I took a desperate lunging dive like a rugby player scoring a try, while bringing the club down on the possum's head … *WHACK!* Again, stunned but not out, it kept running, but it was now much slower and as it tried to get around a fallen tree I dived again full length to grab its tail. *WHACK … WHACK … WHACK* and I had my second possum of the night.

I repeated this process for a kilometre up the McKenzie Creek, hunting around the beautiful grassy river flats before turning and walking back along the beach. While I was running ahead chasing possums, Dad was somewhere behind me, trying to keep up and help me pluck. And Mum and Robin were further behind, also trying to keep up. Above us the Southern Cross twinkled like diamonds hanging from a ceiling and the Milky Way stretched from the mountains in the east to the horizon in the west, cutting the dark sky in two like a gigantic archway.

We didn't get back to the hut until about 2 am. In total we'd seen more than 150 possums and using my speed and stalking skills I'd managed to catch 25 of them. The hoop only worked for the smaller possums and any adults near the bush edge were impossible to catch. But if a possum was sitting on a coprosma bush or sedge grass then I stood a chance. I think this has to be the most sporting way to catch these fluffy little animals that destroy the forest.

After four days our portable transistor radio informed us of an approaching storm, so we stashed our gear under one of the whitebaiters' huts for Roger to pick up on his next visit. After wading across the Awarua River at low tide, we began tramping home to Gorge River. The route traverses rocks that range from the size of a watermelon to that of a house. At low tide a rough bulldozer track that was carved through the boulders around Awarua Point by the mining company in the seventies makes the tramp slightly easier. There are two smaller rivers to cross – the Hacket and Ryans Creek – and at the mouth of Ryans Creek we have a bivvy shelter where we can sleep to break up the 30-kilometre hike.

We managed to get 110 possums on that trip, which equated to about five kilograms of fur, valued at around $300. I used some of the money to buy new traps and a stronger headtorch and saved the rest. I imagined having a rifle, and wondered how many possums I could catch if I didn't have to run them down on foot.

After watching Dad selling his artwork and Mum selling her knitting, I had an idea to add value to my possum hunting. If I could take the skins and tan them, I could use them to make luxury fur products that would be worth much more than the fur I was currently selling. A tramper showed me the skinning technique – it was much more effort, but I could sell the dried skins for a few extra dollars and I didn't mind the hard work. One day when we were in Hokitika I sold 50 skins to Fur Dressers and Dyers and while I was there had a long conversation with the owners, Peter and Carol Grey. They shared some of their extensive knowledge about sewing possum skins and recommended that I buy a specially designed sewing machine.

The machine was expensive and would have to wait, but to get started I began tanning my own skins with a do-it-yourself kit and used Mum's hand-wound sewing machine. It was a lot of work but eventually I produced a couple of cushions that I sold to some passing trampers for $160. That was a lot more than the $60 I would have made from selling the raw skins, and I could see the potential. Next time I sold my skins to Peter Gray, I asked him to tan some for me and a few months later I received a box of beautifully cured possum skins ready for sewing. Now I started to look for a better sewing machine for the job.

Around this time, I often dreamed of being a trout-fishing guide. Occasionally we would be visited by one of the local helicopters taking high-paying customers fishing in untouched rivers throughout the Southern Alps. Everything I've ever dreamed of over the years has eventually come true and one day when I was 15, I had my chance, albeit in my own backyard.

It was a cold spring afternoon after a few days of rain when a blue and white Cessna 185 zoomed low over our house. It turned sharply above the Steeples before descending carefully onto the airstrip in blustery southwesterly conditions. Out jumped Murray Bowes and three American tourists. Murray introduced us to Roy and his wife, Janice, and their friend Frances. It was very cold standing in the wind, so Mum and Dad quickly invited them inside, where Murray explained that Roy was a keen fly fisherman. They had flown down from Hokitika to Milford Sound looking for a good river to fish and because of the recent rain all the rivers along the coast were dirty and flooded. When they saw that the Gorge River was not so flooded, they decided to land. 'Do you know any good places for fishing, Christan?' asked Murray. 'Yeah, I can take him up the river!' I replied, jumping at the opportunity. Roy wasn't interested in a cup of tea and cake, he just wanted to get fishing, so we headed straight out to the plane to unload his gear. I looked in awe at his waders, fishing vest, five-piece rod, landing net and reel, and big box of flies of every shape and size. We climbed into our aluminium dinghy and rowed across to the north side of the river. It was still a dark tannin brown from the recent rain but would be clear enough for some good fishing.

We walked about 200 metres along the riverbank to the place where I would usually set my whitebait net. Most days of the whitebait season there is a huge trout (that we nicknamed 'Trouty') that sits under one specific rock behind my net, waiting to gobble up the unsuspecting whitebait. I didn't tell Roy this though and instead just pointed to the section of river. 'Try along here, I think it could be a good place,' I said, crossing my fingers that Trouty would be there today. 'What fly should I use?' asked Roy, pointing to his fly box. I carefully picked through it and found one made from white feathers about six centimetres long that looked the most like a whitebait. 'This one,' I suggested with a chuckle.

Then I stood back and watched as he started whipping his rod backwards and forwards, casting slightly upstream in the fast-flowing water. The gusty winds made it challenging but at least it meant there were no sandflies. He was a skilled caster and his fly would land in exactly the right place before sweeping through the water across the current, 50 centimetres beneath the surface. He watched the fly intently through the brownish water and once it was back at the riverbank he would repeat the process. After each cast he would take a couple of careful steps upstream along the bouldery riverbank, so as to always be fishing in new water.

After about ten minutes he suddenly whipped his rod up high and I could see the end was bent right over towards the water. 'Strike!' he yelled, stumbling backwards. It was a good-sized fish and it thrashed about in the water a few metres out from the shore. Eventually he guided the trout in and I scooped it up cleanly with the landing net. He jumped in the air, overjoyed at catching his first New Zealand fish. The handle of the landing net contained some scales and, after studying them for a second, he announced the weight: 'Six pounds!' Smiling from ear to ear, he carefully removed the trout from the net and posed for a photograph by the river's edge. Then he produced some pliers from one of the many pockets on his vest and gently removed the hook from the fish's mouth before lowering it back into the water. With one flick of his tail, Trouty disappeared into the river's depths to ambush whitebait another day.

Roy fished for a while longer and although he didn't manage to catch any more trout, he did have another good-sized one on his line for half a minute. We returned to the house victorious, and Murray was extremely relieved to hear of our success. He and the others climbed back into the plane and with a loud burst of power were soon airborne and heading back to Hokitika. 'Wow, that was a fun day!' I thought to myself, but the story didn't end there.

A few months later Murray called in again and, after shaking hands, he unloaded a huge cardboard box from the compartment at the back of the plane. 'Here you go, Christan, this is from Roy!' he said with a chuckle. Over a cup of tea, he explained the rest of the story. For the remainder of his week staying with Murray in Hokitika, Roy hadn't stopped talking about that trout and how it was the highlight of his entire trip to New Zealand. I unpacked the box to find a fly-fishing set with a five-piece rod, a reel, two fly lines and a box full of flies. What an amazing reward for my first venture into trout guiding!

I just couldn't get enough of fishing and hunting through my teenage years. I developed many of the skills I had learned by watching Dad when I was young, and made them my own. Now I could earn some decent pocket money and even help Dad gather food for the family. I was a fast-growing teenager with a huge appetite and these skills were really coming in handy.

CHAPTER 8

Correspondence School

After doing home schooling for primary school with Mum and Dad as my sole teachers, I was beginning to crave more outside influence in my life. Mum was also finding it harder and harder to come up with stimulating lessons to keep me interested. We eventually all agreed it would be beneficial if I was enrolled in the Correspondence School. Based in Wellington, the school teaches the national curriculum and all lessons are completed in workbooks sent out by mail. This way I would have the same lessons as everyone else and I would have a different teacher for each subject. They would send out the workbooks with a supporting cassette and any tools or resources needed for the lesson.

There was a catch, however, in that my teachers were in Wellington and our only contact with the outside world was a mail delivery every six weeks. That led to Mum's biggest challenge: convincing the Correspondence School teachers to send out the lessons in advance. Most of them couldn't grasp just how isolated we were and would send the two-week lessons one by one throughout the year as they would to their other students, most of them living in cities. The packages would arrive six weeks late and I would have to play catch-up. If they agreed to send all the workbooks early, I could work through them at my own pace, sending them off to Wellington whenever they were complete. By the end of a school year, the teachers would have accepted that this worked well, but then I'd have to change to a completely new set of teachers for the following year and Mum would have to start all over again, explaining our situation in letters or in phone calls if we were in town. This cycle continued for five years.

Our one stroke of luck, however, was with my form teacher. Early in my first year of high school, Roger turned up unexpectedly one morning. As he landed, we could see he had two passengers and we were excited to find out who they were. Out jumped a lady in her early sixties, who quickly introduced herself. 'Hello, Christan, I'm Pam Henson, your form teacher!' We couldn't believe it. Pam was a keen tramper and had heard about a family that had been living way down the West Coast for years. She'd hoped every year that we would enrol in the Correspondence School, so when she did finally see my name on the list of new students, she immediately requested to be my form teacher. She stayed with us for a few days and eventually hiked south to the Hollyford Road end with her friend. Back in Wellington, Pam was able to explain my situation to the other teachers and always convinced a few of them to send out my lessons ahead of time. It helped, but we still ran into problems with bureaucracy in the government-run Correspondence School and most of the teachers simply couldn't get their heads around the extent of our isolation.

My favourite place to do my schoolwork was sitting on my bed with a large piece of plywood on my lap for a desk. I would lean back against the bookshelf beside my bed with my tape recorder next to me. A box contained my two-week workbooks, each colour-coded according to the subject. After breakfast each morning I would make myself comfortable and put on a music cassette. Then I would pick through the box to find the most exciting lesson to do first. At any given time, the box would have a green workbook for English, red for social studies, white for science, light green for music, blue for maths and so on. Each workbook contained eight to ten lessons to complete every two weeks. I was self-motivated and knew what schoolwork needed to be done and when I was going to do it. Mum didn't have to nag me very much and mostly left me to it.

One day's schooling consisted of a lesson in each subject workbook and would take me roughly three to four hours – much less than the six-plus hours of a normal school day. Because I had none of the social distractions and forced breaks that everyone has at school, I could focus on completing my work quickly and move on to what I really wanted to be doing, which was possum hunting, fishing and whitebaiting. Being in charge of my own time meant I wasn't obliged to take weekends off and I worked more to a weather schedule. When it was raining, I could work through two or three lessons in each subject a day, and then when the rain stopped I had two or three days completely free to run a long possum line.

If my subject teacher did send out the entire year's studies in February or March, I could get stuck in and get it done early. Then for the rest of the year I would have 40 minutes extra per day to spend outside doing what I wanted in nature. Whitebait season runs from the 1st of September to the 14th of November and in some years I could finish certain subjects by July or August, giving me a clear schedule for whitebaiting. This type of schooling worked perfectly for me, allowing me to complete the same lessons as everyone else while spending most of my life outdoors, where I could have completely different learning experiences.

Although most of the time I would have preferred to be doing something else, I did enjoy some aspects of schoolwork, especially the more practical lessons. Woodwork was one of my favourite subjects and the best part was the huge box of tools that was sent out at the beginning of each year. There were hand planes, long rulers, sharp hand saws, smooth hand drills, squares and many other exciting tools. With these I would build not only the projects in the lessons but also make and fix other things around the house in my own time. Once I built a tray out of wood and thick greenhouse plastic to sort my whitebait, and another time I built a house for Chooky using the saw, measuring tape, plane and hammer from that toolbox.

At the start of the year, I would pick through the box of woodworking projects and choose the most interesting ones to do first. I loved the subject but found the lessons hard to follow. In my very first workbook I had to make a lovely wooden coaster set out of some flat pieces of wood that were included with the toolbox. I had built many things out of wood before and as I opened the workbook I instantly visualised what I was going to make. In the first lesson I was meant to draw eight design concepts and analyse each one before narrowing it down to two and then redrawing them to analyse again, considering all the pros and cons of each. A design process that had taken me five minutes in my head was meant to fill the first five lessons in the workbook! I didn't have the patience for that and skipped straight to the lesson where I could actually do the practical work.

After sawing, planing and sanding for a couple of days, I had a beautiful set of coasters with a lovely wooden box for them to sit in. Mum agreed that the design process was long-winded but it was her job to make sure I completed the workbook properly. Once I had finished sanding, she made me go back and complete the required drawings for each step of the process to send to my teachers. That annoyed me so much. I was ready to get on with the next project and could see no point stuffing around with all these drawings! Eventually even Mum gave up insisting, and we moved on.

Another of my favourite subjects was technology, which was also based around physical projects. One workbook lesson involved designing a tie-dyed T-shirt and in another I learned to bake super-fluffy bread buns. Completing these sorts of lessons at Gorge River always required some improvisation. For example, rather than turn an oven to 220 degrees for baking, I added just the right amount of driftwood to our fire to keep Mum's camp oven at the required temperature to cook the bread until golden brown. In another project, I designed and sewed a pair of black polar fleece pants rather than shorts (we have too many sandflies to wear shorts) from the pattern the school had sent. The pants didn't quite fit me so I gave them to my cousin Leo and next time his family visited Gorge River he was wearing them. These were all just simple problems that required some thinking outside the box.

My next favourite subject in my first years of high school was social studies because I got to learn about the world. I often looked through our atlas and would spend many hours staring out across the ocean, curious about what lay beyond my bubble of Gorge River, the rest of New Zealand and Brisbane. As I opened up each orange social studies workbook, I was instantly transported to an event that had occurred in some far-off land. Looking back, the subjects that come to mind all relate to human inequality, such as the civil rights movement in the USA, World War Two and apartheid in South Africa. Other lessons that stick in my memory involved natural disasters. I would make myself comfortable on my bed and listen intently as the narrator of each tape spoke about the giant volcano of Krakatoa, the Tangiwai disaster or Cyclone Giselle, which caused the *Wahine* ferry to sink in Wellington Harbour. I was absolutely fascinated by these events and would work through these workbooks swiftly. My curiosity for the world was growing and I wanted to learn more.

Once each lesson was complete, I would mark my answers against the answer sheet in the back of the workbook. I could of course copy the answers in the first place but I knew that if I cheated, I wasn't actually learning, so I never did that. Then Mum placed the workbooks into the iconic green canvas Correspondence School bags. The post would build up and when the next plane or helicopter landed, Mum would ask them to send the mail for us. It was usually a couple of months before I received them back and could go through and read my teachers' comments. I already knew the answers, but it was nice to get some extra feedback from someone who wasn't Mum, Dad, or the answer sheet.

As I worked through my lessons, there were always things I didn't fully understand and would have extra questions about. Most Correspondence School students could simply call their teacher on the phone or look up Wikipedia. Since we didn't have any phone or internet connection, I had to use the resources I had around me. Mum and Dad had both been in the top one per cent of their respective classes at school and were highly educated. Mum had completed a degree in pathology and microbiology and Dad done three years of medical school before his change of path. If I had any questions, I could always ask them and they could usually help me. We also had several bookshelves loaded with educational texts on almost every subject; we even had a full set of *Encyclopædia Britannica*.

Mum made sure we had a constant stream of interesting books to read from the libraries in Queenstown or Hokitika, and even the National Library in Christchurch would send us seven books at a time in a blue canvas bag. I loved reading and each morning when I woke up, I would switch on the 12-volt reading light above my bed and open up a book. I would put on my headphones and tune in to Queenstown's More FM on my radio. The signal was usually very weak and I would strain to hear the latest pop songs between the static as I turned the pages. I loved reading Barry Crump's stories of hunting and exploring the New Zealand bush, and those of Ken Tustin as he searched for the elusive Fiordland moose.

But not everything I read about involved hunting or the wild. Another favourite author was David Hill and his novels were about teenagers living normal teenage lives in the city. One that really pulled at my emotions, called *Coming Back*, involved a 15-year-old girl and 16-year-old boy. The story started with them hanging out as friends at the mall, listening to music and stealing alcohol from their parents. As the novel progressed, they ended up sleeping together at a party and soon after she became pregnant. These novels ignited strong feelings inside me and I started to crave the company of people my own age. In some ways these books partly filled the gap of my non-existent teenage social life, but they also made me think more about what I was missing out on.

Throughout my teenage years at Gorge River, I continued to build on the skills I had learned from Mum, Dad and the wilderness surrounding me. As my horizons expanded locally, I started to push the boundaries that my parents had set, and each year I would explore further into the forest with my possum traps, fish further up the river, and catch more crayfish. Those aspects of my life were amazing but on the other hand the absence of a social life was beginning to take its toll. Trips to town were short and I rarely had quality time with people my own age. And once home again, the only contact I had with friends like Cam and Lochie Bellerby was by mail every six weeks.

I began questioning my future at Gorge River and for the first time started looking at other pathways. What was I going to do for work after I finished school? Could I even go right through to Year 13 with the Correspondence School or would the lack of communication with my teachers make it too hard to complete? And if I did move out to Haast or Wānaka, what would people think of me and how was I going to fit into a normal social life when I had never done that before?

I was 15 when I took my first trip away from Gorge River alone. Despite being primarily school by mail, the Correspondence School organises camps in different locations across the country for its students to attend. This is a great way for everyone to meet other students, something they don't experience in their day-to-day school, and it helps them feel part of something. I was regularly invited to these camps, but most of the time the invitation arrived too late or the camp was in the North Island. One invitation, however, arrived in time and was for a five-day camp at the Boyle River Outdoor Education Centre at Lewis Pass. I was really keen to go and after chatting about it with Mum and Dad it seemed like this was probably my best opportunity ever to go to a school camp. We decided we could make it work. Also, since we would be out in town not long beforehand, Mum and Dad would be able to put a few plans in place to help me get to and from Lewis Pass. I would be away for just over a week, so there wouldn't be too much time to get homesick.

Roger and his co-pilot Theresa picked me up one sunny afternoon and, after I'd hugged Mum, Dad and Robin goodbye, we flew down the coast past Big Bay. As we turned inland towards the Southern Alps there were clouds around the mountains and they clung to the hillsides, forming many different layers. I was a little worried, as I really needed to make it out to Queenstown that day to catch the bus to Christchurch the next morning. Would we have to turn back and fly to Haast? And in that case would I make it to my school camp at all? These thoughts flashed through my head as Roger skilfully guided the plane through mountains shrouded in layers and layers of stagnant grey clouds towards Park Pass. We had to hope there was a gap large enough to fly through safely.

We approached the pass slowly, making sure there was always a clear exit route behind us back to Big Bay, if we had to turn around. Suddenly Roger turned the plane sharply in a very tight circle and the centripetal forces pushed us hard into the backs of our seats. 'It's clear,' came his calm voice over the intercom and, after turning a full 360 degrees, the wings tipped in the other direction and we dropped through Park Pass as if popping through a gigantic door in the mountainside. The skies opened up to a beautiful sunny day on the eastern side of the Southern Alps.

I stayed with Roger and his partner, Debbie, that night at their house overlooking Lake Hayes on the outskirts of Queenstown and they made me feel right at home. Debbie cooked a delicious meal of roast lamb and chocolate self-saucing pudding for dessert and they looked after me as if I was their own child. In fact, over the years, Roger and Debbie have been like second parents to me. They are my 'out in town' parents. I tossed and turned in bed that night, unable to sleep, which was very unusual for me. Perhaps it was the excitement, or maybe just the new surroundings. I'll never know.

The next morning at 7.15, Debbie dropped me off at the northbound Intercity bus and eight hours later I arrived in downtown Christchurch right in the middle of rush hour. Only the day before I had said goodbye to my family on our remote grass airstrip, and now, 24 hours later, I'd been transported to a completely different world. Tall buildings surrounded me on all sides and the noise of the traffic was overwhelming. There were people everywhere and they all seemed to be in a hurry to get somewhere. Excitement grew inside me because although I had been in bigger cities before with Mum and Dad, it was far more exciting to be there by myself. I stared in fascination along the streets that seemed to stretch forever in all directions. The names Just Jeans, McDonald's, Samsung and Fisher & Paykel loomed on large signs and billboards against the backdrop of traffic lights, street lamps and glass buildings. I felt a new sensation – a deep-down craving to explore more of this crazy new world, a hunger to see things I hadn't seen before – and it felt like the beginning of a whole new chapter in my life.

All of that, however, would have to wait for another day, as Mum and Dad hadn't sent me out completely alone just yet. They had organised for me to stay with a family friend and soon enough a familiar face materialised out of the crowd. 'Welcome to Christchurch!' said Dave Hill, with a big smile on his face. Dave and his friends Malcolm, Simon and Greg were the hunters who came to Gorge River each autumn for the 'roar' and we had lots of things to talk about as we drove to Dave's house, nestled in the outer suburbs. We discussed how many deer had been shot by other parties of hunters and what fish we had been catching recently. He was as excited as I was about my trip and was intrigued to see me out in the big wide world by myself after watching me grow up over all these years.

Naturally we had venison for dinner, where we were joined by Dave's two kids, who were around the same age as me. One of them, Tom, was quite chatty and I went with him to his dimly lit bedroom. There were many different-coloured LED lights coming from an array of electronic devices and I asked what the big neon green fan was on the side of his computer. He explained how it cooled the computer when he was playing online games. He was very good at electronics and could already pull computers apart, repair them and put them back together again, whereas I could catch a fish or set a possum-trapping line through the dense South Westland rainforest. It was fascinating how our lives were truly worlds apart and yet we could still sit down and have a conversation.

I slept on the couch in the lounge room, near a big TV, speakers, a DVD player and a few other devices. I found all the LED lights, some of which would flash off and on every few seconds, strangely unsettling and for a second night in a row struggled to sleep. Looking back now, I realise most people wouldn't have noticed those multi-coloured lights, but after growing up at Gorge River where our most modern piece of technology was a simple CD player, they were quite a distraction. I still have the same aversion to electronic lights to this day and often have to cover them with tape or a towel before I can sleep.

The next day, Dave dropped me at a special meeting point in the city and someone ticked my name off a list before directing me to a private bus. There were other people my age on board already and I guessed they must be fellow Correspondence School students. The bus wound its way up towards Lewis Pass and eventually pulled into the Boyle River Outdoor Education Centre, tucked away on the edge of the forest, overlooking a beautiful river valley. Everyone was welcomed and shown to the bunk rooms at the back of a large central building. There was a room for all the boys and another for the two girls in the group. We took a few minutes to settle in and were informed that lunch would be served in the dining room in ten minutes. All this time everyone was awkwardly avoiding eye contact, except for two guys who knew each other from a previous school camp. They were chatting away and their conversation broke the ice, encouraging the rest of us to start talking a little, although it was still very awkward for most of us. After a lunch of burgers and coleslaw, we were split into two groups and assigned to an outdoor instructor who would stay with us for the week.

We were led out to a quiet corner of the grassy lawn and sat in a circle under the branch of a huge rimu before taking it in turns to introduce ourselves, say where we were from and what our favourite fruit was. I waited quietly, fearing my turn, and eventually everyone's eyes looked in my direction. 'Hi, I'm Christan. I come from Gorge River, between Haast and Milford Sound. And I like bananas.' Most of them probably didn't even know where Haast or Milford were, but that was fine by me. Then we went back around the circle and introduced the person to our right. That way we started to remember each other's names. Next we took turns tossing a ball across the circle and calling the name of the person catching it. I found it really hard to remember everyone's names and was slightly confused each time it was my turn.

After the introductions, our instructor set us some tasks to complete as a group, an activity that would force us to talk to each other more. She led the way into the beech forest to a three-metre-high wall constructed from planks of wood nailed to solid posts buried in the ground. Our task was to get the entire group to the other side. We discussed techniques and some people loudly suggested ideas while others, including me, remained quieter and in the background. Eventually we made a human pyramid and were able to get some of us to the top of the wall. Then they could lower the first people down the other side while helping the last people up.

In the final activity of the day, we stood in a tight circle with one blindfolded person standing straight as a plank in the middle. They were then pushed from side to side, further and further each time, trusting that those around would catch them. We began to build trust between us, and we would need it in the following days as we moved on to more dangerous activities.

That evening after dinner we sat and played games in the activities corner of the main building. I chatted with a couple of the others but found it hard to find common interests. Almost everyone's conversations were focused on what they did in the city and what TV shows they watched or what comics they read. I understood their conversations and knew what they were talking about but struggled to come up with anything to add. It was quite confusing, because I watched two very outgoing guys chatting away easily and felt that I should be like that myself. Something inside was holding me back.

Over the next few days we learned new skills, including rock climbing, compass navigation through forests, abseiling, and many smaller trust activities. I was naturally very confident in the forest around the camp and would lead the way with our instructor from place to place along the narrow muddy paths. I think the others could feel my confidence in that environment and this helped them to accept me, but socially I couldn't contribute so much to the group. Eventually I started chatting to one of the girls, who was quite curious about where I came from. Her name was Amanda and when we were rock climbing we belayed each other.

Despite being confident in the outdoors, I was terrified of heights and found the rock climbing and abseiling extra scary. I remember at the beginning of the abseil standing with trembling legs at the top of the cliff face, with only a double rope attached to my harness for safety. Despite being assured by the instructor that the rope could lift an elephant, I still couldn't step backwards over the edge. But after encouragement from the rest of the group I slowly leaned back into the harness, allowing the two ropes to take the weight of my body. Then I lowered myself over the edge of the cliff and once

I began trusting the harness it was actually quite good fun. I dared myself to look down the 20-metre rock face to the bottom, where the smooth rock gave way to a thickly forested hillside, but quickly had to turn back to the instructor above. After two abseils and two rock climbs, I began to feel more comfortable with heights and learned to trust the rope and the equipment. I enjoyed the challenge immensely and wanted to do it again.

Time went fast, and before I knew it we were eating our last dinner together. I asked Amanda and another guy called Elijah for their addresses so we could send letters to each other. Some of the others exchanged phone numbers and soon we were on the bus back to Christchurch. I waved goodbye to my new friends and jumped into the passenger seat of Dave's HiLux. He had a surprise for me – lunch on The Strip, a popular area in the middle of Christchurch, with Greg, Simon and Malcolm. They were intrigued to meet me away from Gorge River and asked many questions about where I had just been. We ate delicious steak sandwiches and soon the conversation turned to hunting. It felt good to be around like-minded friends again who also knew where I came from.

The next morning, while sitting on the comfortable Intercity bus back to Queenstown, I contemplated the journey I had just been on. It had been really exciting to be away from home alone and I was starting to learn more about myself and who I could be as an independent person. The next day was sunny and Roger and co-pilot Jess flew me home to my family, who were delighted to see me. Over a big dinner of my favourite yellow-eyed mullet and fresh vegetables, I told them all about my adventure.

CHAPTER 9

Flying the Nest

By the age of 16, my thoughts and emotions were becoming more complex and confusing. There was a lot on my mind. After reading in the evening, I would lie in bed, imagining how my social life would be if I was living out in town. Perhaps I would have a beautiful girlfriend and a group of mates to hang out with and create trouble. I had seen what was out there on my previous trips to Haast, Dunedin, Brisbane and Boyle River and knew full well what I was missing out on. But on the other hand, I was still fully entrenched in my life at Gorge River, hunting, fishing and whitebaiting.

No one ever forced me to live at Gorge River and through my teenage years I never felt trapped. I knew that if I wanted to leave, we could talk about it and work out a way for it to happen. But if I'd wanted to leave during my early teens, then my family would have gone with me and I didn't want to be the one who made us all leave. Now that I was older, things were different. I could leave by myself and they probably wouldn't follow. I knew that eventually I would have to make a tough decision.

In my second-to-last year of high school my lessons were getting harder and we still had no contact with the outside world besides handwritten letters every six weeks. My maths, physics and chemistry lessons were becoming quite advanced and when I asked for help either Mum or Dad would usually have to research the topic before providing a useful answer. This made it very slow going, and it was at this point that I learned to use the answers in the back of the workbooks to help me understand the subjects. When I didn't understand the question properly but had the answer, I could use that to work out the steps in between that I didn't understand so well. It wasn't cheating.

But I still had one more year of school ahead and couldn't see how I could finish that at Gorge River. One solution was to have closer contact with my teachers. Perhaps a satellite phone or satellite broadband internet connection.

During our trip to town in May, we decided as a family to buy our first computer. Robin and I really wanted one and Mum and Dad knew we needed to acquire computer skills eventually, and now was the time. I also bought my first MP3 player off Trade Me and our cousins Elena and Kevin helped me load songs onto it. It was so exciting listening to my own music that wasn't full of radio static. A friend, Neroli in Haast, showed us her amazing digital photography and then taught us how she edited it by adjusting the saturation or contrast to really bring out the beauty of the picture. We soaked it all up and when we got home headed out with a tiny digital camera given to us by Anne Mitchell and took many pictures of the scenery around us. Then on a rainy day we would edit them on our new laptop. Robin was very good at cutting out sections of pictures and placing them into other photographs. In one she shrank an image of herself to the height of a daffodil and placed it in the shade of the flower, which now looked two metres tall.

Yet without an internet connection the computer didn't fix the biggest problem: the lack of contact with teachers and friends. In Haast, satellite broadband from a company called Farmside was becoming more popular. We realised we could power it with our solar panels and receive it, regardless of our extreme isolation, via a dish pointing to the sky.

One day that winter our family friends Andy Woods and Mylrea Bell called in with a friend of theirs in a red and white Cessna 180. It was a beautiful sunny day and they had been on a scenic flight stopping at Milford Sound and Martins Bay, where they had originally met Dad years before. Over a cup of tea and cake, Mylrea told us about an outdoor pursuits programme run at Mount Aspiring College in Wānaka and about the school's onsite hostel. Each year, 30 new students come from all over the country to live in supervised housing on the school grounds. As well as the normal subjects for Year 13, the programme also includes outdoor activities such as rock climbing, mountain biking and skiing every Sunday. Sometimes the students even do overnight hikes to the West Coast or Southland.

Thinking back, it was an awkward conversation between us that day. To me this idea sounded like a dream, and Mum and Dad would have felt the same while acting interested in front of Mylrea. But deep down the idea of me leaving Gorge River would have been terrifying for them, and I knew that too. Therefore, I couldn't appear too enthusiastic, even though I was listening intently to Mylrea's every word. After the visitors left, we talked a little about the idea but I didn't push the subject, as I still wasn't sure it was what I really wanted to do. The thought of going to an actual school was daunting on one hand, but incredibly exciting on the other. I had so many emotions to sort out!

Another option I was considering was going to work on the crayfish boats. Geoff Robson's son Spud, one of the local fishermen in Haast, had already told Dad that if I wanted a job on his 60-foot fishing vessel *Impulse*, then I just had to ask. I started imagining a life in Haast, working six days a week on a fishing boat. It also sounded exciting, but I had no idea how I would cope on the sea. However, one day when we were in Haast, I decided to give it a go. Dad gave me the phone number of Denis Nyhon, who owned the *Southern Legend,* and I gave him a call. 'Hi, it's Christan Long here from Gorge River – Beansprout's son. I was wondering if I could take a trip on the *Southern Legend* sometime?'

'Yeah, sure,' came the reply, 'they'll be in Jackson Bay on Monday evening. I'll tell Gareth to pick you up on the wharf.'

Next day I hugged Mum and Dad goodbye and hitchhiked south from Ōkuru towards Jackson Bay to meet the boat. It was just the second time I'd been away from my parents for more than a day. I quickly got a ride all the way to the bay with Dayna and Ryan, who I knew from Haast School. We chatted about things and they asked me lots of questions about my life at Gorge River before eventually dropping me by the Jackson Bay wharf.

The first fishing boat to return that evening was *Sharcaree*, and Swag and his crewman Paul invited me on board. Having known me since I was a baby, Swag announced, 'If the *Southern Legend* doesn't pick you up, you're coming fishing with us tomorrow!' Just as it got dark the *Southern Legend* came steaming around Jackson Head and pulled up alongside. After thanking Swag for his offer, I grabbed my bag and clambered onto the high back deck of the 55-foot Australian-built vessel. Denis's son Shane had cooked up a huge roast lamb with vegetables and gravy and we washed it down with a can of Speight's as we sat at anchor under a large full moon in the shelter of the bay. I was already feeling I could be a part of this fishing community but there were still a few big lessons ahead. I fell asleep to the gentle *plop … plop … plop* of the waves as they splashed against the outside of the aluminium hull near my head.

At 4 am, long before daybreak, we headed out of Jackson Bay and turned towards the open ocean. Gareth was captaining the *Southern Legend* in Denis's absence and Shane was crew. The sun rose above the far-off mountains and I watched their every move as they started lifting the craypots somewhere off Teer Creek. We slowly worked our way south around Cascade Point and on towards the Barn Islands. Gareth positioned the boat alongside the coloured floats and Shane grappled the pot rope with a heavy iron hook attached to a rope. After the floats were on board, he'd skilfully toss the rope over a pulley and loop it around a hydraulic winch that would haul the heavy steel craypot to the surface with a loud whining noise. I watched in awe as the pot appeared from the turquoise-green ocean loaded with flapping spiny rock lobsters. Gareth went back to help Shane and together they guided the swinging pot onto a slanting aluminium frame on deck. They worked seamlessly in time with each other, tipping the contents into a sorting tray and re-baiting before pushing the pot overboard into the ocean once more. As we steamed to the next pot, Shane sorted the crayfish by size, measuring each for the minimum tail width of 54 millimetres for males and 60 millimetres for females. They explained that they were catching so many that they even threw back many of the takeable crayfish and only kept the medium-sized ones, as these made the biggest profits. The largest and smallest takeable crays were returned to the sea.

This was all incredibly exciting. However, excitement wasn't the only sensation I was experiencing. Each time we stopped to lift a pot, the *Southern Legend* would roll aggressively from side to side in its own wake, and diesel fumes from the 1000-horsepower motor would waft about the deck. I began feeling sicker and sicker, and by the time we started lifting the craypots around the Barn Islands I couldn't hold on much longer. Seeing that I was looking quite green, Gareth handed me a can of Coke. After taking a large mouthful I heaved the contents of my stomach over the portside railing. It was as if a huge weight had been lifted from me and I felt better for the remainder of the day. It was amazing to see Gorge River from the ocean and I thought back to the many days I had spent sitting among the sandflies staring at the *Southern Legend* through my telescope. And now I was finally on board!

We continued pulling in the craypots one by one until somewhere far off Awarua Point we encountered a breaching humpback whale. All of a sudden it came rearing out of the water about 50 metres upwind of us before twisting onto its back. Its huge white flippers flicked across and hit the water, sending a gigantic cloud of spray into the air as it sank back beneath the white-capped waves. 'Do you smell that?' yelled Shane over the wind as a terrible odour of fish wafted over the boat. 'Whales smell bad!'

The large ocean swells passing under us lifted *Southern Legend* like a cork before lowering us into huge troughs. It felt like we were sliding into the bottoms of tremendous valleys in the middle of a landscape of rolling hills. Combined with a moderate northerly breeze, the swells indicated an approaching storm. Eventually Shane pushed the last craypot overboard and as the engine cranked up its revs Gareth announced, 'Right, let's go to Milford!' It was completely dark by the time we pulled alongside the dock in the shelter of Deepwater Basin, and after another roast dinner we headed straight to bed.

When we steamed back towards the open sea at 4 am the next morning, Gareth handed me a little orange jar of seasickness tablets. 'You're going to need these,' he said with a grin. He was navigating using radar and GPS in the pitch black and it wasn't long before I felt the bow begin to lift and fall with the rhythm of the swell. All we could see in any direction was darkness. The waves grew bigger and bigger and soon the bow was being lifted violently upwards before falling just in time to crash into the next one. It seemed like we were going through each giant crest of white water and as we did so the windows turned green for an instant as the entire boat was drenched in heavy spray. It wasn't long before I was huddled in a corner of the wheelhouse battling waves of nausea. I crawled outside and hid in a sheltered corner of the deck with the spray drenching my hair. When I emptied my stomach contents onto the deck, the sloshing water quickly washed it away. It felt like this could be the end and the thought of death started to seem quite appealing. I was so much of a mess that I didn't notice we had turned around until Shane passed a hot cup of tea and a piece of toast with Marmite to me through the window. 'We're going back to Milford,' he yelled over the roar of the engine. 'Thank God for that,' I thought to myself as I slowly returned to the living world. That was the end of my trip, and later that day Shane drove me back around to Wānaka and organised a ride back to Haast for me with some locals.

And so ended my first fishing boat experience. I had loved the excitement of the boat and lifting craypots, but now I had more questions than before. It looked like incredibly hard work in often horrendous conditions. I knew that it would toughen me up fast and I could probably handle it. But only if the awful seasickness went away.

The winter went on and by the time the whitebait season came around I had finished most of my year's schoolwork. Ahead there was a physics and chemistry exam in November that I would sit under supervision in Haast. I was debating what to do with my hard-earned free time and was craving to go to Big Bay to stay with Warrick Mitchell and catch whitebait.

Two years earlier I had built myself an aluminium-framed whitebait net by connecting angle bars from the hardware store and covering them with brand-new netting from the shop in Haast. I bought an electric drill to plug into our generator and assembled the net at Gorge River. To save money, I also used some aluminium bars cut from the wreckage of Eoin Wiley's old plane in the flax bushes near the river mouth. The entire net was designed to be disassembled so I could fit it in Roger's plane; I reassembled it in the shed at Big Bay during our annual stay with the Mitchells. Warrick's brother Grant had bought me some iron reinforcing bars, and Ian Todd and his son Willy had given me a quick demonstration on welding before leaving me to it. In a couple of hours, I'd managed to weld together two 1.5-metre-long metal frames that were then covered in metal whitebait mesh to use as screens to guide the whitebait into my net.

All of this whitebaiting gear was still at Big Bay and I had only used it for a couple of weeks, so I wanted to go back there alone that season. But I had to work out how to broach the subject with Mum and Dad. The opportunity came one day early in September, when Roger and his co-pilot Jess called in for a cup of tea out of the blue one day. They were returning to Big Bay to pick up a load of whitebait from Warrick. This was my chance. 'Can I hitch a ride to Big Bay with you?' I asked. 'Of course!' replied Roger. I turned to Mum and Dad and announced, 'I'm going to Big Bay whitebaiting for a while.' I packed my bag and loaded my brand-new pair of chest waders into the back of the plane. They must have known for some time that this day was coming, but it was still hard for them to watch me fly away with Roger, giving no fixed date of return.

Since Graeme and Anne Mitchell had moved to the North Island, their children Warrick, Grant and Kelly had taken turns doing the whitebaiting. Warrick welcomed me like a brother into their house and introduced me to his mate Fraser, who was helping him to fish their two whitebait stands for the season. Together the three of us caught whitebait, collected firewood, loaded and unloaded Roger's plane with supplies every few days, and zipped out to sea at high tide in Warrick's inflatable boat, with its 30-horsepower motor. One day we borrowed Ian Todd's rifle and stalked our way up the track that leads towards the Pyke River, and I shot my first deer. Warrick showed me how to gut and clean the carcass and we transported it home on a quad bike to hang in the meat safe.

I had left home in quite a hurry and had forgotten one crucial item – my toothbrush. I had to make do for two weeks with an old one found in a toolbox. Thus I learned my first important lesson about travelling: always double-check you have EVERYTHING before leaving.

Warrick had recently installed a satellite broadband dish on the roof and had his laptop connected to the high-speed internet it provided. One rainy day Fraser helped me sign up for my first email address and Facebook account. I added a few people I knew and it was amazing being able to message my friends in the outside world while still being in the depths of South Westland. Although Big Bay had become connected, we still had no internet at Gorge River, so there was no way for me to talk with Mum and Dad. Partway through my stay at Big Bay I wrote them a letter telling them what I was up to then carefully wrapped it in a plastic bread bag tied to a rock. I knew Guy Meads regularly flew his yellow Maule along the coast to the airstrip at Neils Beach and I asked him if he could throw it out the window as he flew past.

Sure enough, he returned a couple of days later and told me he had dropped my note safely onto the airstrip. I was enjoying new experiences while Mum and Dad were at home missing me terribly, and in four weeks this note was the only contact we had. Apparently, Robin actually had it the hardest and was very quiet for the time I was away. The facts of me growing up were starting to sink in for everyone and it was now more obvious than ever that things would have to change.

After two weeks at Big Bay, I said goodbye to Warrick and Fraser and hiked the 30 kilometres back along the coast to home. When I appeared around the flax bushes in front of the garden Mum was standing at the sink sorting out a fresh salad, Dad was sitting at his easel painting and Robin was on her bed quietly doing her schoolwork. They were completely overjoyed to see me and I was really happy to see them too.

Over dinner one night we had a serious conversation and I stated the obvious. If I was to continue to live at Gorge River then we would need to have an internet connection so that I could have more outside influence in my life and also contact my teachers. If I was to leave, then they would still need it to stay in contact with me. Together we decided that the days of Gorge River being completely disconnected from the outside world were numbered.

A few weeks later we all flew back to Big Bay together and stayed with Warrick for a week. One bitterly cold, rainy afternoon I was standing at the river mouth, waiting for the incoming tide, when someone I didn't recognise wandered down the beach and set up a net behind me. He introduced himself as Dave Cassaidy and after a short conversation about the miserable weather I asked him where he was from. It turned out he was the head outdoor pursuits teacher at Mount Aspiring College. Over the next week, he told us all about the college outdoor pursuits programme and what it involved. Warrick had another friend staying, whose name was Jane Hawkey. She was a lovely lady who lived by the Clutha River in Albert Town, ten minutes' drive from Wānaka. Somehow she must have heard that I was thinking of moving to Wānaka, because she mentioned that she had a room for rent if I needed it.

Several weeks later we headed out to Haast to catch the last of the whitebait season and for Dad to sell his artwork. Two years earlier Mum and Dad had bought our first car, a Subaru Legacy station wagon, so we decided to take a family road trip to Auckland for Christmas. Our plan was to drop in on friends who had previously visited us at Gorge River and then stay with Mum's family. On our previous trip to town, I had studied the New Zealand Road Code and passed my learner driver's licence test. So now I used the quiet gravel roads of Haast to practise changing gears and stopping and starting before cautiously moving onto the busier sealed roads around the township. Then I drove on the open road for the first time on my way to complete my NCEA Level 2 physics exam under the supervision of Marion Beynon. After a couple of weeks, we left Haast and our first stop was Andy and Mylrea's house in Wānaka.

Over dinner we mentioned that I had been thinking more about Mount Aspiring College and had even met one of the teachers. We talked for a while and at the end of the conversation they made an incredibly kind offer. If I decided to attend the college, then I could live with them on their small family farm in Maungawera, 20 minutes' drive from school. Suddenly the whole dream became a serious proposition and I knew that a year in Wānaka would be the fastest way for me to adapt to the outside world.

The time had come to choose my direction in life. I could have a future at Gorge River living with my family, hunting possums and eventually working on fishing boats. Or I could dive headfirst into the modern world and see where it would take me. I was facing one of the hardest decisions of my entire life.

Unfortunately I am terrible at making tough decisions and in the heat of the moment I panicked and said no. I couldn't commit to completely uprooting myself and breaking my family's hearts. Mum and Dad were somewhat relieved, but in my head I knew it wasn't the right choice. I had let myself down, just when the correct path was set out so clearly before me.

We continued our road trip up the country, visiting friends along the way and eventually arriving at Mum's brother's house, tucked behind the sand dunes of Bethells Beach on Auckland's wild west coast. Every day, my cousin Leo and I explored the dunes, caves and hidden sandy beaches around the rough coastline. Kevin and Alison joined us just before Christmas Day, and Mum, Andrew and Alison cooked a huge Christmas dinner of a large ham decorated with pineapple and cherries and baked in Andrew's woodfired oven. Grandma told us stories about growing up in Shanghai, where her grandfather worked at the British Consulate.

On Boxing Day we left Bethells Beach and drove further down the North Island's west coast to Dad's family's farm in Kāwhia, where we joined his relatives from Auckland for a memorial service for Nana, who had passed away the year before. Grandad, Annette, Sue and many of the cousins came over from Australia. Together as a family we planted four trees around a statue that Dad's Uncle Lawrence had made to say goodbye to Nana. I hiked over the sand dunes with Nicholas, James, Fraser, Jonnie and Jamie, exploring the farm. It was amazing spending time with them all and I was seeing clearly that I needed to have more human interaction in my life. The decision I had made back in Wānaka was constantly on my mind.

Eventually, we hugged everyone goodbye and began driving back towards home. In front of me I saw clearly the pathway that I was on, realising that unless I made something happen now, I would soon start my final year of school and would have missed the last opportunity to transition easily to the outside world. Mum and Dad had already made plans for the installation of a satellite broadband dish later in January and we had our fingers crossed that the solar panels were powerful enough to run it. This would be an exciting change, but I needed more to look forward to than that. I needed a challenge in life, and I couldn't see that happening at home.

One afternoon I was sitting in the passenger seat as we drove through the rolling green hills of the central North Island. It was sunset by the time I finally gathered enough courage. I turned to Mum, Dad and Robin and said, 'You know that school in Wānaka – I've decided I want to go there.' Mum and Dad listened and quietly agreed it was a good idea. Finally, I had said it. I had found the strength to make the hardest decision of my life and my family had taken it okay. Everyone quietly braced themselves, knowing that the next few months would be a huge challenge for us all.

The next day, Mum called up the college to enrol me and it was confirmed. It was now early January and far too late to get into the school hostel. I needed to organise a place to live before we flew home to Gorge River. I had already said no to Andy and Mylrea and we didn't want to ask them again. However, there was still Warrick's friend Jane Hawkey. I called her and, after telling her about our trip to Auckland, I explained my decision to move to Wānaka. 'Do you still have that room available for rent?' 'Yes, I do!' was her excited reply. The pieces of the puzzle had fallen together and we jumped into Roger's plane and headed home together as a family one last time.

My final month at home flew past. Eamonnd, a local pilot from Haast, arrived one morning with a technician from Farmside, who installed a one-metre-diameter dish on our roof. After tinkering around for a few hours, he tuned the dish in to the satellite and we plugged in our laptop. The little globe icon popped up in the bottom right-hand corner of the screen and, from that moment on, Gorge River was connected to the world. A few days later it was time for our first phone call. We set up Skype and used it to call Roger's cell phone.

'Hi, it's Robert calling from Gorge River,' said Dad.

'What, is this really you?!' came Roger's quizzical reply.

However, it was a bitter-sweet conversation because at the end of it Dad organised for Roger to pick me up a few days later and take me away. Mum insisted there was no way I was leaving alone and decided to go with me to Wānaka and stay a couple of days to help me settle in.

Before I knew it, the day had come, and early one morning I quietly finished packing my bags. The morning seemed to drag on forever. Outside the window everything was normal. The waves emerged from a sky-blue ocean and crashed onto the beach, wetting my toes as I stared past them at a seagull circling around the bush-covered top of the Gorge Islands. The sun rose above the hill and began travelling across the crystal-clear blue sky, passing momentarily behind a small puffy cloud above Cascade Point. Three tūī played in the rātā behind the house and Chooky scratched her way around the garden looking for worms and maggots from a freshly buried possum. Every second seemed like a minute and the minutes seemed like hours. Waves of doubt flooded over me and questions flashed through my mind. How was I going to fit in?

What would the other kids think of me? What if I didn't like it? And how would Mum, Dad and Robin cope without me at home? Then waves of excitement shot through me – this would be my first big adventure in life. But the excitement quickly passed and I felt hollow inside once more.

Finally, at 11 am we heard the unmistakable low-pitched *nnnnnnnNNNNN* of an approaching plane and within a couple of seconds it passed over the top of the house with a loud *rrrooooooMMMMMMMmm*. No one yelled 'It's Roger!' that day. We all knew it was him and we knew what would happen next. I stood like a statue as I watched the plane complete a long, arcing turn before aligning itself with the airstrip in the light southerly. Usually, I love watching planes land, but this day I wasn't interested. There was just too much on my mind.

We unloaded the plane. Roger had Debbie with him and they stopped for a quick cup of tea. The conversation was normal but the energy in the room was quite different from a usual visit. Dad had his arm around me and Robin sat quietly in a corner. Before long it was time to go and we walked out to the plane. Dad held me in his arms for a long time before I finally climbed into the back seat of the plane, next to Mum. Roger completed his pre-flight checks and I waved a final goodbye to Dad and Robin. With a roar we began rolling down the runway and about halfway along a gust of wind made us airborne. Roger tilted the wings away from the hillside and we turned out above the ocean into smoother air.

Tears streamed down my face and through blurry eyes I saw the *Southern Legend* lifting craypots on the edge of the foamy white water surrounding the Gorge Islands. I could see the beach where I would look for jade, the river where I fished and the airstrip where I walked each day. At the end of the airstrip stood the two small figures of Dad and Robin. I knew they would be crying too and knew they would watch the plane until it had completely disappeared out of sight behind the mountains. At this moment I wasn't just saying goodbye to my family, I was also saying goodbye to a place so deeply ingrained in me that I didn't know if I could survive away from it. A place that was my home and everything I had known for the first 17 years of my life. Suddenly we turned around Longridge Point and Gorge River disappeared from view behind the hillside.

The eagle had flown the nest.

PART TWO

Adventures Out in the World

CHAPTER 10

Adapting to a New Way of Life

The bell rang out across the grounds of Wānaka's Mount Aspiring College to signal the start of the 2009 school year. Mum and I were standing just outside the front gate and I hugged her a long goodbye. That afternoon she would be driving back to Haast on her way home to Gorge River. There were tears in her eyes but I could see she still had a familiar brave smile on her face. Any challenges I was going to face would be small compared to the challenge of living at Gorge River without her son.

I walked towards my form classroom, turning back to wave one last goodbye before I disappeared out of sight behind a building. Around me, other students hurried in different directions and everyone's paths seemed to criss-cross over the school grounds. I was surrounded by a sea of unfamiliar faces and for the first time I was completely immersed in this crazy new world that I had chosen.

After asking for directions, I managed to find my form class and made myself comfortable on a seat near the back. There were about 20 others in the room between the ages of 13 and 17 and most of them chatted in small groups, excited to be back together after the holidays. Three or four of us were sitting quietly by ourselves. The second bell rang and my form teacher, Vicky Ashton, stood up and introduced herself before going round the room asking us to introduce ourselves. When it was my turn, I explained that I was new at school and came from the West Coast south of Haast. It was quite scary to stand up and speak in front of everyone but Ms Ashton welcomed me warmly to the class. Another guy called Felix then introduced himself and I was relieved to find I wasn't the only 'new kid' in my form class.

Soon the next bell rang and it was time to change classrooms and start lessons. In my hand I clutched my schedule showing a long list of times and different places I needed to be. As I stepped outside again into the crowd of hurrying students an image of my Correspondence School lessons at Gorge River flashed through my mind. They seemed like a world away now, as if they had been in a dream. I pulled myself together and with a confident smile on my face said to myself, 'Okay, let's go!' And so began my first day at a normal school.

At lunchtime I ate my sandwiches sitting in the middle of 'the Quad', a grassy field surrounded by classrooms, with a big group of new students who were living at the college hostel. Suddenly I felt a tap on my shoulder and turned to see the familiar smiling face of Nicole Buchanan and another girl. She turned to her friend and said, 'This is Brenna. We're from Haast too, and we look after each other. Just tell me if you have any problems!' It was certainly nice to see someone I knew.

It took me about two weeks to settle into the routine of school and the new surroundings I was immersed in. As far as studies were concerned, I was relieved to be on exactly the same page as all of my peers. With the Correspondence School I had sat the same physics and chemistry exams as every other student in the country the year before, and the only thing I had to get used to was learning in a classroom with 20 others. There were so many more distractions than I'd had at Gorge River, but it was helpful to have a teacher in the same room who could explain things so much better than my Correspondence School answer sheets. I quickly found I was one of the more focused students and felt confident academically.

But studies were only a small part of the reason I'd moved to Wānaka and I was already finding the social life quite challenging. I mostly spent time with the other 120 students from my year and we would often sit around in the common room or out on the grass. About 40 of us were new to Wānaka and this made it easier because I wasn't the only one. However, I still had no idea what to talk about in a group and most of the other new students seemed to fit in much faster. At Gorge River I had learned how to talk with strangers, but they were always adults and the conversations were very different and more natural. This constantly frustrated me because deep down I knew that I was an outgoing person. I had to find a way to fit into these new social circles.

It soon became clear that I was one of the most unique students at school and it didn't take long for people to start talking about the 'new boy from Haast'. I was surprised when my peers were curious about my background and would invite me into their groups. It felt nice to be accepted. But I found it easier to get on with people one on one, especially with some of the quieter students. At the school sports day in my second week, I started talking to one girl who was a little more reserved and she introduced herself as Rebecca. We chatted away for a while and she seemed quite interested in my stories from Gorge River. Rebecca loved hiking and the outdoors, so it gave us mutual things to talk about and she mentioned joining the school rock-climbing club.

After a life of living outdoors I was pretty fit and decided to enter all the sports events that I could, even though I had never participated in any of them before. In the middle-distance running I was competitive and was easily in the top ten, but when it came to swimming I was absolutely dead last. I could swim okay, just very slowly, and everyone else was half a length in front. This didn't faze me and I remembered how at home I had always pushed the boundaries and was never scared of a challenge. Now in Wānaka many different challenges lay before me and I decided to say yes to everything in the year ahead.

A few days later, voting for the student council was held and anyone from Year 12 or 13 could put their name forward. I didn't even know what the student council was, but decided to submit my name anyway. That Friday afternoon everyone from Year 12 and 13 met in an assembly room. All the candidates had to make a speech explaining why they should be on the student council and afterwards the 200-odd students would take a vote. I was quite relaxed and when it was my turn to speak walked straight to the front of the room. As I turned to see 200 faces staring back at me, however, I was filled with terror. I had never stood in front of a crowd like this and it caught me completely by surprise. I pulled myself together just long enough to stammer out a couple of reasons to vote for me and then hurriedly sat back down. I assumed few people knew who I was and didn't expect anything to come of it.

Several days later I walked into the Year 13 common room and Harry McFadden from the hostel was waving a piece of paper at me from within a group of about 12 students. 'Congratulations, Christan, you're on the list! We voted for you.' The 12 student council members had just been announced and sure enough my name was there. I later heard I had received the second-highest number of votes. Even though I was still fitting into Mount Aspiring College and felt like the odd one out, I could now feel a part of something. It came as a big surprise and gave me a huge confidence boost.

My physics teacher, John Hammond, was a keen rock climber and most of the diagrams he drew on the whiteboard were of rock-climbing scenarios, with the students' names included in the pictures. I had loved climbing at Boyle River, so this was much easier to understand than reading my Correspondence School lessons in previous years. It also gave me an idea. After one physics lesson I walked to the front of the classroom and introduced myself. 'Hi, Mr Hammond, I'm Christan. I hear you run the rock-climbing club. Can I join?' 'Of course!' he replied in his friendly British accent. 'We meet at the outdoor pursuits shed after school each Wednesday.'

The next day I was there and everyone piled into the back of the school minivan. Mr Hammond drove us out to Hospital Flat, a popular rock-climbing area to the west of Wānaka. We stopped at Riverside Crag and he set up some ropes attached to anchors at the top of the 15-metre cliff. We took turns climbing in threes, with two belaying from the ground to keep the climber safe. Little bits of quartz jutted out from the black schisty rock face, providing small hand- and footholds. I was still scared of heights and once I was a few metres above the ground my legs started shaking. But with each climb that fear seemed to abate slightly as I learned to trust the equipment and the belayers below. Gradually I gained the confidence to go higher and higher and quickly fell in love with the sport.

Being away from school with a small group of like-minded people made it much easier for me to be a part of the group and I quickly made rock-climbing friends. I got to know Rebecca better and made new friends with Alex, Nia, Tamsin and Mr Hammond, who during the climbing club outings insisted on being called by his first name, John.

Whenever I had been out in town with Mum and Dad, I had never been allowed to go to parties or drink much alcohol. I had never done my own thing. But I was now living in a small room connected to Jane's house in Albert Town, and all that had completely changed. Mum and Dad never asked Jane to supervise me and she never wanted to. She already had Tao, a five-year-old, and spent about a third of the year away from Wānaka. Jane and I were more like friends, and I was her flatmate.

This meant that at the age of 17 I was completely free from all parental rules. There was no curfew set, no one I needed to ask before going out, and no one worrying about me if I wasn't home by 3 am. I did all my own shopping, cooking and cleaning, and made my own homework schedule. I appreciated the responsibility that my parents gave to me and it was good knowing they trusted me to make my own decisions. Before Mum had left me alone in Wānaka, she'd helped me find an old mountain bike at Wastebusters, and this gave me the freedom to go anywhere. I biked 20 minutes to school each morning, and central Wānaka was only another five minutes from there. Some afternoons I would take the mountain-bike trails along the Clutha River and stop under a tall poplar tree to look for trout in the river.

Since I was quite well known at school, I always got invited to house parties and would pedal my way there through the sunset. Most parties were held at the houses of ex-students and some became quite out of control before the police arrived to shut them down. I still found it hard to fit in, but after a few drinks it was easier to make conversation. At one house party in a flat near school the students built a two-storey beer funnel.

I got on quite well with some of the cool kids, who often invited me for a drink or asked me to join a game. Being the new kid from the bush made me a prime target for peer pressure, but I embraced it fully and didn't mind trying new things, within reason. They helped me extend my comfort zones, which in turn helped me to fit in. One night a group of friends convinced me to ask Rebecca to the upcoming school formal. She said yes and that made me quite happy.

As well as the climbing club, I joined the kayaking club for kayak-rolling sessions in the school swimming pool. There I learned how to roll correctly, starting by using the side of the swimming pool before finally learning to use my paddle to right my capsized kayak. One of the highlights of my whole school year was the 'climbathon'. This was a climbing marathon at Basecamp, the local indoor climbing gym, as a fundraiser to buy iPads for the students. The goal was for everyone to climb a combined height equivalent to that of Mt Everest in 24 hours. To top it off, our principal, Wayne Bosley, agreed to spend the entire time suspended on a portaledge attached to the overhanging roof. We all set a goal for the number of climbs we hoped to do and I raised about $500 in sponsorship from friends and family to complete 50 ten-metre rock climbs over the 24-hour period.

A group of the more serious climbers from the club started climbing together from the very start. When we reached our goals within a couple of hours, it became obvious that we had underestimated our potential. 'Okay, so how many can we do?' we asked each other. We started to get competitive and took turns completing ten climbs in a row. The hours ticked over and by 11 pm most people had gone home, leaving just Loz, the manager of Basecamp, Wayne Bosley, who was still suspended from the roof, and our small group of dedicated climbers. By now we were doing 50 climbs in a row, with an hour's rest in between. No one told us to stop, so as the night wore on our totals rapidly increased. First it was 200, then 250, then 300. After comparing numbers at about 2 am, I was surprised to find myself leading by about 50 climbs. Despite being just 12 years old, one climber, Finn, was like a monkey and had even competed at national climbing competitions. I hadn't expected to be in front of him.

We continued climbing all night and into the morning, with just one compulsory two-hour sleep break at 5 am. By 7, we were back at it and the competition was fiercer than ever. I was well in front but Finn wouldn't give up without a fight. At 2 pm, I completed my 500th climb. There were still two hours to go, but I was so exhausted that I was almost delirious, and I was starting to lose my sense of where I was and what I was doing. I was now so far ahead of the others that there was no way anyone could reach my score, so I decided to retire. In the final count my 500 climbs beat Finn's 400 and Tamsin's 350, and I was stoked. To put that in context, 500 climbs is 5000 vertical metres. Therefore, in 22 hours I had climbed over half the height of Mt Everest myself! And most importantly I had made some close friends and received another huge confidence boost. Each of these steps took me closer to feeling more comfortable in the outside world, away from the safety of Gorge River.

One of the main attractions of Mount Aspiring College for me and many of the new Year 13 students was the outdoor pursuits (OP) programme the school runs as part of the curriculum. Each week we would have four lessons of outdoor-related learning. Three were classroom-based, but the fourth was where we had the most fun. We would leave school at 12 pm in the vans and spend the rest of the afternoon rock climbing, kayaking, hiking or mountain biking, and when winter came along it was straight to the slopes of Treble Cone for ski lessons. For someone like me who had spent my entire life in the outdoors, this made school worthwhile and was always the highlight of the week.

My chance meeting with Dave Cassaidy at Big Bay the previous year had helped me to advance directly into the Level 3 class, whereas most newcomers started at Level 2. I would be learning to kayak with people who had started the previous year and I would learn to ski on a steeper mountain alongside people who had been skiing most of their life. This was a huge challenge and I had to work hard to keep up. However, I was already so comfortable in the outdoors as a result of living at Gorge River that I just needed to focus on the hard skills, and by giving my full commitment I learned fast. Unbeknown to me at the time, by accepting me into the Level 3 class, Dave had set me on a fast track into the outdoor industry.

Partway through the school year everyone began discussing what to do after school finished. Many of my friends were planning to go to university or polytechnic, and suddenly I started to think about my options in life. I had never planned to study but now, after taking the most difficult step away from Gorge River, I was ready to venture further into this new world and my previous dreams of working on fishing boats or possum hunting had faded. Hugo, a friend from my year, invited me to join him at the University of Canterbury open day in Christchurch. His mother drove us up and we stayed two nights in one of the halls of residence there. I have always loved building and fixing things with electricity and was curious about the electrical engineering degree on offer.

At the same time, I kept in close contact with my outdoor pursuits teachers and started asking questions about their profession. They pointed me towards the two-year Diploma in Outdoor Leadership and Management at Otago Polytechnic in Dunedin. It was as if this course was tailor-made for me. I could use my previous outdoor experience to gain some formal qualifications and then pass on some of those skills to others. I considered both options but in the end it was an easy decision. Despite Dad's offer to pay for tuition, I decided that I couldn't commit to four years of engineering and therefore enrolled in the outdoor leadership course. I had only taken one step into the world and I needed to explore much more before committing to four years in one place. Mount Aspiring College offered a $1500 scholarship to Otago Polytechnic and I eagerly submitted my application.

My school year had flown past and soon it was exam time. I took my study reasonably seriously and worked hard enough to get some good grades that I was happy with. My year in Wānaka was about so much more than schoolwork and I was most satisfied with my progress in other areas, such as adapting to living in a town and making friends with people my own age. But even after a year, I still felt socially awkward and knew there was a lot more work to do.

During the year, I had been home to Gorge River a few times to see my family and had even managed to do a week of whitebaiting at Big Bay with Warrick. At Gorge River I caught and froze 18 kilograms of whitebait, which I sold around Wānaka to add to my savings. Mum, Dad and Robin also visited me in May and they seemed to be doing okay at home without me. They called me every few days on Skype and being in close contact filled the gap I had left behind slightly. Listening to them talk about their daily life at home already felt like a world away from my new life.

Mum and Dad were always interested in how I was getting on with sewing my possum skins. The year before, I had finally invested in the fur-sewing machine that Peter Gray had recommended and I had it set up in my room. The machine produced a much better product than a normal sewing machine and made my job much easier. Sometimes after school I would sit in the warm afternoon sun streaming through my window and stitch together scarves and cushions, which sold quickly on Trade Me. I can confidently say I was the only kid in my class at school, and certainly the only boy, to own a sewing machine. Some of my classmates gave me curious looks when I told them about it, but they also respected my creativity and were interested in how I made money from it.

Everything I made sold and soon I received orders for two large possum bedspreads, which would sell for over a thousand dollars each. However, because I wasn't spending much time at Gorge River, I didn't have enough good skins to do the job. I managed to finish a small rug for Jane and when I eventually left Wānaka Mum took the sewing machine to Gorge River. Dad attached it to an old bicycle frame, as its motor overpowered our solar system. Later we attached it to a small electric motor taken from Mum's other sewing machine and it was far more efficient.

The last event of the school year was prizegiving, and my family came all the way from Gorge River to attend. Everyone was seated in the school gym and Wayne Bosley stood on stage announcing the prizes. I waited patiently until finally he said the words I had been waiting for: 'The Otago Polytech scholarship goes to ... Christan Long.' I was overjoyed and it was a fantastic way to say goodbye to Wānaka. The next day we drove to Queenstown, where I passed my restricted driving test before flying home with Roger for Christmas.

I had been in contact with Andy Thompson, who ran the diploma at Otago Polytech, and I was curious to know whether I could use my previous experience, combined with the Level 3 outdoor pursuits skills I had learned from Dave Cassaidy, to advance straight into the second year of the course. Eventually I convinced him to let me do that, so rather than taking two years to gain a diploma I would do it in just one! My cousin Elena also joined the course and she too went directly into the second year. Together we moved straight onto how to teach rock climbing, kayaking and other sports, completely skipping the year where our classmates had learned the hard skills. We were super excited but both knew it would be difficult to keep up. It was worth the challenge, though, and that summer before the course started, we met in Wānaka for two weeks to build our rock-climbing and kayaking skills.

My two main goals for Dunedin were simple. First, I needed to get as much experience as possible teaching outdoor pursuits and obtain sound qualifications to take into the rest of my life. Elena and I worked hard on our rock climbing, using everything we had learned at polytech, and we passed our NZOIA (New Zealand Outdoor Instructors Association) Rock 1 assessment in Christchurch at the end of the year. That, along with the Diploma in Outdoor Leadership and Management and 17 years of wilderness experience from Gorge River, made me eligible for many awesome summer job opportunities.

The second reason to be in Dunedin was to completely immerse myself in a city environment. I needed to continue working on my social skills, so I decided to live in one of the halls of residence, City College, with 300 other students. I moved into an apartment with five others, and my room overlooked Dunedin's busy main street. There were other rooms on each side of mine, and above and below. 'I'm a long way from Gorge River now!' I thought to myself.

On my first day I had barely unpacked my bags when there was a knock at the door. I opened it to find a tall, lanky guy about the same build as me. 'Hi, I'm Zach, I'm going to be your neighbour!' he announced. We headed off to play a game of pool together in one of the common rooms and quickly became friends. We looked so alike that sometimes on nights out together people would stop us and ask if we were brothers.

Each weekend, there would be a party in someone's apartment, and before long we had a group of friends to hang out with. At first, I didn't let on about my background, and I was curious to see how well I could blend in. One night we had a big birthday party in somebody's apartment and afterwards we planned to hit the clubs in the city centre. By the time the 10 pm noise curfew came around, all but two of us had passed out. One of my friends, Jenni, and I were the only ones left standing, so we rolled everyone into bed, turned out the lights and headed out on the town together. After that I started hanging out with her friends Jade, David and Morgana and we've kept in touch to this day.

The people I lived with at City College were mostly city people and my escape to the outdoors was through my course. We were always rock climbing at Long Beach, kayaking on the Taieri River, or off on some other adventure or other. Our longest trip away took us to Murchison, in the north of the South Island, for a week of whitewater kayaking. It was an amazing trip, although my kayaking skill level was still well below that of most of the others. Every day I would kayak the rivers, afraid that I would capsize in the next huge rapids, and it was the only time I have ever experienced that much fear in the outdoors. On the last day of that trip, I capsized in a relatively dangerous section of whitewater and all of the practice at the school swimming pool paid off: I rolled straight back up and kept paddling, unfazed. That was exactly what I'd needed and suddenly I didn't fear the rapids any more. I was able to try some more challenging lines through them, following my more experienced course-mates. They were different to everyone I lived with at City College, with a love for the outdoors and adventure sports, and some of them took quite high risks. I often spent time at their flats and afterwards we would search through town for brick walls to practise our climbing skills on.

Compared to the previous year in Wānaka, it now felt easier to blend into social groups. But I still felt more comfortable in a one-on-one situation, still felt like the odd one out and was always slow to speak up. For example, when everyone was talking about their favourite movies or computer games, I didn't really have much to add to the conversation. I was more at ease talking with girls than guys, but it was very awkward to get past just being friends. That said, I did find my first girlfriend, Sanne, who lived upstairs, though we broke up after about a month.

Partway through the year, Dad's book, *A Life at Gorge River*, was published and my family came to Dunedin for the launch. There was a lot of media coverage, including a classic photo on the cover of the *Otago Daily Times* of Dad, mid-stride, crossing a busy Dunedin street. Some of my friends started joining the dots between me and these news stories. Zach and another friend, Josh, came along to the fully packed book launch at Dunedin Library. There were so many people they had to turn some away and Dad returned a few weeks later for a second talk. After many years of encountering negativity for living at Gorge River, it was nice to see people suddenly interested in our lifestyle. Those who had previously criticised Mum and Dad for raising a family away from TV, phones and computers were now coming to have their own personal copy of Dad's book signed.

I loved my time in Dunedin but one year living next to the bustling main street was enough. Towards the end of my diploma,

I got in contact with an old friend of Dad's from Te Anau, Rosco from Rosco's Milford Kayaks. He agreed to take me on as a first-year sea-kayak guide for the coming summer. Not counting all my possum hunting and whitebaiting, this would be my first official job.

CHAPTER 11

Climbing Mitre Peak

Living in Milford Sound gave me another chance to adapt to the outside world, albeit in a more relaxed environment than Dunedin. Milford Sound is a small community of several hundred people and almost everyone knew of my family. 'Oh, are you the one living up the coast?' they would ask. 'You must be Beansprout's son.' I loved the wild storms that passed through Milford Sound and when it was too windy to kayak I would board one of the tourist boats and cruise around admiring the waterfalls thundering down the 1.6-kilometre-high cliffs in one of the most spectacular fiords in the world.

At work, I combined my kayak skills from polytech with my storytelling ability and unique knowledge of the West Coast and Fiordland to guide Rosco's clients around the fiord each day. One of my favourite memories of guiding is of a dark, misty morning when I met my group at the Milford Lodge. After a short lesson on the basics of kayaking we paddled out of Deepwater Basin in heavy drizzle. The bottom of the mountains were like giant bushy feet jutting out from under the dark grey clouds above, and the surface of the water looked greasy where the fresh water from the Cleddau River mixed with the salt water of the ocean. Having paid a lot of money to paddle a kayak in the rain, the clients' spirits were naturally low. However, I had seen the forecast and was quietly confident they would get their money's worth by the end of the tour.

After paddling for about 30 minutes, we stopped and I told them about the fiord and how it had formed, and then introduced myself with the story of how I'd grown up at Gorge River. They were fascinated by my family's lifestyle and I explained how when it's raining in Fiordland you still have to go out and enjoy the experience. 'It's like living in a *Lord of the Rings* scene,' I said.

We carried on paddling and I led the way along the edge of the fiord's almost vertical granite walls. Moss-covered rātā towered above and huge droplets fell from their leaves and splattered onto our bright yellow kayaks. As we were approaching Deep Cove, a slight breeze began to blow in from the ocean and within 30 minutes the rain had stopped and the sky began to clear. Mitre Peak, the guardian of Milford Sound, emerged from the gloom, and the wet cliff faces reflected the sun's first rays. One by one, the jagged, rocky peaks appeared above us and soon the entire fiord was bathed in warm sunlight.

Witnessing this incredible transformation from dark to light completed our kayak tour and for most of my guests it would have been the highlight of their entire stay in New Zealand. For me that moment awoke my sense of adventure and, as I stared up at the knife-sharp ridgeline running to the summit of Mitre Peak, I imagined myself standing up there looking down. I had already become comfortable kayaking around the waters of the fiord and now I felt a deep urge to explore these commanding peaks, which I knew would push my own limits far beyond anything I had attempted before.

I mentioned this to Rosco and he told me some stories about Mitre Peak and explained that, over the years, ten of his kayak guides had stood on the summit. Instantly I knew I wasn't leaving Milford before I was number 11. I asked some of the locals for more information and worked out that there are a few ways to make the climb. Some people opt to do it over two days, camping at around 1000 metres, while others do it in one very long day. Some carry ropes for abseiling back down the scary cliffs, whereas others choose to travel light and fast, which in turn allows more time to negotiate the difficult sections without ropes. I was confident in my climbing ability and had shaken off my old fear of heights. I knew climbing without ropes would be exposing myself to a high level of risk, but I was confident that my experience in the wilderness would guide me to make the decision to turn around before I pushed beyond my limits.

Many of the extreme things I had done at Gorge River I had faced alone, and I decided to continue that approach on Mitre Peak. I figured I would be safest with no one to slow me down or distract me, and decided to attempt the climb solo. I approached the mountain with a lot of respect, as one year earlier someone had fallen 200 metres to their death while abseiling down and their body had had to be retrieved by a helicopter from a steep ravine. With that on my mind, I chose a clear day on the weather forecast and set my alarm for 3.30 am.

At 4 am I was in my kayak and, under a faint light from the crescent moon overhead, I paddled towards the mouth of the Sinbad River, where I would start my climb. Early morning in Milford Sound is a stark contrast to the buzzing daytime activity in New Zealand's number-one tourist destination. There are no boats with motors running, no helicopters landing and no planes circling overhead. Everything is completely still and silent until just before daybreak, when the first tūī initiate the dawn chorus with a long drawn out tune that travels across the fiord's calm waters. I pulled my kayak well above the high-tide mark and disappeared into the thick undergrowth of dense rainforest that covers the first 1200 vertical metres of Mitre Peak. There I found a rough track running directly uphill at about 30 to 35 degrees, with natural stairs formed by rātā roots and mossy rocks.

By the time I could turn off my torch I was already 550 metres above sea level and from there the ridge flattened and the climbing was much more gradual for the remainder of the bush section. There was one large descent of 150 metres and it was really miserable climbing back up the other side knowing I had ascended those metres already. I emerged from the dimly lit forest just as the sun rose above the mountains to the east, and the golden tussocks covering the slopes glowed in the warm morning light. Far below me I could hear the gentle hum of the Milford community as it began to come to life, and a tour boat drew a foamy white line along the middle of the fiord as it embarked on the day's first cruise.

Not far above the bushline, the ridge narrows to become just one or two metres wide for a short 50-metre section. I vividly remember looking down between my legs and seeing the ocean far, far below. For a short while I was petrified and wondered what the hell I had got myself into. But after taking a few moments to focus on the way ahead, I began rebuilding my confidence by taking it one step at a time up the loose tussock stairs that led towards the sky. I hadn't even got to the hard part yet! A little further on, the path widened again and I was able to run along the approximately four-metre-wide rounded granite ridgeline heading upwards towards the crux of the whole climb. My confidence was growing and I began to really feel in the zone.

From around 1300 metres the ridge narrows again and becomes quite steep in sections, and the exposure to heights becomes extreme. There is a rough path worn into the mountainside by previous climbers, which leads from step to step up the loose tussocky ridgeline. The steps were just strong enough to hold my weight and I found the tussocks were useful handholds, but each one had to be carefully tested first. It was scary climbing, so I slowed down and took my time to check that each footstep and handhold was firm. Looking up the jagged ridgeline to the summit, I could see that for the next few hours just one slip or lapse of concentration could send me tumbling all the way down the sheer granite cliffs to the ocean below. I stopped to calm my nerves a little and as I did so my whole world narrowed into focus. Every move was the difference between life and death and needed to be executed correctly, without fail. Nothing else in the world mattered at that moment – and I felt truly alive.

Climbing up this sort of terrain is easier than climbing down and I began to wonder how I would get home safely again. In my backpack I carried a VHF radio and I knew that in the worst-case scenario I could be helicoptered off the mountain. However, I carefully assessed the risk I was exposed to and decided to continue.

As I neared the top, some huge slabs of rock made the climbing really fun and I changed to my rock-climbing shoes to gain extra grip on the coarse, crystallised granite hand- and footholds, shaped by the weather over thousands of years. I continued steadily upwards, all the while keeping an eye on the ocean, now 1600 metres below. Upwards … upwards … upwards … until suddenly I clambered up one 45-degree rock slab to find there was nowhere else to go. I had made it to the top!

I will never forget the feeling of ecstasy and relief that flooded through me at that moment as I stared down upon the world around me. I couldn't believe I had actually made it to the summit and as I stood some 1690 metres above the ocean it truly felt like the top of the world.

The jagged ridgeline dropped away from the summit towards the west before continuing out towards the Tasman Sea; to the north, flanked by glaciers, Mt Pembroke stood proudly behind The Lion and The Elephant. These two mountains are separated by a steep, U-shaped valley that drains into the 160-metre-high Stirling Falls. To the east, the ridge I had just climbed directed my gaze towards the Milford Sound airport and Deepwater Basin nestled at the base of a 600-metre vertical cliff descending from the Sheerdown Range. Far below, I could see the cruise boats of Milford, like small toys, and right in the middle of the fiord one small group of kayaks floating on the ocean's deep blue surface like yellow matchsticks.

After a quick radio call to the 'Paddle-on-Inn', Rosco's kayak base, I knew it was time to face my fears and begin the challenge of down-climbing everything I had just come up. Most of it went relatively smoothly and again I took it one step at a time. I discovered that down-climbing barefoot worked best: as I gently lowered myself down using the tussocks, I could feel the structural integrity of the dirt footholds with my feet. But the exposure was insane! As I watched my feet find the footholds, I could see the ocean sparkling in the sunlight 1500 metres below, and it took all of my previous rock-climbing experience combined with intense concentration to stay calm and control my nerves.

As I got to the hardest, most exposed part of the down-climb, I met another climber. He had left his mates at the beginning of the difficult section and carried on alone. We had a quick chat before I recommenced the descent on some very steep slabs of solid granite. I had already forgotten about the guy when suddenly I heard him call, 'Watch out – ROCK!' At that very instant, a rock about the size of my fist went flying past within a metre of my head. There had been no time to react and I watched it bounce down the smooth rock face for hundreds of metres before vanishing from sight. To this day, that moment goes down as one of my closest shaves with death. The guy was well above me but had been far too slow yelling the warning. And because he had started with 'Watch out' in quite a relaxed tone I hadn't reacted as fast as I could have. Had the first word been 'ROCK!', yelled as loudly as he could (which is standard protocol in the mountains), then I may have had a better chance to brace for impact. I'm quite sure that if the rock had hit my body I would have lost my footing, and if it had hit me on the head there is no doubt I would have tumbled down the mountainside towards the fiord below. Any type of fall in that location could not be survived.

Shaken, but still calm, I carried on. Thankfully the rest of the descent went smoothly and I ran down the muddy track, covering the last 550 vertical metres of forest in 35 minutes, holding onto the strong crown ferns to slow my descent.

As I paddled up to the boat ramp in Deepwater Basin, Rosco proudly acknowledged me as his eleventh kayak guide to stand on top of Mitre Peak. However, I wasn't the first to have done it barefoot – legendary kayak guide 'Horrie' had already beaten me to that!

In total, the 1692-metre climb took me nine hours, up and down. Four hours of that was spent in the most exposed section above the kilometre-high cliffs and I still remember that day as one of the very best of my life. As a child in the wilderness around Gorge River, I was never sheltered from risk and had learned to recognise the fine line between life and death. After climbing Mitre Peak and experiencing risk at a more extreme level for most of a day, as well as a very close shave from the falling rock, I discovered that other dangers in life were clearer to me. I have continued to build on this understanding since, and firmly believe that when you fully appreciate the surrounding risks, you can manage them accordingly and be much safer. I didn't know it then, but that wouldn't be my last close shave.

Experiencing something is the best way to learn, and in this modern world where people are sheltered from risk, how can they ever get the opportunity to build this critical knowledge base? Instead, they learn to fear risk rather than striving to understand it. Eventually everyone is faced with a dangerous situation, and if they aren't familiar with the sensation and can't identify it, then how will they act in the safest way? As successive generations are wrapped more and more in cotton wool, human beings are losing this knowledge. I am forever grateful that I was able to learn to manage risk, rather than fear it, from my own earliest experiences.

I returned to kayak guiding the next day, and as I paddled my group around the fiord, I gazed back up at the cliff face with utmost respect for the commanding peak in front of us. I felt a tremendous sense of achievement as I explained to my clients, 'Yesterday I stood on the top of that mountain!' 'Wow, that's crazy!' one of them replied. I thought that over for a while as we paddled on. To me it didn't feel so crazy. Extending my comfort zone was starting to feel quite normal, and I decided to search for further opportunities to expand my horizons and build on the experiences I already had behind me.

CHAPTER 12

Voyage to Antarctica

On the 5th of November 2011, I woke up at Gorge River. It was just a usual sunny morning and a light breeze was blowing the tall flax leaves from side to side outside my bedroom window. However, I was feeling bitterly disappointed. Just four days earlier I'd had to say no to a last-minute offer of a job ski-patrolling at Big White Ski Resort in Canada. I had been dreaming of skiing in Canada during a ski-patrol course I'd recently done in Wānaka, but the offer had come too late for me to apply for a Canadian working holiday visa. There was no way to fast-track the application, leaving me suddenly without plans for the upcoming New Zealand summer.

At around 10 am that morning I was checking my email on the computer via our satellite broadband when a Skype message popped up from my Auntie Alison. 'Christan, do you want a job on a ship going to Antarctica? If yes, let me know asap!' I quickly typed a reply requesting more information and she put me in touch with a guy called Warren, who passed me straight on to his brother

Duncan aboard the ship. Another few minutes and Duncan's email arrived, explaining a little more about the situation. Some of the Filipino hospitality staff had been denied their visas to New Zealand and could not travel on a Russian icebreaker embarking on two back-to-back tourist voyages to Antarctica. They urgently needed people to fill the vacant positions. Another email arrived from Eric, the hotel manager on board. It sounded too good to be true, but there was a catch:

Hi Chris,

The pay is average, US$1500 per month, but the trip experience is awesome. The staff are pretty easy-going and you can have a lot of fun.

Please note, we do need a decision in the next two hours, I understand this is VERY short notice. The voyage starts in 5 days and there are 120 passengers.

It's an opportunity of a lifetime, the work is so easy, you will have plenty of time to play.

Regards,

Eric

As soon as I read this, there was no way I could say no to such an opportunity. I was looking for an adventure and, having lived in isolated places, felt I would fit into ship life at the bottom of the world just fine. But if the ship left in five days that meant I had just four days to pack up and find a way to Christchurch. As Eric and Duncan were finalising my contract, we started making arrangements for me to leave Gorge River. Thankfully the weather forecast was clear for flying and a quick Skype call to Roger and

Debbie confirmed they could pick me up the day after next. It was all organised within the two-hour window, including returning the signed contract to Eric. I laughed when I thought back to three years beforehand when the only contact we'd had with the outside world was the mail delivery every six weeks. How things had changed.

Everything fell smoothly into place and suddenly the excitement started to hit me. I was going to Antarctica! Two days later, on the morning of the 7th, my bag was packed and I was ready to go. Each time I leave Gorge River we still experience some of the same feelings we had on the day I first left home. My stomach always feels hollow and I dread the sound of the plane flying overhead. However, now that I have been away a few times and have always returned, it is much easier for everyone. Even if I am away for a few months, Mum and Dad know I will come back eventually. So I said a normal goodbye to Dad and Robin and once again climbed into Roger's plane next to Mum before flying off into the distance.

My trip to Christchurch went smoothly and a taxi dropped me at the Port of Lyttelton at the agreed time. The driver unloaded my two bags and pointed to one of the huge vessels berthed alongside the dock. 'That's your ship,' he said. I stood in awe for a moment, taking in my surroundings. Looming above me was a gigantic Russian icebreaker with a tall yellow superstructure the shape of an apartment block, rising above the dark blue hull. Painted on the rounded icebreaking bow was its name in Cyrillic characters: Капитáн Хлéбников (*Kapitan Khlebnikov*). Along the side above the red paint on the waterline were the letters FESCO and above that each deck was painted an industrial shade of green. This would be my first time living at sea and I would cross the roughest ocean in the world four times on this ship. My excitement for the unknown sent chills prickling down my spine. What was it going to be like down there in the mighty Southern Ocean? Little did I know that the life I led on solid land in innocent little New Zealand was about to be turned upside down aboard this mighty vessel.

I was beckoned on board by a middle-aged Russian sailor who was manning the gangway. I said 'Hi' and he replied with a simple 'Hello' before gesturing for me to follow him inside through a solid iron door. Duncan, a Kiwi guy with a short ginger beard and a huge smile, stepped forward to introduce himself. 'Welcome aboard, Chris! Your cabin is this way.' My roommate was already settled in and in a strong Canadian accent informed me his name was Dylan. We headed off to find the rest of the hotel staff and get acquainted with the ship. Dylan and I would be working together alongside Matt, a Kiwi; Alex, another Canadian; and Amanda and MT from New York. The head chef, Walter from Austria, would be our boss. As we casually chatted away, little did we know that together we would experience some of the best days of our lives, alongside some of the worst imaginable.

We were due to depart the next day, so after about ten minutes of introductions everyone was sent straight to work. One of the huge cranes mounted near the bow lowered pallets of food through the hatches on the foredeck and we formed long human chains to unload them into the food storage areas. As I stacked the crates of zucchinis into the chiller, I had to chuckle to myself – this was just like our monthly supply drop to Gorge River, except on a whole different scale. The ship had already experienced horrendous seas on the passage over from South Korea and many of the existing stores had come free, creating a huge mess in all of the dry-food storage areas. The floors were half a metre deep with bags of stores mixed with crushed cardboard boxes of cans of almost every other kind of food item, labelled in one of five different languages. In the corners the mess was a metre deep and there was no way we could tidy it all that day; we'd have to deal with it at sea.

The next morning we were put to work preparing food. There was no training for the job and no one set out a plan for the day. It was my first time working in a kitchen and it passed in a blur of chopping huge quantities of vegetables, with different people giving orders, constantly yelling and pointing to an endless list of jobs that needed doing. The passengers came aboard around midday and by the time we passed under the heads of Lyttelton Harbour it was already quite late in the afternoon. As I lay in bed that night, completely exhausted, I tried to gather my thoughts. I decided to keep a diary of this crazy new adventure and scribbled down my first entry:

Day 1

10th November

We left Lyttelton late and headed south. Worked 16 hours today with just one 10-minute break. Not even a lunch break. Eric saw the Sea-Legs seasick pills I have and laughed. He returned later with some that he says are much stronger. Fingers crossed they work.

By day two I began to feel a routine developing and over the next two weeks this is what it looked like. My day would start with my

5.40 am alarm and as I brushed my teeth the ship would roll from side to side beneath my feet. We started work at 6 am and my first job was to prepare three fruit platters of neatly chopped melon, pineapple and watermelon. Then there were the tinned pears and prunes that first had to be found in the mess on the storage room floor and always seemed to be somewhere near the bottom, beneath huge tins of tomatoes. They would go in serving bowls and everything would be sent from my kitchen on the third floor to the dining room on the fourth, where four Russian waitresses would set the fruit out on the breakfast buffet. The rest of the breakfast was made upstairs in the hot kitchen by Matt, Walter and Dylan, so Alex and I downstairs could immediately start on lunch.

I would prepare three meat platters and three cheese boards, as well as bowls and bowls of chopped tomatoes, lettuce and cucumbers. It doesn't sound like much, but when each of these food items needs to be prepared for 150 people it takes a long time! And I had never prepared restaurant-quality food before, so the procedures were completely new to me. I was quite slow at the start and after being yelled at to 'Chop chop, don't sleep!' by the head chef I tried my best to pick up the pace.

Once lunch was prepared and sent upstairs, I would head directly up to the serving area to plate the lunch orders from the bain-marie. Dylan and I served the food as the scary Russian waitresses took the guests' orders. If we were slow, they would get very angry and start swearing at us in Russian. If we didn't plate the food neatly enough, the unshaven Walter would come charging in and throw the plate aside. He would then do one plate to show us what he wanted, before storming back into the kitchen. If the orders were coming out too slowly, Eric, the hotel manager, with his shiny shaved head, would march in and also tell us to 'Chop chop!' It was a high-stress environment and when the weather was rough everything had to be done with one hand, as the other desperately clutched a railing to avoid being thrown across the kitchen into the opposite wall.

As soon as lunch was served, I would head back to my kitchen, hoping for a ten-minute break. On the way, Walter would hand me a large box containing 80 boiled eggs to peel. 'Appetisers,' he would grunt and wave me down the stairs. At first I wondered when we had our own lunch and then I noticed everyone else was just eating as they worked, so I started doing the same. Once my team became more efficient, we were able to sit down to eat our meals after the passengers had finished, and eventually we even had time for a morning meeting to discuss the plan for the day. In the first two weeks, however, there was none of this and Walter would just randomly yell instructions down the stairs at us.

The eggs were part of the appetisers Alex and I would prepare. We'd place them on a bed of salad and top them with mayonnaise – Walter liked everything smothered in mayonnaise – and to finish we would add red and black caviar with a sprig of parsley and a perfect slice of tomato on the side. Preparing these ingredients for 150 appetisers would take most of the afternoon, and just before dinner we would plate them and send them upstairs about 20 at a time in a small Soviet-style food lift. As well as the appetisers, I would need to prepare another large bowl of lettuce, three more cheese boards, three meat platters, three different salad dressings, and the usual salad condiments. Dylan and I would meet once again at the bain-marie to plate the evening meal and repeat the same chaos as at lunchtime.

After plating, it was straight back downstairs, where all the leftovers had to be put away. We would clean any dishes that the 65-year-old Russian helper had missed and wipe down all the tables and benches. On a normal day we would finish around 10 pm, and if the passengers had a landing the next day – for example, on the Auckland Islands – then we would have to make sandwiches for everyone to take ashore. On those days we finished after 11. With this schedule, I was earning less than $4 per hour. I found that after working that much in one day there was only just time to sleep enough to recover for the next. The highlight of my day would be taking a hot, steamy shower after work. I would brace myself against the motion of the ship by jamming myself between the wall and the sink. The sensation of the hot water running over my fatigued body seemed to wash away the pain and suffering of the day, and I would collapse into bed exhausted.

After living most of my life in the outdoors it was a huge shock to be stuck inside for the entire day below deck, with no view or fresh air. Once or twice a day I would sneak away for a few minutes and stand on the deck sucking in huge breaths of fresh, clean sea air and watching the dark blue ocean slide past the side of the ship. On the evening of day two I watched an albatross swooping, its wingtip almost touching the top of the gentle ocean swell. Looking further into the distance, I was surprised to see land. After the chaos of the previous days it felt like we had been at sea for a week already. 'Surely we should be out of sight of New Zealand by now?' I thought to myself. But it was unmistakably the Dunedin skyline – we hadn't even left New Zealand yet. I felt a shadow of reality fall over me and began to realise just how far it was to Antarctica.

Day 3

17 hours of work today with one 15-minute break.

Today is the roughest day yet, the ship started rolling at around 6 pm right as we were making the appetisers. Four of the plates fell off and smashed into a thousand pieces on the floor. All the boxes of vegetables we had stacked in the cooler fell over and made a huge mess.

Serving the meal was really hard and MT had a tray of cutlets fly off and smash everywhere. Finished by making 100 sandwiches for the landing tomorrow.

We went past the Snares Islands today.

The weather was in our favour and I had avoided seasickness, partly due to the super-strong medication I had been given. However, just as we started dinner service on day five we began punching into the teeth of a powerful Southern Ocean storm. The *Kapitan Khlebnikov* was built to break ice and much of the ship's weight is in the superstructure above the waterline, which exerts downward pressure on ice. But at sea this weight makes it very top-heavy, and as the storm strengthened, the whole ship started rolling 35 degrees to each side. The simplest of tasks became very difficult and when a big set of waves smashed into us, all we could do was hold on to a bench or handrail for dear life and wait. After rolling five or six times the extreme motion would abate and we could continue with the job. My kitchen was near the bow, so we would get thrown around on every wave. Up on the eighth floor of the main superstructure it was just about impossible to stand up, due to the ship rolling so far from side to side.

I hadn't taken my seasickness medication that morning and began to feel really ill halfway through serving dinner; however, I had no choice but to continue. Eventually I was able to sit in a dark corner of the kitchen for a few minutes as the nausea gripped me. My stomach felt like it was tied in a knot and I stayed in that corner staring blankly at the hard tiled floor. The metal trays and piles of plates made loud crashing sounds as they were thrown backwards and forwards with each roll of the ship. This storm was forecast to last three days, and I felt small and completely helpless. Irene, the assistant hotel manager, found me and returned a few minutes later with a different type of seasickness medication and a glass of water. I tried to swallow the tablet and threw it up almost instantly, along with the rest of my stomach contents. From my corner I could see that the leftovers from dinner still needed to be cleaned up and I knew if they weren't done soon the glass bowls could smash on the floor and the whole situation would become much worse. I gritted my teeth and began clearing everything away.

Eventually the expedition doctor turned up with yet another brand of seasickness medication for me to try. I vividly remember looking at the small yellow tablet with the letters BMS written on one side – the same as the registration letters of Roger's plane. My thoughts flashed back to the countless times he'd flown us safely over the Southern Alps through all sorts of conditions. At that moment a little spark of confidence ignited inside me, as if there were greater powers out there looking after me. 'I can do this,' I told myself, managing to swallow the tablet and keeping it down long enough to finish the work. Afterwards I grabbed a bowl of beef stew with rice and stumbled straight to my room. Once lying down, I was amazed to find the waves of nausea had almost completely disappeared and I forced myself to eat some food. The reality was that there were guests to feed and our job had to be done – the bosses didn't seem to care if I was sick. I was experiencing first-hand the reality of working in international waters, where there are few laws covering working conditions.

On day eight there was an announcement over the ship's intercom: 'Iceberg – 15 degrees off the starboard bow!' Everyone dropped what they were doing and raced up on deck for a few minutes to take in this incredible sight. In the distance on the starboard horizon, I saw the ghostly white shape of my first iceberg, surrounded by a glassy calm ocean reflecting the light blue evening sky. The powerful Southern Ocean swells were now behind us and the ship's bow rose and fell ever so slightly, as if in slow motion. There was a chill in the air and suddenly the ship had come alive. The passengers who had been seasick in their cabins for the entire voyage were now on deck enjoying the fairy-tale spectacle. I took a deep breath of cool, clean air and with a fresh spring in my step headed back to the hot, stuffy kitchen.

Soon we started breaking metre-thick sea ice and one evening after work I stood in the soft evening light on the roof of the ship above the bridge. From there I looked ahead at the floating ice floes and watched as the *Kapitan Khlebnikov* threaded its way through the thinner patches of ice. Now I could appreciate the ship's true power. Like most icebreakers, it is driven by diesel electric generators and at maximum power six generators provide a staggering 24,000 horsepower (18.5 MW) to the three hardened-steel propeller blades. That's enough electricity to run 12,000 homes and it provides enough force to break through three-metre-thick ice. When the ice became too thick and we slowed to a stop the captain would reverse a few hundred metres before ramming the floes repeatedly until we crashed through.

One morning as I broke down cardboard boxes, I sliced my middle finger open under the fingernail with a sharp knife. It wasn't too serious and after a trip to the ship's doctor to get bandaged up I returned to work a little shaken. I was annoyed at myself for letting my guard down and it was a very good wake-up call. There were several machines we operated that could cause major injury. I had to use a meat slicer every day and Dylan had already sliced a chunk off his knuckle while cutting meat on a rough day.

As I chopped away at a huge pile of cabbages that afternoon, I thought back to my childhood. Despite growing up in a wild place surrounded by many different risks, I had never had an accident. Mum and Dad had always said, 'We are too far from hospital – you must not hurt yourself.' They taught me to watch the river and the ocean and learn how it all worked, and use that knowledge and my common sense to keep myself safe. Now I was 3000 kilometres away from a hospital, in one of the most isolated corners of the planet, and I needed to do the same. There were many different hazards in that kitchen, such as knives, band saws and meat cutters, but I didn't need someone to identify them for me. I could work that out myself and I vowed that each time I had to use these tools I would make sure every single movement I made kept me clear of injury, no matter how rough the ocean.

One afternoon Duncan came running into the kitchen. 'There's a helicopter bound for an emperor penguin colony leaving in a few minutes – Matt, Dylan, MT and Chris, put on your cold-weather gear and lifejackets and meet at the helicopter pad. Everyone else makes up for your absence and you repay them next time. Go!' Having long been dependent on weather and aircraft, I'm used to being spontaneous, and ten minutes later I was sitting in a Soviet-era Sikorsky helicopter as it skimmed above the ice floes of the Ross Sea before landing on the ice just off Franklin Island. The ice was covered in a thick layer of snow and initially felt more like solid land. From the helicopter we had seen what looked like a grey smudge on the snow, resembling a crowd of thousands of people standing around in a huddle. That had to be penguins.

After receiving strict instructions to be back in one hour, we set off in the direction of the 'crowd'. The snow squeaked underfoot as we walked and the whole landscape seemed to be made up of three colours: white crunchy snow underfoot, the steep black cliffs of Franklin Island, and the monotone grey cloudy sky above. A few hundred metres behind the penguin colony a gigantic iceberg with a crack down the middle rose from a flat, frozen ocean and suddenly a single shaft of sunlight illuminated the glacial blue ice cliffs. One large section of ice perched precariously, as if waiting for the right moment to crash down onto an unsuspecting passing penguin.

After a short walk we found ourselves 100 metres away from a colony of emperor penguins. There were adults standing about one metre tall, with their creamy yellow fronts and black backs and flippers. The chicks were about 60 centimetres tall and grey and fluffy all over, except for their black head with its big white patches around each eye. Some chicks stood with an adult while others gathered in small crèches, perhaps with an adult supervising nearby. The emperors had just finished a long, dark, cold Antarctic winter and hadn't had many visitors recently (not that they ever do). Consequently, they were curious and took turns coming over to investigate us.

They didn't seem to be afraid and one walked straight towards where I was sitting in the snow. Its head swayed from side to side as it walked and it reminded me of an old man who had lost his walking stick. It stopped about a metre away and stared at me inquisitively with its small, beady eye for about a minute. Then it ruffled up its feathers and shook itself, before dropping onto its belly and sliding like a sled towards Matt and Dylan, propelling itself with its clawed feet. I always thought penguins walked, but in reality most of their travel is done on their front feathers, sliding like a toboggan, which requires much less energy.

After 30 magical minutes, we returned to the helicopter pad and the rotor blades churned up a large cloud of loose snow before carrying us safely back to the ship. For one hour, almost like a dream, I had been transported to a world of raw nature and rugged beauty. As I stepped back into the galley to complete the remaining eight hours of my shift, the dream was shattered and I was brought back sharply to the reality of ship life.

Day 13

Today the ship was parked in some thick ice and we were allowed off to walk around under the huge bow. There were emperor penguins playing in the water and sometimes they would launch themselves onto the ice to say hello.

We had the polar plunge! When it was my turn I looked into the black water, saw an emperor penguin swim past, and then jumped into the –1.8°C water. What a magical moment. Afterwards a Russian sailor handed me a shot of vodka and I had a 20-minute hot shower to warm up.

Worked 17.5 hours today preparing for Thanksgiving, with a 1.5-hour break.

A few days later it was my turn to go ashore again and I climbed back into the helicopter. The pilot turned and flew directly south until the *Kapitan Khlebnikov* was a speck in the distance. Below me I could see a small, green, twin-cabbed vehicle driving on a long, straight road on the sea ice. There was a little green hut at the end of the road, set near the front of a glacier that ran down the flanks of the mountain above. Mt Erebus (3794 metres) is the world's southernmost active volcano and on this particular day was capped by a huge lenticular cloud resembling a sombrero. Thirty minutes later I found myself standing on the sea ice in front of the sprawling buildings of McMurdo Station. In summer the station can house over a thousand scientists and support staff, and in good weather there are regular flights back to New Zealand by C-17 Globemaster or C-130 Hercules ski plane. I could see these aircraft parked at the end of a runway on the sea ice in front of the station.

Since it was Thanksgiving we were not permitted to visit McMurdo Station and instead visited Discovery Hut, which stands on Hut Point peninsula nearby. This wooden Australian-style hut was built by Captain Scott during his first Antarctic expedition.

Walking inside was like stepping back to 1902, when Scott and his men spent the winter in their ship frozen into the sea ice in front of the hut. There were old biscuit tins, a fireplace where they burned seal blubber, and even the carcass of a sheep hanging in one corner.

At Scott's hut I met a guy from McMurdo Station who was out for an afternoon stroll. He explained that he was spending the summer there working as a carpenter. We chatted away for a few minutes, and before long I was flying back to the ship in the back of the helicopter. However, I couldn't get that conversation out of my head. I knew New Zealand's Scott Base was just a few kilometres away. Could I work there and make this world of rock, snow and ice home? Perhaps I could even drive one of those strange vehicles across the ice?

Day 18

27th November

Today we drove along under the sheer cliffs of the Ross Ice Shelf.

We then turned north and set course towards Hobart.

On the evening of day 21, I was standing in my favourite position on the roof of the ship. This, along with the sauna, had become my happy place away from the chaos of the kitchen below. About a kilometre off our starboard bow, I could see a black, rippled line, the end of the sea ice that had kept us safe from the huge Southern Ocean swells beyond. After years of staring out at this ocean from Gorge River, I could read the ominous sky and deep down inside feel an approaching storm. Before going to bed I walked through the kitchen and made sure there was nothing that could come loose when the ship started rolling again. Late that evening after everyone went to bed we exited the safety of the sea ice and began punching towards Hobart through horrific ten-metre swells. I slept very well in the rough conditions and experienced the craziest dreams.

The next day in the kitchen all hell broke loose. The ship was rolling heavily, 35 degrees to each side, and the bow heaved up and down in a corkscrewing motion. The simplest job, such as walking across the room, was hard work and every movement had to be made in time with the swell. Even though I had secured the kitchen the night before, some things had come loose and there was broken glass all over the floor. In one of the cooler rooms a large tray of goulash had tipped over and coated the entire six metres by six metres chiller floor.

I ate only a little breakfast and within an hour had already started throwing up. I felt my stomach cramp and raced out of my warm, stuffy kitchen to the door at the back of the accommodation block, where I sat on the step in the biting ice-cold wind and spray. There I heaved the contents of my stomach into a wax-paper sick bag. Afterwards, a wave of euphoria washed over me, and that combined with the ocean spray felt so good that I even cracked a smile. Around me huge, black, menacing waves were literally throwing this 12,000-ton, 122-metre-long ship around like a bath toy. Yet above the angry crests of the giant swells, the albatrosses of the Southern Ocean continued to glide, using their 3.3-metre wingspans that had evolved specifically for these horrific conditions. After a couple more minutes contemplating the power of nature, I braced myself once more for the waft of odours in the kitchen.

I repeated this routine every hour or two. In the few minutes after throwing up, I would feel well enough to eat some dry crackers and drink water. We still had another seven days at sea until Hobart and I had to keep my energy up. I have experienced a few horrendous days in my life, most of which have been at sea, but looking back now, that day at the mercy of the Southern Ocean swells was by far the worst of my life. Thankfully, after a rough start the next day, I was able to keep my lunch down and quickly overcame the seasickness. The conditions took a few days to improve, but now at least I could face the chaos with a strong body.

Finally, after eight days at sea, we pulled alongside the Hobart docks. After one last breakfast the passengers departed for the airport and a group of us was allowed to go ashore. As we walked down the wharves towards town, the concrete seemed to move beneath our feet and the solid land felt unfamiliar and foreign. In the hustle and bustle of Hobart everyone was going about their normal routines, yet I felt so far removed from it all, as if I was watching everything in slow motion from a distance. We found a grassy park and soaked up the warm sunlight, marvelling at the long green blades of grass as they tickled our skin. After working 12 to 16 hours a day for 30 days straight, it felt like heaven and we just couldn't get enough of it. Three hours flew by and suddenly our time ashore was over. With heavy hearts we pulled ourselves together and turned back towards the ship. That evening we waved goodbye to Hobart and a course was set due south back to Antarctica. It was time to do it all over again.

CHAPTER 13

Possuming at Ryans Creek

After my time in Antarctica, I headed back to Gorge River to see Mum and Dad and spend some time in the wilderness. I contacted the local helicopter hunters in Haast, Ken and Jeremy, who offered to drop me at home on their way past the next morning. We lifted off in their Hughes 500C from the helipad behind Haast township and in the first light of dawn flew south towards the Cascade Valley. Ken guided the helicopter along the Cascade River flats in search of elusive deer, which leave the safety of the forest at night and in the early morning to eat grass. When one was spotted, Ken would dive towards the ground, flaring the helicopter right above the running deer with a loud chattering of blades. I held on tightly to my seat, feeling like I was on a rollercoaster, and watched intently as Jeremy started shooting, before leaping off the skid into the long grass to recover the carcass.

After watching the helicopter hunters fly past for so many years, this was the first time I had ever been in a helicopter as it hunted, and it was really fun to see them working from up close. We continued the hunt over into the Pyke, then past Big Bay, and by the time we made it to Gorge River we had a load of deer hanging from the cargo hook. They dropped me on the airstrip in front of our house and then, with a loud whirring of rotor blades, lifted off and disappeared up the river valley. I stood on the end of the airstrip for a moment feeling as though I had just woken from a dream, before turning to hug Mum and Dad, who had stumbled out of bed as the helicopter landed.

After the hustle and bustle of the previous travel days and the adrenaline-filled deer-hunting flight, Gorge River seemed so calm and peaceful. While I had been away, Robin had left home and moved to Wānaka to complete her last year of school, just like I had done. Mum and Dad were now living at Gorge River alone and it would take a year or two for them to adjust to life without their kids. Little else had changed since I had been away, however, and they still went about their daily routines of lighting the fire in the morning, collecting firewood, digging the garden and creating artwork to sell. Probably the largest difference was that with Robin and me gone they needed 70 per cent less food, so Dad set the net only every once in a while, Mum's vegetables from the garden now lasted through the winter, and much less food needed to be flown in from the supermarket.

Dad had always been very cautious around firearms and when I was growing up we'd never had a rifle. From the age of 12, I began to dream about the possums I could hunt if I could shoot them rather than run them down or use traps. I knew Dad was not interested in shooting and I never pushed the subject with him. After moving to Wānaka and finding myself independent from my family, I'd decided to get my firearms licence. A year later I'd used some of my savings from possuming to buy the strongest air rifle I could find. With this I could shoot quite a few possums, but it lacked the power to knock over the big ones and hunting them still required a lot of running. Eventually I bought a .22 single-shot rifle for $100 from a Wānaka policeman, and now this was the first time I had been at home with my new weapon. I decided it was time to push my possum-hunting limits to find out just how many I could shoot. After studying some maps, I planned my first serious possuming trip as an adult. I could see a route over the 700-metre mountain behind our house to the Ryans Creek catchment and Dad told me about some grassy river flats there, five kilometres upstream from the ocean, that might have a few possums.

I had also upgraded my torch since our previous trips to Big Bay. I now had a homemade headlamp with a 30-watt halogen bulb mounted on a piece of wood held onto my head by some elastic. It was powered by 12-volt motorcycle batteries, which I could charge with two five-watt solar panels. Batteries are not light, and together with my sleeping bag and camping equipment my backpack weighed 29 kilograms. This would be my first multi-day trip into the forest alone and I chose a nice fine spell of weather after a week of torrential rain to set out.

After hugging Dad goodbye partway up the hill, I headed off into the rimu and beech forest, following deer trails along the ridgelines in the general direction of Ryans Creek. I double-checked with my map and compass until I found a safe ridge that curved down into the creek in a place where I knew there would be no dangerous bluffs. Eventually the ridge dropped into a nasty canyon, which soon opened out onto the river flats I had been aiming for. It was almost dark by the time I found a hunters' campsite and a large sheet of black plastic I could use for shelter. It was much larger than the small tarpaulin I was carrying, so I strung the plastic up between some small beech trees on the edge of the forest. Underneath, I laid out my sleeping bag and foam mat, away from the dew that started to settle over everything. I was starving after the hike and set about making dinner.

For food I had pasta, rice and vegetables and my plan was to cook over a campfire, so I hadn't packed a gas cooker. The fire would also be used to make hot water for drinks to keep me warm through the frosty winter nights. During the day there had been a strong southwest wind blowing and the sun had been shining from a clear blue sky. However, the winter sun had been on the river flats for only a couple of hours and everything in the area was still soaking. The West Coast bush gets extremely wet during rain and there are very few dry corners to be found. After ten minutes of searching under logs and trees for anything dry, I had a few handfuls of leaves, grass and moss that were dry enough to use as kindling. But it wasn't much and there were no dry sticks over two centimetres in diameter anywhere to be found.

Nevertheless I decided to give it a go and the fire crackled into life, starting with a sheet of toilet paper before catching on to the leaves and grass. Shortly, however, the dry bits had all burnt and the larger wet sticks had not caught alight. The fire died away, leaving a sad pile of steaming wet sticks. 'Okay,' I thought to myself, 'this is going to be harder than I expected.' So I searched around again and came back with a few more bits and pieces of dry kindling. The fire built up again but no amount of blowing could light the wet sticks and after five minutes the last yellow flame disappeared. As I contemplated my predicament it was obvious that no fire equalled no food and warmth and that equalled a miserable night with no possum hunting. I needed to use everything I had ever learned in the wilderness to get that fire lit.

I took a moment to look around and take in the full beauty of the valley. The icy-cold creek tumbled down its bed of rounded sandstone cutting its way through the grassy river flats on each side. The grass gave way to tall rimu, beech and rātā that towered above like shadowy giants clinging to the steep hillsides that rose several hundred metres on all sides. In the sky the deepest shades of purple left over from sunset were fading to black and the first stars were beginning to twinkle in the crystal-clear night sky. A fantail flitted by, catching the last sandfly, and as a light puff of wind tickled my cheek I could feel the energy from the wilderness calming my thoughts. Although I was far outside my comfort zone my mind was clearer than it had ever been before. I was completely alone and everything I needed to solve the problems before me had to come from within. I had not carried a 29-kilogram backpack over a 700-metre mountain for nothing, and knew there must be a way to get that fire going.

I scoured around the river flats again, this time looking further into the forest among the larger trees. There were a couple of small hollows that the rain had not soaked and there I found a few small, dry twigs and some bark. One coprosma bush was sitting in an exposed corner of the river and the wind had dried it slightly more than the others. Under a huge log in the riverbed I found one larger stick that was dry and after breaking it in half I now had two dry sticks three centimetres in diameter. After 15 minutes I studied the small pile of dry kindling and carefully built it into a perfect teepee shape so that the fire from each dry piece would catch on to the next. Then came the smallest wet sticks and finally the larger ones on top. The fire built up slowly and I blew on it as hard as I could for five minutes until my head started spinning. Slowly the damp sticks started burning and little by little the fire grew. Once the smaller wet sticks were burning they began to dry the larger ones and after ten minutes I had a healthy campfire crackling away in front of me.

When the flames were 40 centimetres high I put my billy on to boil and added some pasta. During the 15 minutes it took to cook, I grabbed my rifle and did a quick circle around my camp, looking for the possums I hoped would be there. Within five minutes I had already shot five big fluffy possums and sat down to pluck out the fur. This many possums was really bad for the bush, but it was going to make for a very productive hunting trip! Excitedly I finished off my hot dinner and prepared for a big night of spotlighting.

I hunted along the river flats upstream from my camp. There were many possums out in the open eating the moss and grasses, and by scanning my torch along the tops of the trees for the red reflections of their eyes I could spot those that were eating leaves high above the ground. Then it was just a matter of stalking up to within 20 or 30 metres of them, from where I could take a shot. The possums in the trees seemed less afraid and most of them would stay put until I was directly below them. One accurate shot to the head and the possum would fall cleanly to the ground in front of me. Every now and then one would become stuck between some branches and I would have to climb up the tree to retrieve it.

On the steep mountains on each side of Ryans Creek are huge slips where the trees have fallen away, leaving massive grassy scars through the forest. Possums love these 45-degree slopes and with good aim I could shoot them and let gravity roll the carcasses down to me. Occasionally one would get stuck in the tussock grasses and I would have to climb up 30 or so metres to get it, balancing on the narrow deer trails cut into the steep, crumbly hillside. From there I would again shoot above me until another became stuck and I would eventually find myself a couple of hundred metres up the mountainside, clinging on to tree branches while chasing possums with my torchlight. Once I had three or four, I would stop and pluck the fur before the carcasses cooled down, and soon my bag began filling up. I splashed backwards and forwards across the creek in my sandshoes and in some places the water would be thigh-deep with a very swift current. I was moving so much that I didn't even feel the cold and I kept going until 3 am. I finished with a tally of 35 possums and, after heating a hot chocolate in the last embers of the fire, crawled into my sleeping bag tired and exhausted but extremely satisfied. All my childhood dreams of possum hunting were finally coming true.

In the daytime as I slept, the batteries charged just enough from the solar panels to give me power for the next night. Late in the evening I walked three kilometres downstream to the end of the river flats and passed three deer standing out in the open. They watched me curiously for a while before turning and running along the bush edge and around a bend of the river. I began hunting again just as the first stars came out and by 2 am I had shot and plucked 35 more possums and had worked my way back to camp.

Having finished hunting the entire river flats, the next morning I packed up my camp, attached the large bag of possum fur to the outside of my backpack and began the walk out to the river mouth. This part of the river runs through a gorge as it cuts through the mountainside to the ocean. The riverbed itself contains huge boulders the size of houses and sometimes it's easier to climb under them than it is to go over. The crystal-clear creek forms waterfalls and tight rapids as it flows through the mountains and there was one crossing that I found quite scary. It was only four metres wide but the water was waist-deep and moving swiftly. I had with me a small emergency locator beacon that Mum and Dad had bought me, but in this sort of terrain I still couldn't afford to make a mistake. Very carefully I studied the flow of the water until I had worked out a route. I stepped in confidently and ran with the current for a few large steps and was safely across. Not far downstream, the creek went under a huge boulder and around a large log. I had to be careful not to slip, or I could be sucked under a boulder not far downstream and drown. Eventually the large boulders gave way to stony gravel and I emerged onto a steep, sandy beach. Angry waves were crashing where Ryans Creek meets the ocean.

Tucked away in the forest nearby is our bivvy built from tarpaulins and long lengths of driftwood. Here I met Dad, who had walked the eight kilometres south from Gorge River to set a possum trap line. My batteries charged faster with the stronger sun and that night I set out along the coast to the south. Dad came with me to help pluck the possums and we hunted five kilometres of sandy beach all the way to the Hacket River mouth. The next night we found a dry sandstone creek bed that ran all the way up a hill through the forest. Where the creek meets the beach there was a large stand of tutu trees and in one of them five large possums were chewing the juicy green leaves. Further up, the trees hang over each side of the creek bed and every hundred metres or so there would be another pair of possums sitting in the branches. A few years later I returned to this creek and the whole patch of tutu around the creek mouth was dead. Sadly, with that many possums eating their leaves, the trees have no chance to survive and eventually become skeletons.

By the end of the four-day hunting trip I had shot 131 fluffy winter possums and had 8.5 kilograms of fur stuffed into my bag. The price of possum fur had risen over recent years and was now $140 per kilogram, earning me over a thousand dollars. I was satisfied that by spotlighting I could combine my fitness and bush skills from my childhood with a rifle and a stronger torch to push the limits of what I was capable of in the wilderness. I was coming closer to reaching my full potential in possum hunting. The only problem was that in four nights I had covered all the easy ground for shooting in the area. I needed to find a place where I could hunt for many nights or even weeks on end.

After a few weeks at Gorge River, I walked out to Haast. Mum and Dad had agreed to lend me their car, which was parked at Roger's hangar in Queenstown, and I drove it north to Porters Ski Field to work my first winter as a ski-patroller. Here I continued to develop my mountain-rescue and first-aid skills. I worked on skis each day and my job included constantly monitoring the slopes for hazards. Sometimes after heavy snow I would join the snow-safety officers as they commenced avalanche bombing high on the mountain at sunrise. During the day I would often be called to the scene of an accident. In my time at Porters I attended five life-threatening ski accidents and used my first-aid experience to safely package and transport each patient down the mountain in a toboggan to a waiting rescue helicopter. I also quickly fitted into the group of 30 staff members who worked on the mountain. I made many new friends from all over the world and our conversations would cover the ski fields in Norway, Sweden, Switzerland, France, Canada and the US.

While growing up at Gorge River, we had always been very interested in the outside world, including not just New Zealand but the whole globe. I remember as a 12-year-old having competitions with Robin to see who could name the most countries, and we could each recite almost the entire 190 listed in our atlas, and knew most of their populations and geographic locations. Since I had taken the hardest step away from home, I felt nothing was holding me back. Now that I was surrounded by people from all over the world, it felt natural to want to expand my horizons.

One evening after ski-patrolling I clicked 'buy now' on an Air New Zealand ticket to London, leaving in November. I barely even thought about what it meant and just knew that I was following my intuition. I had some savings from patrolling and possum hunting, although most of it had gone towards paying off my student loan, and I knew I could visit some of my new European friends from Porters. Apart from that, I had no idea where I was going, what language I would need to learn, where I was going to stay or who I would meet in the far-off lands of Europe. The less I knew, the more the idea excited me!

This decision marked the end of my three-year transition from Gorge River to the outside world. I was now totally confident in social circles with people my own age and felt a strong part of any group of friends. It had taken a long time and I'd had to work hard to get this far. The last big step in the process had happened a few months earlier, following my voyage on the *Kapitan Khlebnikov*. After leaving the ship in Perth I'd found a job doing face-to-face fundraising for the Red Cross and Médecins Sans Frontières. For three months I'd constantly approached complete strangers in an effort to strike up conversation, using my storytelling ability to make friends with everyone, and if it went well they would make charitable donations.

My team travelled throughout Perth and on to North East Queensland where we would spend ten hours a day, six days a week, talking to strangers. Eventually I was utterly exhausted from this, but the last of my social awkwardness from growing up in the wilderness had completely gone. I was comfortable talking to anyone of any age or ethnicity, anywhere, anytime. I had finally built myself a good foundation of social experiences and could move forward into the future, where I would embrace my differences and use them to my advantage.

I realised that the skills from Gorge River combined with what I had learned in the outside world could take me literally anywhere. I could now live in the wilderness, hunting and fishing for food, just as easily as living and working in a developed urban society. There was only question left in my mind. How far could I really go?

CHAPTER 14

Twenty-one and Off to Travel the Globe

On the night of my twenty-first birthday party, the shadows started to lengthen and the blustery southwest breeze abated, leaving a silent, calm evening. I had been at Big Bay whitebaiting with the Mitchells, and Roger and Debbie had flown Mum and Dad down from Gorge River for the event. We were joined by local helicopter pilot Jason Laing, Grant Mitchell and his mate Nathan. As the sun slid towards the horizon, Dad and I collected some large logs of wood using a quad bike and trailer on the long sandy beach and we built up a huge pile in the sand dunes in front of the DOC hut. We lit some dry gorse under the logs and as the flames began to lick at the larger logs above, the first of the Big Bay whitebaiters appeared from the flaxes to join the party.

Right on sunset a red and white Cessna 185 zoomed low over our heads and after a steep, banking turn touched its wheels down on the sand below the high-tide mark. 'That's the Cascade plane,' said Dad and down the beach we could see Dobbie, who has been whitebaiting at Big Bay for over 50 years, drive up to the plane on his four-wheel motorbike, towing a trailer. Soon enough Dobbie's bike came up the trail through the sand dunes with Simmo, the four Cascade guys and a large pile of Speight's loaded on the trailer. The guys who whitebait at the Cascade are famous for enjoying a beer or two and they would be welcome guests at my birthday party. Not far behind them came Guy and Davida Meads along with Barry and Cliff and Trevor on their three-wheelers.

Jason and Grant threw a heavy log of rātā on top of the fire and a large cloud of sparks flew up into the evening sky around the circle of hardy whitebaiters. The conversation covered all topics, from the recent lack of whitebait to the large number of possums and deer in the area. It was really special to see all these people in one place and by the time the Southern Cross was circling the clear night sky above, there were 30 of them congregating around the huge driftwood fire at Big Bay, 60 kilometres from the closest permanent civilisation.

The next day I flew back to Gorge River with Mum and Dad to spend my last two weeks in New Zealand with them before leaving for Europe. While I was at home, we had the enjoyable week-long visit from Ben Fogle and the Channel 5 film crew that I mentioned in Chapter 4 and then, before I knew it, I found myself in the cramped seat of an Air New Zealand 777 bound for London. I still remember the plane doing a banking right-hand turn above downtown Auckland and seeing the Sky Tower lit up in blue, standing proud above the Viaduct Basin. The roads criss-crossing the city were lit up by thousands, maybe millions, of orange street lamps. Moments later, New Zealand disappeared from view and I settled in to my first long-haul flight. I had no idea where this new adventure would take me – I had no commitments, no car, no mortgage or student loan, and I had no idea where I would end up or even when I would come home. A chill went down my spine and I suddenly felt truly free.

On a cool autumn day, I stepped out of Heathrow Airport. The flight had been very good despite the lack of legroom. At 187 centimetres tall, I was never going to be very comfortable flying, but I'd still managed to get a little sleep. Sean, the assistant producer from Ben Fogle's TV crew, had kept in touch with me and had ordered a taxi to pick me up and take me straight to his house in Brixton to spend my first night. He was out for the day but had left me strict instructions to make myself at home until he got back. I will be forever grateful to him for his hospitality and although I only stayed one night it had to be one of the most important nights to have a place to stay – my first night on the other side of the world, in a city of millions.

As 12 am in New Zealand had become 12 pm in London, my body clock didn't know if I should be sleeping, waking up, going to bed or something else, and I felt quite out of place. The streets were really busy and people seemed to be in such a hurry to get places. Some people on a street corner urgently wanted to talk to me and I recognised them as face-to-face fundraisers, the job I had done in Australia. On another street corner someone else wanted to sell me a copy of the latest *Big Issue* magazine and I politely refused as I ducked through the mobs of people wearing black woollen winter jackets and jeans.

Everything appeared different from what I was used to: the buildings were about five floors high in all directions. Even the cars looked strange, yet also strangely familiar – maybe because of a *Johnny English* movie I had watched with my cousin Leo when I was young. Even the language spoken in the street was not always English, as Brixton is so multicultural. There were people of all different ethnicities and I found it fascinating and exciting as I soaked in my surroundings. It wasn't long, however, before it all became too overwhelming for my jet-lagged self and I crashed into bed at Sean's house in the mid-afternoon.

And that's how my life as a traveller started. From London I spent some time in the UK before backpacking across Europe towards the east. I found Western Europe quite similar to New Zealand in some ways, but as I travelled further east by bus and by train, the cultures became more different from my own and therefore more interesting. After spending Christmas with a friend, Jana, in the Czech Republic, I continued east through Poland, Hungary, Romania, Bulgaria and Turkey.

By travelling alone, I learned much more about myself. For example, in each place people would recommend a long list of sites to visit and I never found these very interesting. There were only so many churches I could photograph before they all looked the same. I wanted to meet people and experience the local culture through those who lived there. I started couch surfing and instantly found it the easiest way to connect with people in each city. Also, rather than visiting the main list of recommended cities, I would simply look at a map, choose a route through a random list of places, and stop where I could find a couch-surfing host.

Sometimes I would stay with them, but other times I would just meet them for a drink. They would always proudly introduce me to their country's food and language and often I would end up meeting all their friends as well. Most cities would have a meet-up at a bar once or twice a week, where all the foreigners and locals could gather. It was such a fantastic way to meet people along the way and although I was travelling alone I didn't go a day without talking to someone. I have always been used to meeting strangers and at Gorge River, despite our extreme isolation, we welcome everyone into our house. As I travelled across Europe, I was making connections with strangers every single day. All of my social awkwardness as a child had reversed and I had become outgoing and constantly found new friends in each city that I visited. I always added them to my social media and have kept in touch with many of them to this day.

In Istanbul I was at a couch-surfing meet-up one evening with about 50 other people from all over the world. An American girl in the crowd seemed to be the most travelled person in the whole group and we eventually got talking. Her name was Graceie, and she was inviting everyone to join her at a friend's house south of Athens. I had already planned to head in that direction, so a few days later I met her and we stayed for a week together in a deserted, wintry Greek tourist town. One day we decided to hitchhike from Athens through the Balkan countries and on to Barcelona. We packed our bags and set off on our first adventure together. We had no idea where we would stay, but as we each had a sleeping bag and some winter clothing, I figured we could just go and find accommodation wherever we ended up each evening. In the following nine days we hitchhiked 3200 kilometres through 12 countries, meeting countless kind locals along the way.

Once we reached Barcelona, Graceie went travelling with her mother for three weeks, leaving me to explore Spain by myself. I toured around one of the most fun countries in the world, surrounded by fun people, couch surfing and partying wherever I wanted, but most of the time I felt unexpectedly lost. Graceie and I were both very adventurous, resourceful and afraid of nothing, and she had stolen my heart away. This was a new feeling for me, as I had never properly fallen in love before and it caught me quite off guard. It was a very happy day three weeks later when we were reunited in a park in central Barcelona. While lying on the grass in the shade of a fountain we hatched the plan for our next adventure: Morocco.

By this time we had a proper tent, and although the camping gear was heavy it gave us complete freedom. We could hitchhike and just go with the flow, meeting the locals as we went, and in the evenings we would look for a place to sleep the night. Many people in Morocco invited us home to stay with their families, but sometimes we'd ask to be dropped off in country areas, where we'd wait until no one was around before slipping unnoticed into a forest or desert at sunset.

One evening, as we hiked out of a remote mountain village towards forested wilderness, we found ourselves walking with an older-looking lady who had two kids and a goat. As we passed their house, she beckoned us up the rough, muddy path through the long

Off on a hike in the Haast Pass with my outdoor pursuits class from Mount Aspiring College

On a mountain-biking trip with Mount Aspiring College, in the Pisa Range near Wānaka

The *Kapitan Khlebnikov* parked in thick pack ice in Commonwealth Bay, Antarctica, 2011

In the kitchen of the *Kapitan Khlebnikov* with my coworker Alex, displaying some of the 150 appetisers we had to prepare each day

A sunset in the Craigieburn Range, when I was working as a ski-patroller at Porters Ski Field, in 2012

Graceie (second right) and me with our host family in the mountains of Morocco, 2013

Carrying a huge backpack full of possum skins, weighing around 40 kilograms, from the Pyke River to Big Bay in 2014

At Big Bay with, left to right, Robin, Willy Todd and Steve Dobson

Welcoming visitors from Queensland and Wānaka during a stay at Gorge River with Graceie

Showing off my catch of two butterfish and two blue cod, after a successful spearfishing trip to the Gorge Islands in 2015

SV *Hawk*, in which I sailed for three months (July to September 2015) through the Northwest Passage. Here the yacht is moored amid icebergs at the mouth of the Ilulissat Icefjord in Disko Bay, Greenland.

Guiding *Hawk* through icebergs from the top of the mast, just off Ilulissat, Greenland

At the bow of *Hawk* in front of a glacier in Lancaster Sound, in the Canadian Arctic

At the helm of *Hawk* during 10-metre swells in the Bering Strait, from where we could see the United States and Russia at the same time

Left to right, Jérémie, Graceie, me, Shanan and Joe in the cockpit of *Hawk*, towards the end of our successful transit of the Northwest Passage

Visiting Scott Base in Antarctica for the first time, in 2016 while on a voyage with Heritage Expeditions. Little did I know that this would soon be my home for ten months.

My first experience of the brutal cold of Antarctica: teaching a field training course when it was minus 42 degrees Celsius, 2017

Sitting on the ice with majestic emperor penguins, near Scott Base, Antarctica, 2017

Leaving the house at Barn Bay while tramping to Gorge River with Tamsin Lane, 2017

Back at Scott Base, working for Antarctica New Zealand in the summer of 2018–19. The green Hägglunds behind me were our main form of transport on the sea ice.

In the back of a helicopter with Jamie (left) and Morgan (centre) on a flight to collect penguin guano samples from Cape Adare with Antarctica New Zealand

Camped with a science group next to a huge Adélie penguin colony at Cape Hallett, in the Ross Sea region, Antarctica, 2019

Heading out of the Tromsø Villmarkssenter in northern Norway on a sled ride, with two guests and nine excited huskies, January 2020

Zircon and Rubin patiently waiting for the day's sledding to commence

Receiving an enthusiastic doggie hug from one of the craziest huskies of all, Thermos

Ski touring near our home at Villmarkssenter, with Nat (left) and Andreas (centre)

Sitting by a campfire under a full moon: husky Ali, Malthe, Nat and Andreas

Sea kayaking with Nat around the southern tip of the Lofoten Islands, in northern Norway, on what must have been one of the calmest days of the year, summer 2020

Walking along the exposed ridgeline of Vengsøya Island, near Tromsø, with Andreas, 2020

The last rays of the sun light up my home for the winter of 2020–21, at Nordreisa in northern Norway. You can see the lake, the barn, the house and the 60 dog kennels.

Out on a 60-kilometre training run in the forest near Nordreisa after a welcome snowfall, with the temperature around minus 20 degrees Celsius

The Aurora Borealis (Northern Lights) danced across the sky each night above Nordreisa.

With my favourite husky, Is, at Sommarøy near Tromsø. Is lived with me for eight months and she was one of the hardest things to leave behind when I decided to return to New Zealand.

grass. We were prepared to camp but after she became quite insistent we agreed to join her and curiously followed her into her simple home. We could barely speak a word of each other's languages, yet she excitedly introduced us to her mother, husband and three kids aged from four to sixteen. 'Bonjour', 'bonjour', 'bonjour!' was about the extent of our French.

The house was very traditional and consisted of an uncovered concrete courtyard measuring about seven metres by seven metres, with grass growing in the corners, enclosed by a four-sided, single-storey concrete building. Each side was divided into separate rooms and there was a bathroom with a squat toilet, a kitchen, one living room with a small TV and a bedroom. The other rooms were for the goats and a cow and chickens. This family was obviously very poor compared to others we had met in Morocco but they were rich in hospitality and insisted we stay the night. The kids were extremely curious and taught us a few words of French as we drank cups of hot freshly brewed Moroccan mint tea.

Aside from the TV, they had much the same amount of technology as we'd had at Gorge River when I was young, and it was so nice to see how these people lived off the land and were not obsessed with smartphones or computers. We communicated predominantly through sign and body language that evening, but it didn't stop us from having a slow conversation about where we were from and how we had hitchhiked all the way from Athens. We gave them a large chunk of goat meat that we had with us for dinner, and the mother cooked it with freshly picked vegetables in the most delicious tagine. Afterwards we sat with them on colourful mats on the floor and drank more of the sweet mint tea. Eventually they gestured for us to sleep on a pile of soft blankets on the floor in the

TV room and we fell asleep to the gentle hum of crickets singing in the grass outside. In the morning we said goodbye and they waved to us from their front gate as we walked down the road and into the distance.

The whole experience was really special and it made me think of home. As a child I had lived in a quite similar way to this family, while the rest of New Zealand led much more luxurious lives with cars, nice houses, ample electricity and various technological devices to make life easier. Our life was much more comparable to that of the developing world than the first-world country we lived in. And yet the values and skills I learned at Gorge River have helped catapult me to wherever I want to go. I feel no limitations on what I can achieve if I set my mind to it. And I want this to be an example to people in the developing and undeveloped world that it doesn't matter where you come from, you can achieve ANYTHING if you put your mind to it.

When I was little my parents' income of only a couple of thousand dollars a year was well below the poverty level, yet now I have travelled to 60 countries on six continents. I have never received a cent towards my travelling from my family and every single mile I have journeyed has been funded by my own creativity, ingenuity and hard work. However, what my family did give me were the basic skills and a self-reliant mindset, and those values have nothing to do with what borders you live within or your family's yearly income or the people who live around you.

Soon Graceie and I had been travelling together for three months and were becoming very close. We shared much of the same curiosity for different cultures and were both happiest when expanding our knowledge of the world. Every day we set out to meet new people and were constantly searching for fresh experiences to extend our own comfort zones. We wanted to continue exploring the world together, so I invited her to return home with me to Gorge River. With her enthusiasm for new experiences, I knew she would be a perfect adventure partner around South Westland. A couple of days later we booked tickets to New Zealand and after the flights were confirmed we had a good laugh. It would be my first time taking a girl home to meet Mum and Dad!

CHAPTER 15

Bringing a Girl Home

Mum and Dad were happy to see me and very curious to meet my new girlfriend. As I had expected, Graceie adapted smoothly to our way of living at Gorge River and fully embraced most aspects of it. Now that she was so eager to explore my own backyard I finally had an adventure partner to share my knowledge of the wilderness with. Over the next three years we returned several times to Gorge River for three to five months each New Zealand summer and together we explored deeper into South Westland. Graceie got along with Mum and Dad very well and fitted into our life more easily than I'd ever imagined anyone could. We did everything together, and she would do it all while wearing my old Swanndri jacket and a dress over her sandfly-proof thermals.

Graceie jumped at the opportunity to learn more about our way of eating food grown in the garden and collected from the chemical-free wilderness around us. She had come from a childhood of incredibly unhealthy eating in the US and over the years had improved her own asthma by eliminating some foods from her diet. I bought a .223 rifle for deer hunting and every two weeks we would stalk through the bush together in search of deer. By now export prices were so low that the helicopter hunting was almost non-existent and the deer numbers were high. Usually, we would return within an hour or two with a backpack of fresh meat and would hang it on hooks in our fly-proof meat safe in the cool forest behind the house. After maturing the meat for three days, we would begin eating some each day for a week until eventually the outside of the legs would start to mould a little. We now had no freezer, so we would process the remainder of the meat in one go. Some of the nice muscle bundles were cold smoked to help them last another two weeks, some were cut into strips and dried to make jerky, and the rest was minced. The mince would stay in a pot in a cool part of the house and as long as Mum brought it to the boil each evening it could last up to a couple of weeks.

Every day we ate food that we'd caught, which allowed Dad to take a break from fishing and possum hunting while we were there. When the weather was good we would eat fish, and when it rained we ate the venison. Graceie and I helped with jobs around the house and built Mum a new woodshed that we then kept full. The ocean had been eroding the middle section of our airstrip in recent years and Graceie spent days helping me trim the flax bushes and sedge grass to keep the airstrip safe for pilots to land on. When it was raining, we would pick through Dad's jade offcuts and polish up nice pieces to take as gifts on our next travel adventure.

Summer at Gorge River is relatively warm but the ocean is still a chilly 12 to 16 degrees Celsius, so we both bought good-quality wetsuits. When the weather was settled and the sea had calmed down, we would go freediving for crayfish, and I bought a hand spear for blue cod and butterfish. After years of staring out to sea as a child, studying the ocean, I had still never been out to the Gorge Islands. It was always dangerous to row our dinghy through the constantly crashing waves on the river bar and I had been to sea only once with Dad, on an exceptionally calm day. But now I was ready to try going out there and one calm day we kicked our way out to sea on our body boards, with a fishing rod and mask and snorkel in a backpack. Since we were not in a boat we couldn't be capsized, and after timing a lull on the bar we only needed to punch through a couple of smaller breaking waves before reaching the glassy ocean beyond. In the deeper water the swells passed safely below us, and we were out of the main danger zone.

There are strong rip currents around the river mouth and in the channel between the Gorge Islands and the shore. I had studied these currents all my life and had played out many scenarios in my head already. Therefore we were able to use these currents to push us swiftly out to sea, and after paddling for 15 minutes we neared the islands. Here the waves surged over a metre up their sides and the foamy water crashed backwards and forwards. I carefully watched the rhythm of the ocean and chose a lull in the surges to paddle in close. A smaller surge lifted me high up and as it drained away I carefully hung on to the razor-sharp rocks. Using the few seconds before the next surge, I scrambled to safety above the water's reach. Then it was Graceie's turn. I carefully guided her in and she made it safely onto the rocks during the next lull in the swells.

Now that we had reached safety, we set up our fishing rods and began casting into the deep water around the islands. It didn't take us long to catch a blue cod and eventually we had three or four large enough to keep. Next, I dived back into the surging waves to search for crayfish in the cracks and crevices around the islands' rocky walls. I was amazed to find many of the small caves full of crayfish and on future trips I would explore the underwater world around the Gorge Islands further. There were so many crayfish that I quickly became bored with catching them and each time I returned I would try to catch something different. Usually, the water visibility is only a few metres, but after a week of calm weather it would be ten to fifteen metres and I could stalk blue cod through the large seaweed-covered boulders on the ocean floor. They were quite curious and eventually would turn to look at me for a second, giving me the chance to aim my two-metre Hawaiian spear powered by a rubber sling.

During these trips to the Gorge Islands I would practise freediving deeper and deeper and eventually on one breath could make it to a maximum depth of ten metres before returning quickly to the surface. Five metres was easy and there I could spend 30 seconds exploring the maze of cracks, caves and channels around the jagged limestone outcrops that make up the islands. There were crayfish in most of the places I looked and there were always deeper places I couldn't get to, so I kept pushing my limits. It was lots of fun and my new wetsuit and freediving equipment really helped. I also learned to read the risks around me and use the rips and waves to my advantage while in the water. However, there was another risk that I was exposed to and without even knowing it I was pushing into very dangerous territory. Eventually I received a warning from the heart of the ocean itself.

One day, after catching a few blue cod, I left Graceie to continue fishing and jumped in with my hand spear to try to find a different fish species on the vertical rocky walls of one of the Gorge Islands. The sea was glassy calm and the surges around the rocks were only rising and falling one metre, which is calm for that particular island. It's always spooky to freedive around and from the surface you can only see the walls disappearing into the murky gloom, with no sign of the bottom. A few nervous chills travelled down my spine but I was used to diving where I couldn't see the bottom and quickly calmed myself. After a few dives to about five metres, I saw a huge blue moki, a really good eating fish that is rarely seen at Gorge River. I followed it down and down, equalising my ears every metre or two as the water pressure increased. At about ten metres I stopped and watched it glide off into the gloom. For the first time I saw the flat bouldery bottom of the ocean, another few metres below me.

I dived down again and this time there was a school of smaller fish that I had also never seen before. Calmly I waited for them to come around me and lined up a good-sized one to spear. I released the white fibreglass hand spear and the black rubber strap propelled it through the water. It hit the fish I was aiming for, but in the process the strap slipped through my fingers and the spear slowly glided down to settle on the bottom of the ocean, out of reach in front of me. I really needed oxygen, so I kicked powerfully back to the surface. As I sucked in huge breaths of air, I decided to have one attempt at retrieving the spear. I had no idea how deep it lay, but knew it was deeper than I had ever freedived before.

After taking my time to recover, I sucked in as much air as I could and duck-dived towards the bottom. Down I went, down, down, down. As the pressure increased, I equalised my ears and soon the bottom appeared out of the gloom with the white hand spear clearly in view. Suddenly, about three metres from the bottom, my ears stopped equalising and the pressure built quickly. The spear was just one metre away now and my ears were becoming very painful. As I reached to grab it, my head felt like it was going to split in two and my vision started to narrow. But the spear was in my hand now and I needed to breathe. I pushed off the bottom and kicked as fast as I could towards the surface. The rock wall in front of me seemed to go on forever and now my lungs were contracting uncontrollably in an effort to breathe. Still I kicked upwards and upwards until finally I burst out of the water, gulping down huge deep breaths.

I was quite shaken and lay on my back for a couple of minutes rising and falling with the surges, calming myself with deep breaths of sea air. Eventually I kicked towards the island and pulled myself out of the waves, back onto the sharp rocks above the seaweed line. I didn't feel well and was still a bit dazed from what had happened underwater. There was a dull pain in my ear and when I spat some salt water from my mouth, I noticed it contained a small amount of blood. I made my way over to Graceie, who was still fishing on the other side of the rock. She hadn't noticed anything out of the ordinary, but I told her that I had gone too deep and didn't feel well. All I wanted to do was return to shore, but first, out of curiosity, I dropped my fishing line to the bottom to measure the depth. It confirmed I had dived 14 metres. Shaken and subdued, I kicked the 500 metres back to shore on my body board with all my gear in my backpack. I didn't tell Graceie the full extent of what I'd done until later that night, and I didn't tell Mum and Dad until a year or so later, to avoid scaring them.

Lying in bed that night, my head was spinning with thoughts. Fourteen metres was about four metres deeper than I was used to, and I realised that because I'd been wearing a weight belt I would never have floated up to the surface if I had passed out. Even if Graceie had noticed something, she couldn't dive more than two metres under the water herself and all she could have done was swim to shore and report me missing. I was furious with myself for having succumbed to the temptation of retrieving the spear, when I knew it was too deep and I should have left it. This is an extremely common trap to fall into in the outdoors and I learned a valuable lesson in that regard. But no matter how much I thought about it, there was one huge question that I had no answers for. What had happened to my body down there and how much danger had I been in? I needed to learn more about the dangers of freediving.

Since then I have completed two freediving courses, in Egypt and Bali. Through these courses I learned that the danger of running out of air near the surface that day at the Gorge Islands was much higher than that of the pressure I felt in my head at 14 metres. The main injury from excess pressure is usually a perforated eardrum: as it breaks, the pressure is relieved. This causes long-term damage but does not usually lead to falling unconscious underwater. As for the blood I spat, it may have been caused by a small pressure squeeze in my sinuses or throat, and although it was scary, in reality it was probably the least of my worries.

The training also helped me to freedive more efficiently and on the final day of my last course I reached a depth of 30 metres while holding just one breath. That is deeper than many people even know it is possible for humans to freedive and is twice as deep as most people are allowed to scuba dive. I have used these new-found skills to spear fish on the incredible coral reefs of Hawai'i and Tonga, where I could comfortably dive to 15 metres and spend 20 to 30 seconds stalking fish for dinner.

Whenever I am at home during calm weather, I return to the Gorge Islands to continue exploring the seafloor. As I swim the 500 metres from the shore to the main island, I search for butterfish hiding in the seaweed. On arrival I wait a few minutes for my heart rate to slow, then take a deep breath, duck-dive and kick powerfully towards the bottom, following the seaweed-covered walls. The pressure increases and I calmly click my ears every two metres. As I descend, the light dims to a deep blue colour. When I arrive at the bottom, I stop and hang there relaxing, just above a large boulder the size of a car. At this point my lungs are compressed to less than half their normal volume and it feels like the ocean is wrapping itself tightly around me in a huge, watery bear hug. I give a gentle kick forward into a gloomy cave under the rock and, as my eyes adjust to the light, 20 or so crayfish emerge from the gloom. Every time I return, there are more and more of them, and in some places they are stacked two or three on top of each other. When I reach out to grab them with my old leather ski glove, it's almost impossible to miss.

From the cave, a crack runs all the way back to the surface and I gently pull myself up the vertical wall with my hands as if rock climbing in slow motion underwater. Yet more crayfish are stacked in the crack and I pick through them, choosing a couple that are takeable size for dinner and placing them in my number-8-wire, hand-stitched catch bag. I become more aware of my body and feel the first lung contraction, which tells me I have used roughly 60 per cent of my oxygen – it's time to return to the surface. Three powerful kicks send me gliding swiftly upwards. Soon my head breaks through the shimmering barrier between air and water and my eyes take a second to adjust to the blinding sunlight.

On the Channel 5 documentary Ben Fogle had asked me, 'If you bring a girl home will you make her skin a possum?' 'No,' I replied, never imagining that I would find a girl who would want to. That line was one of the most iconic in the documentary and it always made people laugh. When Graceie and I started possuming, I suggested she could pluck them while I did the skinning. However, she insisted on playing a part in every step of the process and I eventually taught her how to skin a possum herself.

After catching the local possums around home and Ryans Creek, it was time to search further afield. I had always dreamed about spotlighting larger river flats. I knew Big Bay had a lot of possums and after studying some maps we decided the Pyke River flats offered the best chance of success in the area. There were just a couple of problems – we would need a lot of equipment to camp for two weeks, and the Pyke River was two days' walk away. If we could find a ride it would make it much easier.

For Mum's fiftieth birthday we organised a surprise party at Gorge River and we collected crayfish, pāua and smoked fish and shot a deer for the occasion. We invited the local pilots by email, choosing a day in the middle of a fine spell that was settled enough for flying. Mum had a huge surprise when our friends Geoff and Pat Robson, Roger and Debbie, Ian and Sue Todd, Max and Lisa, and Blair all landed on the airstrip one sunny evening, their planes loaded with beer and birthday presents. Most of them slept the night in the DOC hut and we celebrated Mum's special day with everyone squeezed into our small house. We ate so much food and Graceie baked a huge cake in the camp oven for dessert to go with another sent in by Casey Todd.

I had been studying the 14-day forecast on the internet and there was a long spell of fine, settled weather on its way. Before the party, Graceie and I had organised all of our possum-hunting gear and asked Roger if he could take us to the Pyke. Just after sunrise the next morning, Roger skilfully landed the plane on the short grass airstrip in the middle of the upper Pyke River flats behind Big Bay. We had a plastic tarpaulin for shelter, rice, pasta and vegetables for food, two new lithium-powered headtorches and two solar panels.

The first night we headed several kilometres south down the Pyke to the end of the river flats near Lake Wilmot. I had maps and aerial photos of the area and the plan was to hunt every bit of open river flats and catch every last possum we could. The flats were quite grassy and any possums sitting out on the grass or within the first line of trees were easy to spot with the torch. As darkness fell, possums began appearing along the bush edges and as we hunted into the night I went ahead, shooting through the maze of grassy clearings, stands of beech trees, toetoe and flax bushes, and leaving behind a trail of possums for Graceie. She plucked them, and any with nice shiny coats and no missing fur we took with us to skin. Eventually our bags became too heavy and we hung them up in a tree and covered them with a fly-proof bag to skin the next day.

As we worked along the river flats we frequently crossed the Pyke. Usually it was about 40 metres wide, thigh-deep and sometimes quite swift. It was very cold and I remember one crossing was a bit deeper than I anticipated and we started floating along for a few metres before we regained traction on the rocky bottom and continued towards the other side. All of this was by torchlight, in the middle of the dark, starry February night. I was in my element, testing myself in the wilderness, and Graceie was up for the challenge, always two steps behind me. For energy we chewed on venison jerky that we had made at home.

We spotlighted until about 4 am. After shooting 50 fluffy possums we fell asleep exhausted just as the first rays of sun began to show the outline of Red Mountain above us. We slept under a large tarpaulin shelter with some mosquito netting draped across the top of the sleeping bags to keep off the sandflies. However, about 30 minutes after we fell asleep, I awoke to a sandfly bite. 'That's strange,' I thought, 'it must have crawled its way around the mesh somewhere.' Then there was another, and another. This continued through until morning and we struggled to sleep in between the constant bites. Once we woke up properly and investigated the problem, we found the mesh we had was not sandfly-proof at all. We watched as the pesky little flies tucked up their wings and squeezed straight through a mesh designed for mosquitoes. Anyone who has camped in Fiordland or the West Coast will understand the situation we were in. On a bad day, there can be swarms of hundreds or thousands of these sandflies and each one wants to suck your blood. They don't cause any long-term harm and they don't carry diseases, but each bite hurts and is super annoying. Now we were two days' walk from home and we'd planned to be here for two weeks.

Once we got out of bed around midday, the sandflies joined us for breakfast, lunch and even dinner and only disappeared the moment it got dark. Having grown up with sandflies, I knew what I was in for. However, poor Graceie was not so used to them. She put up with a lot on that trip and the constant exposure to sandflies was probably the hardest part of the entire experience.

In the afternoon we walked back through the area we had spotlighted the night before to skin the possums we had left hanging. Everything looks different in daylight and I had to use all my bush skills to find the way back to the hanging bags, using a rough map and no GPS. Mum had agreed to pay $18 for the good-quality possum skins, which was much more than the $8 we could get by plucking the fur. However, skinning is incredibly hard work and even after years of practice it still takes me a couple of minutes to skin a large, tough possum. As she'd promised, Graceie did her share of the skinning. Each day we did about 30 possums and within a couple of days we had multiple cuts on our hands from their sharp claws and the prickly bush lawyer plants and our backs ached. On return to the camp we would lay the skins out on a sheet of newspaper to dry for a couple of days.

By the end of ten days we had spotlighted the entire length of the bush edge around the Pyke River flats and covered everywhere I thought there could be a possum. Each morning I had to soak my stiff, swollen hands in a cold creek to get them moving and stretch my back over a log in order to stand up straight again. We were exhausted and decided to carry all our equipment back to Big Bay, from where Roger could fly it to Gorge River on his next supply drop. This turned out to be quite an ambitious idea. After packing up our camping equipment, possuming gear and six huge bags of fur and skins, we each had about 40 kilograms on our backs. The distance is only six or seven kilometres, but it was a long, painful day walking along the Pyke tramping track. We arrived at Big Bay just before sunset and collected some mussels for dinner to go with the last of our pasta.

We hiked the 30 kilometres back to Gorge River the next day and finished the trip with 450 possums shot over nine nights. Finally, I'd had the chance to use all of my bush skills, fitness and know-how, exactly as I'd dreamed of doing since I was young. And it was amazing to share all these skills with Graceie, who was able to contribute her own energy to the trip and seemed to be fazed by nothing.

Over the next three years, we searched Google Maps for other large areas of river flats and did similar trips into the Cascade, Waiatoto, Pyke and Rakaia rivers. Geoff Robson helped us with his R44 helicopter and other times we were able to use four-wheel-drive access. Together we caught thousands of possums and the money we earned always went towards our next overseas adventure.

By now, Mum was processing hundreds of skins each year with the fur-sewing machine. I had always wanted to make fur hats, so one rainy day Graceie and I pulled apart a cheap aviator hat and made a cardboard pattern from all the pieces. We then cut the same shapes out of possum skin and, after sewing them together, lo and behold we had an incredibly warm, fluffy hat. After making a couple more we product-tested them in winter conditions up the Rakaia River and found that they were significantly warmer than anything else on the market.

The next summer we guided with Heritage Expeditions and due to my previous experience aboard the *Kapitan Khlebnikov* I was asked to guide on a 30-day expedition to the Ross Sea in Antarctica. This was an incredible opportunity: I had finally moved up from the galley into a position that actually excited me. Because I would be spending much of the time outside, I decided that I should make myself the warmest fur hat possible. I chose the fluffiest skins and salvaged some waterproof oilskin fabric from Dad's old raincoat for a lining. It was so warm that I decided to make two more. It turned out I wasn't the only person with a cold head and they sold on board within minutes.

CHAPTER 16

Sailing the Northwest Passage

In June 2015, Graceie and I had just finished a possum-hunting trip up the Rakaia River when we got an email from a guy called Joe from Alaska. He asked if we would like to join him as volunteer crew relocating his yacht from Baltimore to Alaska, through the notorious Northwest Passage. Fewer than 150 small vessels had ever transited this dangerous sea-ice-riddled passage and the chance of making it through in one summer was about 50/50. After reading about our experience in wild and remote locations including Antarctica, Joe was desperate to get us on board. We couldn't actually sail, but personality and experience in high-consequence situations were more important, and he could teach us to sail once on the water.

Two weeks later, jet-lagged and exhausted, we stumbled aboard *Hawk* at its berth in Baltimore, late on the 10th of July. Our journey had taken us halfway around the world and included days of travelling on planes and buses and a week's stopover in Malaysia, which was the only country in the world where I could fast-track the US travel visa required for the voyage. We were greeted by a relieved captain who, after looking at us over his reading glasses, introduced us to Shanan and Jérémie, who were also volunteering as crew for the passage. He gave us a huge bear hug and a welcome tour of his 13-metre aluminium yacht. *Hawk* was not only going to be our home for the next three months, it would also be our lifeline to the world, and we would need a combination of everyone's skills and experience to keep us safe at sea, hundreds of miles from help.

SV *Hawk* was a well-proven sailing vessel and had already circumnavigated the globe with her previous owners, Beth and Evan, who wrote a popular sailing blog while on board. With a hull of eight-millimetre-thick aluminium, she was designed for expedition cruising to remote locations, and her eight centimetres of foam insulation and diesel heater would be necessary in the Arctic. Graceie and I had a double bed in the bow which was very comfortable until we started sailing and the boat sat on a 20-degree lean for several days. The person at the top spends the whole time trying to stay there while the other is snuggled comfortably into the wall below!

Over the next ten days we prepared the yacht for departure, checking and double-checking all the rigging, equipment and provisions until we were satisfied they were sufficient for a safe passage. Graceie and I had the most to do with the provisioning and in total spent around US$10,000 on four to five months' worth of food. One of the shopping receipts from Costco was over a metre long and this is a list of the staple items we loaded:

1100 eggs, 20 cabbages, 30 kg potatoes, 30 kg onions,
15 pumpkins, 20 kg carrots, 80 cans tuna, 60 cans salmon, 60 cans
chicken, 80 cans olives, 100 cans tomatoes, 15 litres almond butter,
10 kg bacon, 25 kg cheese, 5 kg butter, 60 cans milk, 8 kg crackers,
100 apples, 60 oranges, 15 kg salami, 25 kg oats, 25 kg rice, 30 kg
pasta, 30 kg flour, 40 kg fruit and nuts

My experience of shopping for months at a time for Gorge River was invaluable and I explained to everyone some of the basics of provisioning and looking after food: 'Everything has to last as long as possible. The vegetables need to be treated like babies, otherwise they rot and die. But when they do rot, you cut the rotten part off and use what's left, otherwise we go without for months.' Graceie had learned fast at Gorge River and took charge of nurturing the vegetables and inventorying the food for most of the trip.

On the 22nd of July, under a partially cloudy sky, we cast away from our sheltered berth and began navigating the busy shipping channels through Delaware Bay towards the open sea. We decided on a watch schedule where we'd all take turns in pairs to sail and watch out for dangers, night and day. Each of us including Captain Joe would do six hours on in the daytime and six hours off, then four hours on and eight hours off during the night. Everybody's watch would be offset by two hours so that each watch would be shared with first one crewmate and then another. That way, over the three months, we were less likely to fall out with each other. We sailed out of Delaware Bay that night amid huge cargo ships, barges and tugboats and the lights from a nuclear power plant lit up the land. It was stiflingly hot and an incredible contrast to the freezing and desolate Canadian Arctic for which we were bound.

We exited the safety of the canals and as the wind caught in the sails the boat heeled over to one side and the bow began rising and falling through the swells. We came out into the ocean at the end of a tropical storm and the first few days were absolutely horrific as we were lashed by 45-knot wind gusts and five-metre-plus seas. There were occasional breaks in the weather for a few hours and then all hell would break loose again. Tossed at the mercy of the ocean, I was terribly seasick and it felt like the nightmare of the Southern Ocean all over again. I started to wonder what I had got myself into and how I could cope for three months. But the *Kapitan Khlebnikov* had taught me to grit my teeth and dig in for the long haul through anything the ocean throws at you. Only then can you gain the reward of visiting some of the wildest and most inaccessible places on earth.

Joe had plenty of sailing experience and through the storm he taught us how to sail. At the same time, this was his first voyage sailing *Hawk* and it was a steep learning curve for us all. Shanan and Jérémie had some sailing experience but never on the high seas. Only Graceie and I had known each other for more than ten days, but neither of us had sailed at all. We were all thrown in at the deep end and learned fast between bouts of seasickness, lightning storms and hailstones. One day somewhere off New York we enjoyed a few hours of sunshine and calm seas and even went for a swim and caught a small tuna. As we ate dinner, however, a gigantic wall of black clouds rose into the northern sky. The sun set to the west and slowly we slid into the blackness that seemed to rise from the peaks of the waves to the heavens above.

I knew what was going to happen next and decided to save my energy for my watch later in the night. I crawled into the darkest corner of my bed and wedged myself in with cushions to avoid being thrown out onto the wooden floor. Soon the waves increased and for the next few hours *Hawk* was being tossed like a cork by the horrific storm. Sleeping in conditions like this is like trying to sleep in a washing machine. The very bed I lay on would be lifted sharply, with the *Hawk*'s bow hanging almost weightless on each crest, before crashing back down into the next trough. I would be thrown against the cabin wall before sliding back down in time for the next wave. Despite this process repeating every few seconds, I actually slept surprisingly well and felt okay when I was lying down.

Above me I could hear the high-pitched scream of the wind through the rigging and the constant creaking and groaning of the 22-metre-high mast as it transferred the force of the wind in the sails to the hull of the boat. It was a strong test for *Hawk* before the remote Arctic, and in that storm she was leaping over the swells, sending huge clouds of spray and water streaming across the deck above my head. But even capable boats still have things break and we were about to face our first challenge as a crew.

Sometime just after midnight I heard a loud crack followed by the deafening flapping of a loose sail. Joe was shouting and the engine rumbled into action. My adrenaline kicked in and I braced myself between the mast and a cupboard while yanking on my wet-weather gear. The motion of the boat was so violent that I had to hang on tightly to the handrails and slowly inch my way to the stairs out of the cabin. Once outside, I attached myself with a lanyard and Joe motioned to me to take over the wheel. 'Point the bow directly into the wind!' His words were whipped away by a drenching wall of spray as I carefully felt the wind direction on my face and used the power from the engine to point the bow straight into the weather.

Everyone was on deck now and together the others carefully clambered up onto the foredeck to lower the mainsail, which was flapping uncontrollably from side to side. I had never steered a boat in conditions like this, but it wasn't the first time I had faced such a challenge and there was no room for mistakes. Calmly, I worked out what needed to be done, while squinting into the spray and watching the others slowly lower the mainsail until it was strapped down out of harm's way. Joe and Jérémie raised a smaller storm sail and as the boat heeled over to one side we began to sail forward under wind power once more. Suddenly all my adrenaline from the moment disappeared and I felt very seasick again. I hung my head out of the cockpit, heaved my dinner over the side and retreated to my bunk in a wet and sorry state. I still had a couple of hours until my 4 am watch started. Luckily the damage to the mainsail turned out to be minimal and there was only one broken attachment. In daylight we worked together to fix it with some Dyneema twine.

Doing any simple task when a boat is heeling 30 degrees in a heavy swell is incredibly hard work, and cooking food or doing the dishes takes two or three times longer than normal. However, going to the toilet is the greatest challenge of all. To truly join me in this scenario, imagine standing on the back of a galloping horse, pulling down your pants and attempting to relax enough to do your business. Heaven forbid you should get thrown off halfway through your bowel movement! Flushing requires putting the lid down, pumping a lever for 30 seconds and hoping like hell this isn't the day the pump decides to break, sentencing the entire crew to use a bucket for the duration.

Then comes washing your hands. The bathroom tap is only saltwater and you have to use a footpump to make it work, while somehow balancing on your other foot and jamming your body in a corner to stop yourself being thrown to the ground. If you are lucky, the water will squirt out of the tap at the same instant as your hand is actually under the nozzle. But where does it go next? When sailing, a yacht generally leans heavily to one side, so if the bathroom is on the uphill side of the vessel, the sink will empty normally, with gravity, as you are above sea level. But if you are on the downhill side, you may be below sea level, and if you open the sink valve the water will empty back into the sink, often bringing with it the last person's toothpaste or some other surprises that have been waiting to reappear. Sometimes a yacht might stay on the same course for 12 to 24 hours, with the level in the sink slowly rising as each person takes their chances and manages to open the valve just as the yacht crests a wave. But inevitably this fails at some point, and after a day or two the bathroom sink is a disgusting mess that will make you feel like vomiting even in calm weather.

After five days at sea, we stopped in Halifax, Nova Scotia, and then again in Newfoundland to repair a broken steering wheel, before finally pulling into the safety of Nuuk, the capital of Greenland. After the first few days the weather had been much more favourable and we had sailed along at six to seven knots in relatively calm seas.

It was comfortable sailing and we were able to really familiarise ourselves with *Hawk* and hone our sailing skills before the Arctic.

In Nuuk we met the first of our fellow Arctic explorers. One yacht was heading up to 80 degrees north in Greenland in hopes of finding a safe harbour to winter over in. Another, from Poland, had already sailed the Northeast and the Northwest passages in previous years and was now exploring the coast of Greenland. We suddenly felt a part of this remote sailing community and spent each evening sharing stories and gathering vital knowledge about Arctic sailing from those around us. From this point, we were very much on our own. If something serious happened, rescue could be up to a thousand kilometres and a few days away, and I was never going to continue with the voyage unless I had complete faith in the crew and our vessel. Nuuk was our final 'easy out' and I spent my last few watches thinking this over until concluding that I was comfortable to continue. If something were to happen to Joe, I was confident that the rest of us knew the boat well enough to sail safely to the closest port. I ran through all these mental checklists in my mind as I prepared for what might lie ahead.

From Nuuk we sailed up the west coast of Greenland in favourable winds to a place called Disko Bay, known as the 'home of the icebergs'. The Ilulissat Glacier flows from the Greenland Ice Cap at an astounding rate of 20 to 35 metres (66 to 115 feet) per day, resulting in around 20 billion tonnes of icebergs calving into the bay every year. During the night, Graceie, in her possum-fur hat, and Joe had used the radar to navigate *Hawk* through icebergs as large as shopping malls, and we had crossed the Arctic Circle. The bitterly cold katabatic winds descending directly from the Greenland Ice Cap were whipping up small whitecaps and the salt spray stung our eyes as we squinted into the distance looking for bergs. The offshore winds made for perfect sailing and the steady breeze filled the sails, propelling us through the relatively calm ocean. With the yacht heeled over 20 degrees, it was Arctic sailing at its best, even though the temperature with wind-chill would have been well below minus ten degrees Celsius. As the twilight brightened, we witnessed our first Arctic sunrise and pulled into a sheltered anchorage below a long line of rocky cliffs. Far in the distance we could see an unmistakable rounded mountain of ice, the shape of an upturned dinner plate – the edge of the second largest ice cap in the world. Moments after anchoring, I had already pulled up a good-sized cod and filleted it for breakfast.

When villages are a thousand kilometres apart it's important to refuel whenever possible, so that afternoon we spent four hours motoring through a thick scattering of icebergs, searching for a way into the town of Ilulissat. There wasn't a breath of wind and the Arctic sun was high in the clear blue sky. From sea level it looked impossible to penetrate the ice floes, but after being hoisted to the top of the mast I could see a way through. I perched there for three hours on top of the world, yelling directions down to Joe, who manoeuvred *Hawk* through the chunks of ice while trying not to bump them too hard. Someone else stood on the bow yelling back directions as well, and we guided the ship safely through the ice as a team. Eventually, as far as I could see in all directions, icebergs hung suspended in the clear, deep-black Arctic water. Some were tabular like gigantic floating houses with straight sides while others had a rounded appearance from melting, and some had jagged sides, probably from a recent calving. Occasionally there would be a huge noise like a clap of thunder, caused by a massive chunk breaking off a tall berg, which would then sway backwards and forwards for a few minutes until it found its new balance point. In the distance, the houses of Ilulissat village, painted the distinct Scandinavian colours of red, blue, yellow and green, slowly drew closer.

We were following a local fisherman weaving between the bergs in his small fibreglass fishing boat, thinking he might know the way through to the harbour. All of a sudden, the guy pulled out a rifle and for a moment we wondered if he was going to shoot at us, but he took quick aim at a seal whose head had poked above the water about 90 metres ahead. *CRACK!* A loud shot cut open the sky and the seal rolled over in the water as the fisherman used the full power of his 200-horsepower engine to reach it before it sank below the surface. By the time we motored by, he had the seal on a rope and gave us a big wave. From above, I could see a cloud of blood surrounding the small boat.

Eventually we slid gently into the Ilulissat boat harbour and made our way to the refuelling dock. I had never in my life encountered such a chaotic harbour. There were hundreds of small fishing boats like the one we'd seen earlier, all with enormous outboard motors. The locals drive these boats through the icebergs at full speed, literally bouncing off them as they go. Jammed in among the boats were 17 icebergs, the largest of which was the size of a small fishing trawler. As we tied on to the fuel dock, I could see a seal skin floating in the water next to us and a nearby fishing trawler had a whale harpoon mounted on the bow. Halfway through our refilling, a small fishing boat came in for fuel and there wasn't space for both of us. The local guys simply revved their engine and pushed another boat out of the way to get near enough to the hose.

It's normal to buy whale or seal in the meat markets in Greenland, and hunting food from nature is a really important part of the culture. It has been a way of life for these people forever. Any other food requires ships and planes to transport it from somewhere else in the world. There is also a lot of cod and halibut fishing going on and many of the boats had deep buckets with long rope fishing lines coiled inside. Being so close to the mouth of the Ilulissat Icefjord, where the bergs come from, the port is notorious for getting trapped in. You can go in one day and that night there might be a big calving event and the ocean outside the harbour is then completely full of ice. Understandably, Joe was restless that night and early the next day in the soft morning light we quietly slid out of that chaotic harbour with full freshwater and fuel tanks and headed north through Disko Bay, bound for Canada. To be extra safe, we tied six 20-litre jerry cans of diesel and two extra cans of water to the front deck.

Partway through the day, we decided to stop for some fishing. We had found fishing in Greenland difficult due to the deep water, so we stopped at a place very close to shore that was only around 60 metres deep. Shanan had never caught a fish before, so I suggested she drop down a cod jig with six hooks. Instantly she got a fish and began to pull it up from the depths, complaining about how heavy the rod was. We gave her a hard time for not being strong enough and it took her quite some time. On the end of her line were five huge cod! Beginner's luck certainly played its part that day and as we motored past more gigantic icebergs on another calm afternoon, I explained to everyone how to fillet fish on the back deck. Inside, Graceie rolled the fish in flour and fried them in a pan and we ate them with her freshly baked bread for an early dinner. For me the food we could catch tasted significantly better than any other food we had with us, and this was one of my favourite meals. Despite spending days fishing throughout the rest of our voyage, sadly that was the last fish we caught and I had to be content with the provisions we had on board.

Our first stop in the Canadian Arctic was at Pond Inlet, one week after we left Disko Bay. Pond Inlet is a small Inuit community in Navy Board Inlet at the top of Baffin Island. None of the Canadian Arctic villages we visited were anything like the Greenlandic villages. Sadly, most of the Inuit culture seemed to be subject to unhealthy American and Canadian influence and we watched them lining up in the supermarket to pay US$200 for a small box of overpriced junk food that was the only thing available to them. The locals do still hunt and fish, if only as a secondary food source, and while walking around these towns it's not uncommon to see a polar bear or caribou skin hanging out to dry on a washing line.

Anything that moves is fair game for them that far north and the locals are allowed to hunt 130 narwhal a year. A few years ago, this was the location for a controversial culling of 500 narwhal trapped in sea ice, an event that captured world attention. It's a complicated scenario because on one hand you have locals trying to hunt food from the land around them, just as we do at Gorge River. On the other hand, people living in cities are telling them they can't hunt their only local food supply and instead must ship food into their remote villages by barge or plane. As we walked up the main street we encountered an old Inuit guy sitting on a wooden box carving whalebone to sell to passing yachts and expedition ships. We started talking and he reminded me strongly of my own father carving at the kitchen table each evening. It was nice to observe his innovation, utilising the resources around him to make beautiful jewellery.

That night at bedtime we pulled anchor and slipped away from Pond Inlet into the never-ending twilight. The sun still set at about 11 pm but we were now so far north that we wouldn't see darkness for the next month. Over the next few days, we continued through Lancaster Sound to Beechey Island, the overwintering site for the lost Franklin expedition of 1845, officially known as the British Naval Northwest Passage Expedition, in which 129 men perished after their two ships became trapped in sea ice and were crushed. The weather was absolutely perfect, with the clear Arctic sky reflected off the mirror-calm ocean around us. We motored past glaciers that flowed down from incredibly desolate stepped mountains reminiscent of the Grand Canyon. There was almost nothing growing onshore besides a few hardy mosses here and there among the boulders.

Since Nuuk, we had been scouring the shoreline for anything resembling a polar bear. Finally, one afternoon, we spotted two white dots in the distance and after studying them through binoculars decided to change course. As we motored towards them, the dots grew larger and larger and we saw they were moving. Excitement grew – we thought this could be our first sighting of these elusive bears. However, we had been fooled by the difficult perception of distance in the Arctic and as we drew closer another look through the binoculars revealed we were unmistakably staring at two very fat white Arctic rabbits!

That evening as we anchored at Beechey Island we saw another white dot on the shoreline that resembled a chunk of snow positioned near the high-tide mark. We debated launching the inflatable boat, but after some deliberation agreed it was most likely a snowdrift. Because of our 24-hour watch schedule it was rare for us all to relax together at the same time and while at anchor we took this opportunity. The full moon appeared above the island's tabletop mountains and rose into the deep pink and blue sky that held the colours of twilight throughout the entire icy-cold night. Inside we fired up the diesel heater and played board games while drinking whisky together in the cosy saloon. Dinner was a delicious pot of chicken soup with Graceie's freshly baked bread.

The next morning a quick scan of the beach revealed that the chunk of snow was gone. However, a sand bar obscured part of the beach so we jumped into the Zodiac to get a closer look. After checking the sand bar from a distance for bears, we landed and dragged the inflatable a few metres across the isthmus to a bay on the other side. From here we could plainly see a polar bear standing on the shoreline about 800 metres to the north. We approached cautiously in the Zodiac to within about 100 metres of the bear, which looked to be quite young and in a very healthy condition. It was standing with its toes in the water, casually sniffing the air, not the least bit concerned by or curious about our presence. As we sat at a latitude of 74 degrees, watching the young bear, we recorded the farthest north position of our entire voyage. Later that day we saw an adult bear walking along the sand bar that we had crossed.

From Beechey Island, we headed south through Peel Sound, and from there we were committed to finishing the passage, having passed the point of no return. Usually, this area is hard to navigate due to heavy sea ice. In the 2015 summer it had mostly melted and we encountered only some minor floes that we could motor through easily with little navigational effort. We downloaded an ice chart each day via our satellite phone and could monitor where the sea ice was and how fast it was moving. The golden rule is that you must never get between a large area of ice and the shoreline. If you do and your vessel gets trapped, then you really are at the mercy of nature. You could be released if the floes pull apart, or crushed if the wind and tides squeeze the ice together.

This far from civilisation, we couldn't afford any mistakes and studied our daily ice maps carefully, making all of our decisions as a crew, with Joe having the final word. Joe was an amazing captain and was happy to step back and allow everyone to have input. Thus, I was able to contribute much of my knowledge from leading other trips to remote locations and could learn things like marine navigation and sailing skills from him in turn. For the most part, our passage was almost entirely ice free, and after a short stop at another Inuit community, Gjoa Haven, we continued with strong following winds through the maze of islands and shallow channels that winds its way across the top of Canada to Alaska.

Before departure, we had calculated that 1100 eggs should keep us going for the majority of the trip. From my experience at Gorge River, eggs will keep for at least two months without too many problems, but just to make sure Joe decided we should also oil each individual egg to help them last. We took care to stack the eggs in cool, dark places and for the first two weeks enjoyed lots of fresh eggs. However, unbeknown to us, there was a flaw in our plan to enjoy fresh High Arctic omelettes.

Unlike the rest of the world, the US is so paranoid about food safety that all eggs are refrigerated. It is basically impossible to find an unrefrigerated egg without squeezing the chicken yourself. When an egg is refrigerated, it undergoes an irreversible change, and if it is removed from the refrigerator will last no longer than a week or two. After just a couple of weeks we found our precious egg supply was deteriorating rapidly. At first, we would crack one bad egg for every five good ones, and everyone was okay with that. But by the time we made it to the Canadian Arctic it had changed to five bad eggs for one good one, and only Graceie persisted in searching for the elusive good eggs, cracking them up on deck in the fresh air. However, the remaining eggs started to smell under the beds even without being cracked, and when we finally reached Nome in Alaska, Jérémie and I had to remove the last cartons and carefully drop them into a huge dumpster before running away quickly for fear of explosion.

Halfway between Gjoa Haven and Tuktoyaktuk, hundreds of miles from the nearest help, we narrowly avoided disaster. The wind was blowing from behind, but due to the land formations we were often experiencing radical changes in wind direction without warning. Due to being near the magnetic North Pole, our compass and autopilot didn't work for about a month, and on this particular afternoon I was hand steering. Suddenly a gust of wind hit the wrong side of our mainsail, pushing us in the opposite direction.

We were prepared for this to happen and had a preventer rope set up to hold the sail in a safe position but the rope must have been old. As I fought to change direction, the rope holding the boom broke and in the blink of an eye the boom and mainsail flew from one side of the boat to the other with an almighty *CRACK!* It was the scariest single second of my life as the attachment between the mainsail and the deck disintegrated in front of me and ball bearings went flying around the cockpit. We were incredibly lucky that no one was standing up on the main deck at that moment or they would have been killed in an instant by the heavy swinging boom. Miraculously, the sail hadn't split with the impact and we crafted a new attachment for the main rope from the boom using a solid metal handrail and a lot of rope. Our fix-it job held for the rest of the voyage and the whole ordeal was a strong reminder of the risks of sailing and the importance of double- and triple-checking all the equipment.

As we sailed south through the Bering Strait we also encountered a large storm, but we were better prepared this time. Forty-five-knot winds and ten-metre swells surfed us along in the right direction, and we made strong progress. We crossed the Arctic Circle again and during our night watches peered out through clouds of spray to watch the Northern Lights dancing across the clear night sky above. After 14 days at sea without stopping, we left the Bering Sea gales behind and motored into the calm, sheltered waters of the Nome boat harbour. The feeling of being back on land after so long was amazing and the reality of what we had just achieved finally hit us. We had sailed successfully across the remote Arctic to complete the Northwest Passage. It had been five weeks since our last shower in Nuuk and we decided to celebrate our nautical achievement with a trip to the local gym for a long, hot, soapy wash. After scrubbing for ten minutes, dead skin was still coming off!

Moored alongside us in the harbour were five other yachts that had been a few days in front of us as we transited the passage. It was amazing to meet these other hardy sailors, and over a few beers that evening in the cabin of the largest yacht we traded tales of the challenges and highlights we had all encountered. One yacht, *Salty Kisses*, had an entire family on board, including three kids below seven years old. We felt a sense of community among us and despite the distance that had separated each vessel it was as though we had travelled through the remote Arctic together. By looking into each other's sparkling eyes, we understood the tough times and incredible moments that we had all been through. This is the type of community that forms in the hardy conditions of the Arctic or Antarctic, and it's what draws people back to the high latitudes over and over again.

After we'd spent four days socialising with the locals of Nome, the weather gods blessed us again, with following winds through the Bering Sea. After rounding the western tip of the Alaska Peninsula we were on the home straight to Kodiak. On our last night we anchored in Geographic Harbour in Katmai National Park and in the morning went ashore to watch nine grizzly bears catching salmon in a stream flowing directly from the spruce- and birch-covered volcanic mountains above. Four cubs were leaping into the river after their mothers as they learned to catch fish themselves.

Finally, on the 22nd of September, we turned one last corner and entered Kodiak harbour. This was Joe's hometown and, after 10,000 kilometres of sailing, his mission to bring *Hawk* home was finally accomplished. We had learned from Joe how to be sailors and had literally been to the end of the earth together. Despite living in such close proximity to each other for three months, we were still friends, and it was with heavy hearts that we hugged each other goodbye and went our separate ways. Graceie and I headed to her home in Minneapolis. A few months later we broke up and went in different directions.

We had spent a pretty intense three years exploring the globe together and had really given it everything. My personal journey continued with another voyage to Antarctica and a one-way-ticket backpacking trip through Asia and Europe.

After a great deal of troubleshooting, as I had never studied any sort of web design, I managed to build myself a website where I could begin sharing my adventures with the world. I added an e-commerce shop to the site and once Mum and I agreed on a price for the possum hats I began selling them online. She would sew the hats and post them from Gorge River while I managed the online side of things and got a percentage of the profits. Once my site was built, a sale required little effort on my part and Mum would receive an extra order. Eventually I increased my range of possum-fur products and even added Mum's and Dad's books to the shop. Life at Gorge River had taught me how to think outside the box and I had learned this type of innovation from them. It felt very satisfying to apply these same principles to the modern world, and my online store has provided me with a small side income to fund my never-ending adventures.

CHAPTER 17

Working at Scott Base

My Scott Base dream started when I was about 20. I had recently returned from my voyage on the *Kapitan Khlebnikov* and was spending some time at home with Mum and Dad. One stormy West Coast day, two trampers knocked on our door and one introduced himself as Doug Henderson from Arrowtown. We started talking about Antarctica and he told me some stories of the extreme blizzards and changes of seasons he had witnessed while living at Scott Base through winter. Scott Base is operated by Antarctica New Zealand and is the country's main presence there. During my time aboard the *Kapitan Khlebnikov* I had witnessed a snapshot of Antarctica and I felt a yearning to experience more.

It took a few years before I had the experience to apply, and in the meantime I visited Scott Base for two hours while on a voyage with Heritage Expeditions. Our brief tour of the long maze of interlinked green buildings was a teasing peek into what my future could hold. I headed overseas after the voyage and proceeded to spend one year living in South East Asia and teaching outdoor education in China before travelling for another three months in Eastern Europe. It was my longest trip away from New Zealand and after about a year I had started to feel a little homesick. It felt like the right time to send in my application to Antarctica New Zealand.

I was surprised to receive an offer for an interview with Tracey Bean, who oversaw the summer field operations at Scott Base. It turned out that she had tramped through Gorge River, so she could appreciate the similarities between living in isolation there and working on a research station 3800 kilometres south of New Zealand. A short time later, I was offered a standby role for the field positions for the upcoming season. This most likely wouldn't get me to Scott Base that season, but it was still a good start.

After spending six weeks at Gorge River, I headed to the Pacific to live on a remote tropical island partway up the Tongan archipelago, eating coconuts and spearing fish. One day I was checking my emails through the low-quality mobile connection from a neighbouring island and was surprised to see one from Tracey: 'Chris, a position has opened up last minute for summer field trainer. When can you get to Christchurch?' Most of my craziest adventures have required a spontaneous decision and once again my flexible lifestyle allowed me to leap at the last-minute offer. Being on quite a remote island, it was a week before I could hitch a ride to Nuku'alofa on a lovely catamaran owned by New York author Hugh Howey and his partner, Michelle. Dripping with sweat in the 30-degree heat and wearing nothing more than flip flops, a T-shirt and shorts, I boarded the next plane bound for New Zealand.

Eight days later, after a whirlwind week filled with medicals, dentist check-ups, search and rescue training and a flying visit to Gorge River, I stepped out of another plane into a completely different world. The temperature was 70 degrees colder than in Tonga and as I inhaled my first breath of minus-40-degree Antarctic air my lungs contracted violently from the shock. Behind me the modified Airbus A319 engines screamed as the plane sat on the Phoenix Runway constructed from heavily compressed snow on the surface of the McMurdo Ice Shelf. At these temperatures the pilots can't stop the engines for fear they won't restart. All around was a dazzling world of flat white snow and in the distance I recognised the peaks of Mt Erebus, Mt Discovery and the distinct conical shape of Observation Hill near Scott Base.

I was wearing eight different layers of extreme-cold-weather clothing and on my head my fluffy possum-fur hat and buff kept me cosy and warm. I was part of a 15-member group who were all new to this environment and we were ushered over to a convoy of Antarctica New Zealand–branded Toyota Troop Carriers waiting with their engines running a safe distance from the runway. We piled in and slammed the doors closed behind us. In the back of the Troop Carrier my goggles fogged up instantly and we were soon driving along the icy road towards our new home. Finally, the reality of my situation hit me and as we bounced our way across the ice shelf, I realised my dream of living in Antarctica had come true.

Life inside Scott Base is relatively easy and comfortable. The station consists of ten buildings connected by linkways and we could walk from one end to the other without stepping outside. The buildings are painted a distinct shade of Chelsea Cucumber green and positioned 40 metres back from the shoreline of Pram Point at the southern tip of Ross Island. The original part of Scott Base was built in 1957 for the Commonwealth Trans-Antarctic Expedition and has been expanded and then rebuilt over the years to support New Zealand's scientific and territorial endeavours in Antarctica.

In some ways, Scott Base is very isolated. In summertime there are regular flights back to Christchurch every couple of days, but due to the extreme weather delays are common and sometimes it can be two or three weeks between flights. If someone needed urgent medical attention, they could have a long wait. As far as keeping in touch with family and friends back home goes, there is a good phone connection through satellite as well as a slow internet connection for Facebook and email, but no public wi-fi on base. I lived very closely with the rest of the 40-odd staff members and everyone grew to know each other well. For me that was 36 more people than I lived with at Gorge River, so personally I didn't find Scott Base so isolated!

In good weather America's McMurdo Station is a three-kilometre drive away. With a population of between 300 and 1000, it always reminded me of an Alaskan mining town. There are social events, gyms and even three bars that us Kiwis were always welcome to visit. Each Thursday at Scott Base the Kiwis returned the favour and there was an open invitation for the Americans to join 'America Night' at our bar called the 'Tatty Flag'.

For the first couple of weeks until we did our field training, my group of new arrivals were not allowed to leave the station without being escorted by a fully trained winter staff member. I was a part of the field team along with Sam, Kat, Cole, Bia and Jon. We were all new that season and had a couple of weeks to learn the ropes before the scientists came south. As a field trainer, one of my tasks would be to teach the overnight survival courses required for everyone who comes to Antarctica. They cover everything required to live and work safely outside in extreme temperatures and provide a thorough rundown of the survival equipment we carry everywhere. When there were no field training courses, I would be driving scientists on the sea ice to special locations, setting up remote field camps, or escorting scientists and media personnel to different locations by helicopter.

After two weeks on the continent, we ran our first field training session. Here, 18 of the new base staff would learn what they needed for the coming season and, as new field trainers, we would have our first chance to teach the course under the close supervision of veteran Tom Arnold. Tom had come south for one month to teach us everything we needed to know for the summer ahead. The weather had been unstable with regular blizzards, but eventually a calm day was forecast, before a fairly intense storm the next afternoon. That would give us time to sleep in a tent overnight, and we would return to base the next morning. The biggest challenge for everyone would be the temperature, which was forecast to be minus 40 degrees Celsius.

A light breeze was blowing from the northeast as we loaded up the bright green all-terrain Hägglund vehicles. The sun was shining in the northern sky and a small plume of smoke rose from Mt Erebus sitting 40 kilometres from Scott Base. We drove about five kilometres to a place called Windless Bight and stopped near to the Square Frame, a small heated cabin sitting on the ice shelf, which acts as a weekend getaway or bach.

Our tents consisted of four poles that stood like a pyramid. They were modelled on the original tents that Scott used on his Antarctic expeditions over 100 years earlier. In pairs we pitched our tents and buried the snow flaps to keep the wind out and anchor the tents to the ground. Combined with lots of guy ropes, that can hold a 'polar pyramid' tent firm against the vicious Antarctic weather. We set the tents in a line about five metres apart with a toilet tent at one end. Then we made a huge camp kitchen area for everyone to sit in and make food, sheltered from the wind by a two-metre-high wall constructed from large snow blocks cut with a snow saw from the surface around us. When done correctly, this provides lifesaving shelter from the freezing winds that can cut through you like a knife and give you hypothermia. All this was a lot of fun and we laughed and told jokes as we pitched in to shovel, saw and shape the snow into a fantastic kitchen shelter. In the middle we set up our bright red food boxes and pulled out dinner, consisting of dehydrated meals requiring only hot water to prepare. Every time someone took a step the snow underfoot would squeak loudly like styrofoam.

Nothing was normal in the ever-present minus-40-degree temperature. We were practising using the issued extreme-cold-weather clothing and none of us besides Tom had ever experienced these conditions before. I noticed that even while shovelling and moving about, people were still becoming cold and would have to go inside the Square Frame to warm up for a few minutes now and then. With my clumsy orange and black jacket on, I felt as flexible as a robot but at least my body was warm. My possum hat kept my head toasty, but hands are much harder to manage and the thick mittens made it impossible to work. The leather-fingered gloves offered more dexterity but slowly my fingers became cold, so it was a fine balance between the two. My goggles fogged up every 30 minutes or so, making it hard to see. I stashed a second set of eyewear in my jacket to swap with the fogged goggles, which could then go deep inside my jacket to defog.

After dinner we drove up the nearby mountain to the top of Hut Point Peninsula and climbed onto the side of Castle Rock, an old lava core jutting above the glacial surface, to see the view. The ridgeline was exposed and a bitterly cold wind cut straight into any exposed skin. Our calculation of the wind-chill put the temperature somewhere around minus 60 and to this day that was the coldest place I have ever stood. I was wearing every layer of clothing and still the end of my nose started to freeze if I let my possum buff down. Breathing in the wind was almost impossible and hurt my lungs, but by breathing into the fur buff the air was warmed slightly first.

Since it was the very end of September, 24-hour daylight hadn't yet started and as darkness fell we headed to our tents. Climbing into bed took about ten minutes and we took turns de-layering as there was not much space inside the tents. I went to bed first and after taking off my many layers of jackets and fleeces I slid down into my sleeping kit. On the inside I had an extremely warm down sleeping bag and on the outside was another thick synthetic bag. Getting in between the right layers was quite tricky but once I was inside all the layers puffed around my body, keeping me warm – though at minus 40 I was not cosy. Tom came to bed after me and I pulled my possum hat down over my eyes and tried to get to sleep in my icy surroundings.

Shortly after midnight I was woken by Tom's concerned voice. 'Chris, the wind has changed to the south.' I could hear the tent walls flapping and as I woke a small shower of frozen condensation fell down from the roof, chilling my warm face. I poked my head out the door into the gloomy three-quarter darkness and shivered as a gust of wind blew spindrift down my exposed neck. The flags marking our campsite were fluttering in a different direction from earlier and there was already a fair amount of snow being blown by the 15-knot wind.

'I think tomorrow's storm is coming early. The wind wasn't meant to change until at least 9 am. Either we go home now or risk being stuck here for the full storm cycle.' Tom's words chilled me to the bone as I hurriedly dressed, trying to find all of my layers where I had left them. We had enough emergency food for the storm, but the thought of being stuck in the small two-man tents for days on end was not appealing. At 12.30 am we woke the rest of the group and gave each pair a simple instruction: 'Get dressed, pack your sleeping kit and jump into the Hägglunds. We're going home.'

We were now in a completely different world. The temperature was slightly warmer, but the wind made it feel colder. The sky was grey in all directions and the snow surface seemed to blend with the sky. The only thing we could see was the long line of flags marking our safe route home disappearing into the gloom a few hundred metres away. That would be enough to lead us safely back to Scott Base. Most of the group were now well out of their comfort zones. People fumbled with their sleeping kits still half asleep, extremely tired and quite cold. One guy was able to pack his sleeping bag and walk to the vehicles, but there was no way he could help the others.

A couple couldn't even pack their sleeping bags in the cold and needed assistance to complete the simplest of tasks.

Bia, Jon, Cole and I had all experienced wild environments before, albeit in slightly warmer places in New Zealand, and this was the type of high-consequence situation we thrived in. We were finally experiencing real Antarctic weather first-hand and could see how it affected the others in our team. We warmed up the Hägglunds with the built-in diesel heaters and strapped down the ski trailers. After assisting those who needed help with their belongings it was almost two hours before we were ready.

Once inside the Hägglunds, we left the ten empty tents to weather the storm and turned towards home. Each flag on the road was placed 30 metres apart and a small reflector on top lit the road like a highway. These reflectors not only reflect light but also radar, and even though we could see only a couple of hundred metres with our eyes, we could see several kilometres using our radar signal combined with a GPS chart. It reminded me of sailing on the *Hawk* at night, when we navigated with these same tools.

At 3 am we left the world of blowing snow and ice and slammed the door of Scott Base behind us. Inside the warm and cosy locker room we quietly untangled ourselves from scarves, hats, jackets and boots. We had a couple of days to reflect on the experience as the storm increased in strength outside. In conditions like this, no one is allowed outside, so we watched the storm through the base windows. We only occasionally saw the vehicles parked outside, and the outer building and storage containers 100 metres away were rarely visible through the blizzard.

At Gorge River I'd grown up in windy and wild weather and in the mountains of New Zealand and the Northwest Passage I had experienced some horrific storms. It had all prepared me for this steep learning curve, which now took my survival skills to a whole new level. On this particular field training course, I learned more about extreme weather and its effect on people than at any other time of my life. Now I was ready to share that knowledge with the next arrivals at the base.

Teaching in such an unforgiving environment was very satisfying. I remember explaining about cold hands to a group one day. 'When I take off my gloves, I put them inside my jacket so they stay warm and don't freeze. When I'm finished working with my hands, my gloves will warm me back up again.' But no matter how many times you say something, nothing beats experiential learning. Shortly after, I noticed one of the guys put his gloves down in the snow and continue shovelling with bare hands. About ten minutes later the same guy came to me with frozen gloves and cold fingers. Patiently I demonstrated how to jump up and down while swinging the arms to increase blood flow to the fingertips. Sheepishly he said, 'Now I understand why you put your gloves inside your jacket.'

Scott Base is like Gorge River in some ways but on a much larger scale. During my childhood I had learned to build, fix, invent and problem-solve almost anything. I had learned to wire up electricity, build things from wood, combine several broken motors to make one that works, limit food waste, how to plumb, sew ... etc. We had to do all this because there was no one else to do it for us and nowhere to buy supplies. At Scott Base, you will find a person from most professions – for example, there are always plumbers, mechanics, engineers, carpenters, cleaners, science technicians and so on. Each one of these people is highly skilled in their area of expertise and they work together thousands of kilometres from the nearest shop as a strong, resourceful team.

It's expensive to bring vehicles backwards and forwards to Antarctica on the yearly supply vessel, so it's important to be able to maintain and fix them well. Likewise, the tents we used for sleeping would occasionally be damaged by shovels, ice and wind, and would need repairing. We had an industrial sewing machine and a huge assortment of fabrics to patch the tents back together, and if the damage was bad we might use bits from two or three tents to make a new one. That tent would be no good for sleeping, but rather than send it back to New Zealand we would use it as a toilet tent for another couple of years. Few challenges are new and most have occurred before at some time or another. Therefore, it's important that the knowledge is passed down from senior staff to the newer members of the team. I remember any time we had an unusual load to transport or a strange request from a scientist, we could always ask Johnno. He had worked in the Antarctic for many years and could always figure out a solution. In that way he reminded me a bit of Dad.

Everyone works six days a week at Scott Base and many work primarily inside, almost never going outside while on the job. After work, there are hiking trails, fat bikes, gyms, cross-country skis and even a small ski field for people to enjoy. However, due to the surrounding crevasse fields and sea ice, people are only allowed to do these activities along proven safe routes and many of the best sites require more knowledge to visit safely. Each Sunday someone in my field team would organise a familiarisation trip ('Fam Trip') to one of these sites, and leading these trips was one of the most satisfying parts of my job.

Partway through my second five-month summer I organised a Fam Trip to Cape Royds. The sea ice had been unstable that year and we had only managed a couple of trips there by Ski-doo. But now, following settled weather, the 1.5-metre-thick ice sheet had stabilised and I knew this was probably our last opportunity to make the trip before the summer melting.

We met at 8 am in the Hillary Field Centre. Some people had made sandwiches for the trip, while others had organised survival bags, sea-ice drills and hot water. There were 24 of us in total, 11 in each Hägglund and two driving Ski-doos. As leader of the trip, I was responsible for overall safety and I stared at the cloudy morning sky thoughtfully. The view to the south was pretty gloomy, but after studying the forecast I made the decision to go. We headed out onto the sea ice in front of Scott Base and soon McMurdo Station, with its sprawling suburbia of large coloured buildings, passed a few hundred metres off to our right. To our left, on the far side of McMurdo Sound, rose the Transantarctic mountain range, which is home to the McMurdo Dry Valleys, one of the driest places on earth.

In the front cabin of the Hägglund, Hue, Dan and Ruby were telling stories as we rounded Hut Point Peninsula. Gazing north towards Cape Royds, we could see the clouds lifting above Mt Erebus, then the sun broke through onto the tangled mess of crevasses and glaciers flanking its slopes. 'Yes – the forecast was right!' I exclaimed to Dan. The flagged route guided us over the sea ice and past the Erebus Glacier Tongue, jutting 13 kilometres out into the ocean, and soon we were passing between Tent,

Inaccessible and Big Razorback islands, with their towering, jagged peaks formed from eroded basalt.

Due to the extreme cold during winter and spring, the ocean here is covered by a solid one- to two-metre layer of ice and as the glacier tongue moves forward a large crack forms. It's critical to check that crack before driving across, so I parked the Hägglund on one side. We jumped out and I demonstrated to everyone how to drill a series of holes across the crack with an aggressive two-metre-long auger connected to a power drill. It would have been easy to mistake our surroundings for solid land or a snow-covered glacier, but as the drill broke through, salt water gushed out, forming a puddle around our feet and confirming that we were indeed standing on the ocean. Using a measuring tape attached to a chunk of metal dropped down the hole, we measured 1.5 metres of ice – 1.8 metres of good-quality ice is enough to land a jumbo jet on, so 1.5 metres was more than enough for our Hägglund, and we continued bouncing along towards Cape Royds at 25 kilometres per hour.

Soon we saw what looked to be a group of people standing out on the ice and as we came closer everyone's excitement increased. 'That's emperors!' announced Dan from the back seat. Because we were not allowed to approach the penguins, I suggested everyone should lie on the ice and see what happened next. Sure enough, the emperor penguins' curiosity was piqued and soon eight majestic emperors waddled their way towards us. The emperors, along with Adélie penguins, Antarctic skua and Weddell seals, are the only forms of life that we see in this desolate landscape until the whales return in late summer as the sea ice breaks up.

I was lying away from the group a little and one particularly curious penguin waddled right up to me and stopped 50 centimetres away. I looked up at this incredible creature with its black head and soft yellow neck glistening in the sunlight. Its oily feathers created a speckled pattern that seemed to flow right down over its white belly and black back to its scaly feet that wouldn't look out of place on a dinosaur. It is on top of these remarkable feet that the male penguins incubate a single egg throughout the darkest and coldest months of winter. The penguin cocked its head to one side to peer down at me with one eye before bending down to curiously peck at my finger with its long black beak and sandpapery tongue. I have been lucky enough to see quite a few emperors over my time in Antarctica, but this was the first one that had pecked me. Truly a once-in-a-lifetime experience!

The penguins hung out with us for 15 minutes before losing interest. One by one they flopped down onto their smooth bellies and with a few kicks of their back feet slid away across the emerald-green sea ice. We continued driving and soon arrived at Cape Evans, which Scott chose in 1911 as the site for the prefabricated hut that served as a base camp for his fateful expedition to the South Pole. Over 100 years later, and after a huge preservation effort from the Antarctic Heritage Trust, this hut is a time capsule from the past.

The first thing that hits as you stoop inside the weathered front door is the distinct musty odour made up of coal smoke, charcoal, wood and chemicals mixed with an overwhelming smell of old fat. In the outside part of the hut that served as stables the source of the fat smell is revealed. In one corner is a pile of semi-mummified, extremely rancid blocks of seal blubber. This would have served as food and fuel for the polar explorers and their husky dogs. Near the pile of blubber is a box of two dozen broken Adélie eggshells and some names are stencilled on the walls above, most probably those of Scott's infamous Siberian ponies, which failed to be as efficient as Amundsen's Arctic huskies in their race to the South Pole. A bicycle hangs from another wall and at the very back of one of the stables lies a dog skeleton.

Stepping inside another door brings you to the main part of the hut. It feels quite large but it's still hard to imagine 25 people spending an entire winter in here. To the right is the kitchen area, with dozens of tins lining the shelves and wooden packing cases stacked on the floor. Down the middle of the room is a long dining table and beyond stands a fireplace with a large snow-melting pot mounted permanently on top. At the back of the hut to the right is the laboratory, where hundreds of glass test tubes and pipettes lie scattered on the table like pick-up sticks. To the left a mummified emperor penguin lies on a table below a shelf bearing small bottles of medical supplies. One clear bottle contains some white crystals and a label which reads 'Camphor Flowers'. At the sides of the room are wooden bunks where the men slept, and the reindeer skin sleeping bags lie as if waiting for the returning explorers.

After 30 minutes in the hut taking photographs and breathing the rancid air, we enjoyed a quick snack of cheese and crackers before continuing towards Cape Royds. We passed between the towering icy cliffs of the Barne Glacier and a grounded iceberg the size of a huge football stadium and the shape of a boiled lolly. As we arrived at our destination we were greeted by the distant squawking of penguins. Cape Royds is the nesting site of hundreds of Adélie penguins and the location of Ernest Shackleton's 1908 hut. This has also been restored and the interior is much smaller and tidier than the Cape Evans hut.

After slapping on thick layers of sunscreen to protect from the extremely strong sunlight, we split into groups and spent two hours exploring Cape Royds. Standing on the cliffs above, we watched the Adélie penguins leap backwards and forwards from the ocean and with our telescopic camera lenses and binoculars could see the heads of the newly hatched baby penguins protruding from under the bellies of the parents. Antarctic skua circled above, awaiting any opportunity to snatch one of these chicks. From Cape Royds north is open ocean, and waves crash in, forming huge terraces of ice where the spray splashes ashore. Despite being built near the sea, Scott Base doesn't offer many sea views due to the sea ice, and these trips to Cape Royds are the only opportunity for us to see the open ocean. Having grown up near the sea at Gorge River, I missed the salty wind and waves and therefore Cape Royds was one of my favourite places to visit in the Ross Sea region.

By 3 pm everyone had taken enough pictures to last a lifetime and some were becoming cold. Everyone who rode in the back now shifted to the front of the Hägglunds and after warming the engines for ten minutes we were off. After a long day of exploring and the previous six days at work, many people were pretty tired and the motion of the vehicles put most to sleep. However, I was still at work and it was my job to drive everyone home safely. As we bounced along at 25 kilometres per hour, my thoughts drifted back to my Sikorsky helicopter flight seven years earlier and an image of a small vehicle crossing the sea ice rose in my mind. I had imagined that could be me one day and now here I was leading my own trip along that very same route.

Working at Scott Base is not only about the snow and ice. There is a strong sense of community that forms each year between the staff and scientists, and this camaraderie extends to McMurdo Station as well. The living quarters are pretty close and everyone shares a room with one other person. I always explain to people that 'you share a room with someone in a building sleeping forty people, you have breakfast with forty people, lunch with sixty people, dinner with about ninety and then relax in the evening with ten'. All other aspects of the isolation were minor compared to my childhood at Gorge River. I quickly got to know Sarah, one of the base domestics, and we hit it off from the very start. Being in a relationship while living in such a busy station with very little privacy had its challenges, but it was also really amazing to share some of the unique Antarctic experiences with someone special.

One of the social highlights of the summer is 'Icestock', a music festival held in the main car park of McMurdo Station for New Year's Eve. Since it never gets dark and fire is the largest hazard in the driest environment on earth, it is impossible to celebrate the change of years with fireworks. The resourceful folk of McMurdo Station work together to produce this festival with ten hours of live music. Imagine a few hundred friends partying, drinking and dancing under the midnight sun. Most of us Kiwis at Scott Base would join and throughout the evening volunteers ran shuttles with the Toyotas so everyone could have a turn to enjoy the festivities.

I have never performed anything in my life and completely missed out on that experience at school by growing up at Gorge River. However, in my second summer at Scott Base my friend Hue joined the hip-hop club at McMurdo and I decided to give it a go too. About 25 of us practised each week in the McMurdo fitness room after work and I did my best to make it to the practices between my schedule of field trips, overnight field training and nights away camping with science groups. I managed to pick up the routines and at New Year Hue and I excitedly dressed up in hoodies and fake gold chains. The performance was short but intense and was over before we knew it. Everyone enjoyed the show and, for many, watching a group of Antarctic explorers dancing hip-hop was the evening's highlight. When the music finished at 1 am the party moved inside one of the buildings. Bulldozer drivers danced alongside mountain guides and chefs danced with engineers.

Three times a year there is a craft market in one of the McMurdo accommodation buildings and I decided to take along my possum hats. Due to the extreme cold, I knew they would be popular, so I'd asked Mum to send down a large box of them. Everyone arranged their tables and waited for customers to come along. Slowly a trickle of people wandered over from the communal dining room and began looking at the unique arts and trinkets that people had crafted from odds and ends around the station. Good fur clothing outperforms everything else in harsh Arctic and Antarctic conditions, and there was a constant line of people trying on my hats, scarves and mittens. By the end of the market, I had sold 11 hats and a few scarves and pairs of mitts. It was the most profitable day of my possum career and throughout the rest of my time in Antarctica people would often approach me and say, 'My friend has one of those possum hats – do you have one left for me?'

During my time in Antarctica, I felt fortunate to be part of such a strong and unique isolated community. The random and intense experiences are magical and I was privileged to have a role where I could pass on my knowledge of extreme nature and share the stunning raw beauty of this unique environment with the people around me every day at work. For many of us, it's these intense experiences that create some of the best days of our lives and lure us back to the frozen continent year after year.

CHAPTER 18

Living with Huskies in Norway

'I'm off to Norway to work with husky dogs,' I told Blair as he waved the wings of his yellow Piper Cub to Mum and Dad. Gorge River slowly disappeared into the distance behind us as we flew north towards Haast. I had been home for a week to say goodbye and top up the firewood shed before I left. 'Husky dogs? Ah ... but what do you know about dogs?' came his reply. His remark could not have been closer to the point. I thought dogs were quite smelly creatures and the nearest I had come to working with animals was shooting deer and hunting possums. However, after working in Antarctica, I now desperately wanted to work in the Arctic, and dog mushing in Tromsø, in northern Norway, looked to be my best opportunity. With a reference from a mate and my previous experience guiding people in cold environments, I had a contract in my hand within a week. During my interview with Bente from dog-sledding company Tromsø Villmarkssenter she assured me, 'You will learn the dogs!'

I left springtime in New Zealand and after saying goodbye to Sarah, soaking up the heat in Thailand for three weeks and catching up with a few of my many friends scattered around the globe, I touched down in Tromsø on a late October evening. I was met by two young guys, Andreas and Malthe, in the small airport arrivals area and greeted with enthusiastic licks from Skar, a four-month-old puppy with a broken leg they were nursing. It turned out we were all living in cabins at the kennel and after 30 minutes driving along Kvaløya Island we arrived at my new home, Tromsø Villmarkssenter. Andreas showed me to my accommodation, where I crashed into bed exhausted and quickly fell asleep to the distant howls of the 300 huskies.

My room was half of a cosy temporary work cabin and another guide, Nat, lived next door. It turned out we'd both been recommended to Villmarkssenter by our mutual friend Whitey. Nat had also been adventuring across the globe for many years and we had both taught outdoor education in China and Hong Kong at the same time but hadn't crossed paths. He hadn't worked with dogs before either and in our new world where everywhere we looked there were dogs, dog hair or dog food, we decided to keep our cabin a dog-free zone. Because we lived near to the dog yard, we could always hear the huskies and sometimes at night we would have to run out into the darkness to capture a loose dog or break up a nasty fight.

It was snowing heavily in the morning, and our commercial sledding tours were starting the following day. I was thrown straight onto a sled for training with one of the senior mushers and as I entered the dog yard for the first time was met by the sight, sound and smell of 300 Alaskan huskies. There were kennels as far as I could see in the floodlit dog yard. Each was shared by two huskies whose names were inscribed in tags screwed to the wood. Every dog seemed to be jumping and barking in excitement, begging to join us on our sled for training. The noise was deafening. As the barking turned to a spine-chilling synchronised howl, Linas, the manager of the dog yard, waved a yellow Post-it note with a list of names on it at me and explained, 'This is our team. You can grab Snapp, the black one over there standing in the third house back.'

I made my way over to Snapp and the other huskies whined imploringly, waggled their fluffy tails and jumped up and down seeking attention. Snapp, a tall, thin black husky with bulging muscles, was leaping so excitedly that his feet barely touched the ground. As I unclipped his chain he lunged forward, almost knocking me into the snow. I wrestled him towards Linas, who swiftly grabbed his collar and then, holding Snapp firmly between his legs, demonstrated how to fit the harnesses. Clearly, he had done this many times before. 'Okay, he goes in wheel position. That's at the back of the gangline. And next you can grab Karry and Oregano.' We repeated the process until the full team was harnessed and attached to the long wire gangline connected to the sled. As we lifted the heavy snow anchors for departure, every single husky pulled into its harness and barked loudly in anticipation.

'Okay ... Yip!' Linas pulled the quick release – attached to prevent a runaway sled – and we were off. The barking stopped instantly as the dogs leapt through the deep fluffy snowdrifts, towing the wooden sled effortlessly behind them. We accelerated up the slight incline and were soon surrounded by rolling hills dotted with isolated clumps of pine and birch trees illuminated in the last of the daylight. Linas used a powerful headlamp and his commands of 'Gee' for right and 'Ha' for left to guide us through the wilderness while he explained the rules of driving a sled. 'NEVER walk behind your sled. If your dogs pull at the same time, they can rip out the metal snow anchor and will leave without you. That is the worst mistake you can make as a dog musher. NEVER LOSE YOUR TEAM!' I made a mental note of that: 'Never lose your team ...'

Over the next few days, I quickly acquired the skills of sled driving and before long I was given my own guests to sit on the cosy reindeer skins for our 45-minute tour of the wilderness. I was always following the other more experienced mushers along our trails, so if there were ever problems with the dogs there was always someone to help me. The snow continued to fall and soon we had almost a metre of soft, fluffy snow, making sledding hard work for the dogs and mushers but incredibly rewarding and beautiful at the same time. For a few days we saw the sun on the horizon around midday and the soft light sparkled off the snow puffs draped like cake icing over the entire landscape around us. Then all of a sudden the sun was gone – and it would be almost three months before it returned. My mate Lochie – whose family had stayed with us at Gorge River when we were kids and who I'd kept in touch with since – heard I was in Norway and offered to send me his powerful Petzl dog-sledding headtorch. All those years of spotlighting possums in the dark around Gorge River had prepared me well and for the next few months Lochie's torch guided me safely around the Norwegian wilderness.

One clear evening the Northern Lights danced across the clear Arctic sky above our little wooden cabins and as the temperature plunged below minus ten degrees Celsius, Nat, Malthe, Julian, Andreas and I rugged up in our warmest Arctic clothing to snowshoe into the wilderness for a campfire. Someone brought hot chocolate in a thermos and as we drank it from traditional birchwood cups we realised that at those temperatures even drinking hot chocolate required some technique. The first sip would scald your tongue while the second would be perfect. The third sip would be cold and the fourth would be frozen. While the fire crackled, we shared stories of our different adventures around the globe, and as the winter months passed by, we all became close friends.

Driving a sled turned out to be quite easy. However, learning the names and personalities of 300 different huskies at the same time as making friends with the 60 human staff members was overwhelming, to say the least. One day I was helping to organise the teams with Torkil, son of the owner, Tove, and he was pointing to different dogs to make up the team. 'Can you get Sau – he's the black and white husky standing in the house over there,' he said, waving vaguely towards the dog yard.

I walked between the kennels, scratching each dog on the head while searching for Sau's name tag. I found it on a kennel with Får, and was greeted by two extremely excited identical black and white huskies that both responded to the name Sau. I stared at them mystified for a moment. Which one was Sau? Moments like these were common in the first few weeks until eventually I was assigned to one of the five sections of the dog yard. Then I could focus on learning the names of 60 dogs, and by February I knew the personality and preferred position in the team for almost all of them. As for the rest of the dog yard, it seemed impossible to know them all.

One dark, cold evening in the middle of winter, Nat and I finally brought our favourite dogs to our cabin and soon our dog-free area was shared with Gaia, Tinder, Cane, Troffle, Roma, Karry, Oregano and many of the others. They all loved their turn escaping the cold winter nights and most of them leapt straight into our warm beds, leaving snowy footprints on our duvets. Nat had grown to like Snapp and one day brought him to our cabin. Snapp was extremely excited to be inside and ran between our rooms sniffing the smells of the other dogs that had been there before him. Without warning he cocked his right leg and pissed all over my door frame. We threw him straight outside and after a few minutes of emptying his bladder on the walls of our cabin he was allowed back in. All went well until he found another interesting smell and, showing poor judgement, pissed into Nat's clothes box. Snapp was quickly returned to his kennel in the dog yard, where he proceeded to piss excitedly on his own doorstep and into his straw bed.

Hera was a super-cute husky from a litter named after Greek gods and goddesses, and one afternoon I took her into my cabin. I smelled something rotten while working on my computer and turned to find she had done a huge, steaming shit right in the middle of my floor. That was the last time I invited her inside. My favourite husky was a black and white four-month-old puppy called Jane, which I looked after while her sister was injured. Jane loved to lick and I would push her down towards the bottom of the bed to avoid her tongue while I fell asleep. That only worked for a while, and sometimes in the early morning I would be woken by her drooling, wet tongue cleaning my cheeks. She was the first dog I ever fell in love with.

The island we lived on was mostly mountains, and Nat and I decided to buy ski-touring equipment. There is only one small ski field in the Tromsø area and almost all of the skiing is walking access. Some days we would work from 7 am to 6 pm and then, as soon as we finished dog sledding, we would squeeze into Malthe's car with Andreas and another dog musher, Helene, and head off to ski. We ascended the 900-metre mountains entirely by torchlight using skins on the bottom of our skis to hike efficiently uphill. Access to the mountains around us was so easy that we could climb and ski a challenging slope after work and be home in time for a late dinner. As we became familiar with the area, we searched further afield for adventures, and after three weeks of miserable rain in the darkness of January set off on a road trip to Finland. Here, away from the ocean warmed by the Gulf Stream, the temperature was below minus 20 degrees Celsius and we skied for three days over huge frozen lakes to stay in cosy wilderness cabins, carrying our warm clothes, sleeping bags and food in heavy backpacks.

The winter continued, our sled tours were fully booked and we were working hard. As the sun returned and the days lengthened, we started to hear reports of a new virus spreading in Asia, and after contacting my friends in China, Thailand and the Philippines who were all beginning lockdowns, I could see things were going to get interesting. Life carried on as normal in Tromsø and every day we received between 300 to 400 tourists from all over the world, mostly from the UK, Germany, France and Italy – the very countries that were the first in Europe to record Covid cases. One evening shortly after Italy had entered Europe's first lockdown, I introduced myself to my guests in the dog yard and asked where they were from. 'We are from Milan,' came the enthusiastic reply. They spent the whole evening coughing as we played with the huskies and watched the Northern Lights, and I awkwardly tried to keep my distance as best I could.

One day we had a cruise ship in Tromsø and I spent ten solid hours sledding guests from the ship until my team of dogs was completely exhausted. I trudged through the deep snow pushing my sled up each hill to help the dogs until I too was worn out. Everyone was making the most of the high season of sledding, despite new Covid cases popping up in Norway daily. The next day we arrived at work early, ready for another busy day, only to be greeted by a notice from the Norwegian government. The entire country was going into lockdown and all tourist activities were suspended. Our busy winter of dog sledding ground to a screeching halt.

Suddenly my employment was in doubt. I was over 17,000 kilometres away from home, on the opposite side of a world where flights and the movement of people were rapidly diminishing. To make matters worse, no one had any idea how bad it could get. Were global supply lines going to collapse? Stories were coming in from around the world of empty supermarkets, bankrupt airlines, stock markets crashing and border closures cutting people off from jobs and families. Pandemics have happened before but not in a modern world where many countries depend on the global network of trade and technology. The city of Tromsø relies on almost all its resources coming from further south, and as I looked around at the Arctic wilderness I knew that few people could survive off the land here. It's hard to grow anything outside a greenhouse, and the area's only natural foods are reindeer, fish, whales and wild berries. The Sami people did live off these resources in the past, but now there were cities full of people who would need to share the food.

If I stayed in Norway, I knew there was a small chance society as we knew it could collapse and I might never be able to fly home, but the other option was to pack everything up and leave immediately. I knew without a doubt that Gorge River, where we can live entirely off the land around us, was the safest place to be, but the thought of travelling through the chaos of airports, flight cancellations and differing Covid restrictions in multiple countries was not appealing. I talked with Tove and she said I could stay and care for the dogs as long as I needed to and even reduced the rent for lockdown. Therefore, while most of our staff bought last-minute tickets to get home, I committed to the more adventurous option of staying put.

Nat stayed as well and together we formed a really fun, hard-working team with three crazy French guys – Marin, Crouzet and Mika. We still had 300 huskies to feed and care for each day and in the first few weeks of lockdown we had a blizzard each night, bringing record amounts of fresh snow that would be blown into every corner of the dog yard. We took turns clearing snow from the kennels at night, and one morning I came to work to find all the dogs standing in a flat snowy field – every single dog house had been buried. We had to shovel all morning to clear the kennels from the deep, wind-packed snowdrifts. In the afternoons we would harness team after team to run through the epic sledding conditions to keep them from going crazy.

One day someone had an idea to temporarily adopt our huskies as quarantine buddies for people living in lockdown. It would be fun for the dogs and would reduce the number we had to manage. I filmed a 'Borrow a Buddy' promo video and it went viral. Overnight we received hundreds of emails and within two weeks had reduced our huskies from 300 to a more manageable 120. Photos poured in on Instagram of our beloved dogs walking in the mountains, playing with families and sleeping on couches all over northern Norway. As the pandemic worsened through Europe and the tourists failed to return, most of these huskies were permanently adopted. The programme was such a huge success that it was used as an example of the right way to downsize a kennel – the opposite to one large kennel in Finland that was trying to put down their dogs to avoid the effort of rehoming, arguing that it was inhumane to keep huskies in homes. Our dogs had proven how wrong that was.

By now the majority of the world's population was living in lockdowns and the world 'isolation' had become common in almost every conversation about the coronavirus. One of the hardest parts of my childhood was the lack of social contact at Gorge River and I found it very interesting now chatting to people I knew around the world who were confined to their home alone, or with a partner or family, and had never experienced such isolation before. My family had been practising this for decades, and now life at Gorge River continued relatively normally while the rest of the world shut down.

Throughout the six-week lockdown the Norwegian government never restricted our movement in nature, provided we didn't meet new people and avoided overnight trips. We made up for the three months of darkness by skiing every day and exploring the never-ending wilderness of Kvaløya Island by dog sled.

Soon we were allowed to go on overnight trips again and my friend Sussi and I ran our favourite huskies into the heart of the mountains. From our campsite our entire world looked black and white, with snow and ice completely covering the rocky mountains that towered around us in all directions. We pitched camp and built an Antarctica-style snow wall to defend against the biting-cold wind. The huskies in their cute red jackets dug into the snow and slept quietly all night, before waking early next morning to bark at three passing dog teams.

One evening after work, Nat and I joined our mate Manu for a kayak adventure. With our skis attached to the decks of our kayaks, we paddled 12 kilometres down Ersfjord, an incredible fiord flanked by jagged-edged mountain ranges. Manu chose one 850-metre mountain to climb and on a small, snowy, bouldery beach we changed out of our kayaking gear, pulled on ski boots and clipped into our skis in hiking mode. We reached the top at 11 pm and as we skied back down the 40-degree slopes the sun bathed the snow in soft orange light. Far below us the fiord was the deepest, darkest aquamarine I have ever seen and the sun skimmed along the northern horizon, kissing the sea before slowly rising into the morning sky. We paddled home, crunching through a thin layer of ice that had formed in some parts of the fiord. At 4 am I pulled my thick curtains closed to block out the bright sunlight before crashing into bed exhausted.

Northern Norway was able to control Covid relatively quickly and once life returned to normal we never had another lockdown. The Norwegians tend to keep to themselves and when there were small outbreaks it never spread far into the community. I was very impressed with the access to nature around Norway, which reminded me of a large problem back home. I am lucky to come from Gorge River, a rugged and beautiful part of New Zealand, with wilderness on our doorstep. However, in many parts of the country, access to publicly owned conservation land is blocked by private landowners and large areas are off-limits. Deeply embedded in Norwegian culture is a saying that nature is 'Allemannsretten', which translates to 'All men's right', and it is therefore illegal to prevent people entering wilderness. Instead, the emphasis is on respecting the land as you use it.

After sitting a practical test for my Norwegian driver's licence, I bought a car and with the 24-hour sunlight the whole of northern Norway opened up to me. The Arctic mountains are flanked by a vertical 300 metres of sparsely scattered forest that gives way to tuffets of spongy tundra made up of hardy plants including blueberries, cloudberries, lingonberries and juniper. It was possible to hike almost anywhere, and once the snow had melted I headed into the mountains at every opportunity.

The highlight of the entire summer was completing the Ersfjord traverse along the knife-edge ridgeline above the fiord I had kayaked previously with Manu. For two days, Nat and I ran, abseiled, clambered and climbed above sheer cliffs that dropped away to the calm waters of the fiord 800 metres below. Tiny crystals sparkled up from the granite as we climbed. Lichens and mosses grew here and there, forming the most beautiful intricate patterns, and the whole experience reminded me of climbing Mitre Peak many years before. We had almost the same skill level and it was amazing to test ourselves in a spontaneous but well-calculated way where one simple mistake could result in severe injury or even death. Some places required some safe but extremely exposed rock-climbing moves and we completed it all in hiking boots, only using our rope twice when the ridge dropped away for mandatory abseils.

Since the nights were warm, we travelled light and fast and slept in our down jackets above Grøtfjord at roughly the halfway point of the 17-kilometre traverse. In the morning we were woken by a herd of reindeer running backwards and forwards majestically along a patch of snow. What they were doing hundreds of metres above the vegetation line, I don't know. Perhaps they were also enjoying the view. By the end of summer, I had hiked, climbed or skied almost all of the 16 large mountain peaks on Kvaløya Island – more than many of the Tromsø locals manage in a lifetime.

After three months of high-consequence risk-taking in the mountains, I suffered the worst accident of my life so far. However, rather than a fall hundreds of metres down an exposed cliff face into a fiord as you might expect, it was something that occurred inside a building at work. I was stacking bags of dog food into a cupboard when I sliced my finger open on a piece of glass protruding from a broken lampshade. I went straight to the emergency room and had surgery on it three days later to repair a cut tendon.

While recovering with my hand in a brace for three months, I needed to have some company, so I cautiously headed for the dog yard. Many of the dogs, especially Jane, were too enthusiastic and unpredictable and I was afraid they could damage my hand further if they jumped at the wrong moment. I unclipped one of our older lead dogs called Is (pronounced Eece) and she ran straight to my cabin, jumped onto my couch and proceeded to fall asleep. She was a medium-sized husky, mostly white with a black nose, greyish black ears and patches around her beautiful sapphire-blue eyes. When I called her name excitedly, she slowly opened one eye to look at me, as if saying, 'What do you want – can't you see I'm sleeping over here?'

Together we hiked over the tundra, picking blueberries and cloudberries from the bushes carpeting the ground – and by that I mean that I would pick berries with one hand while she curled up in a ball to sleep in the warm sunlight. Her reserved personality was typical of her Norwegian countrymen and it took months for her to completely open up to me. At last, one day in the tundra, she came up and gave me a single wet-nose kiss on the cheek. It was the first time she'd shown me open affection and I felt she was finally accepting me. That single kiss meant as much as Jane licking my face for 20 minutes solid.

One evening in September, I was lying in bed with Is when I received a terrible email from Mum and Dad. My mate Lochie was missing at sea in a typhoon after the cargo ship he was working on had capsized off the coast of Japan. In the following days, two people were pulled alive from the ocean and I sat helplessly glued to my phone for weeks, praying for a miracle that never came. Eventually it had been too long for anybody else to survive and I had to accept that Lochie was never coming home. Although I was devastated, I found peace knowing that he had lived a life of constant adventure and had disappeared near the eye of a Category 5 typhoon in what was probably his craziest experience of all.

Lochie's disappearance hit me very hard and it took a long time to bounce back from it. It had been his first time working on ships, and looking back at the horrendous oceans I had crossed I felt I was far more likely to have disappeared in a storm at sea.

It reminded me like a punch to the stomach that life is short and we don't get to choose our accidents. Although people like Lochie and me regularly expose ourselves to risks while searching for adventure, it's ultimately those moments that make us who we are and what people will remember us for. I knew that as soon as my hand healed I had to continue chasing adventure more than ever, in memory of Lochie.

Eventually my sick leave was over and I returned to the dog yard. My working holiday visa was about to expire and I had to change to a seasonal work visa so I could stay for another winter. I had been living in Tromsø longer than any other place since leaving home 11 years earlier, and although over the years I had become very comfortable being unsettled, I was enjoying the new feeling of greater stability.

Now that I had experience with the dogs and Tove knew I had grown up in an isolated place, she invited me to her autumn training camp in the Nordreisa Valley, four hours northeast of Tromsø. Here I began training the huskies in the surrounding forest with ATVs, using the wheels to increase their fitness for the coming winter. Nat was there as well and for three months we lived together, often by ourselves, working from a remote wilderness house during the day, sleeping in a caravan at night, all the time surrounded by 80 dogs, tall mountains, endless trees, an old creaky barn and a small frozen lake.

Since we were inland, the temperature regularly dropped below minus 20 degrees Celsius and the sun disappeared for the winter. Darkness crept in and no matter how hard we stared into the distance there wasn't a single light to be seen. I worked by the light of Lochie's headtorch much of the time and on the way to bed each night I would stop for a few minutes to gaze at the shimmering curtains of the pink and green Aurora Borealis dancing across the clear starry sky. Soon I would start shivering and a thin layer of snow would crunch beneath my feet as I ran the last few metres to our icy caravan.

After turning the heater on full to reduce the ever-present chill, I would climb into bed next to Is. At eight years old she was tired of running, and chose to spend most of the day keeping my bed warm, only rising once or twice to steal a block of frozen meat from the barn. Despite her lack of enthusiasm, she was still one of our best leaders and sometimes we would need her help to train an inexperienced team. However, she had the final say in the matter and one day attempted to lead 20 huskies through the front door of the house. Finally, after she tried to take a shortcut to the caravan and tangled Nat's entire team in a thicket of birch trees, we got the message, and after that we only ran her on very rare occasions to stretch her legs after days of sleeping.

Each day we took turns training the dogs in teams of 20 through the forest and soon we knew each animal well enough to build a 20-dog team in about 15 minutes. The energy of the huskies on a cold morning would be electric and as we wrestled each pair to the gangline, all 80 dogs would be going totally stupid crazy. Once attached to the gangline, some would chew loose from their harnesses and start running around the dog yard. No sooner had we caught them and replaced the harnesses, another would have done the same, and no matter how many hands we had, it never seemed to be enough. I found it amazing practice for staying calm while surrounded by chaos, and it reminded me of working under the beating blades of a helicopter. Every time the dogs created trouble, I practised taking a deep breath before calmly solving whatever problem they had thrown at me.

Once the team was ready, I would jump into the seat of the ATV while attempting to pull on my huge winter jacket. 'Okay … Yip!' I would yell as I removed the quick release from a solid tree. Once the dogs were running, they were easier to control, and for hours we would follow the winding, bumpy trails through the forest. Ice crystals fell from the trees and steam forced from the lungs of the huskies rose in clouds as they trotted along at a steady 15 kilometres per hour. If it was Tove's racing team, we could train for up to 80 kilometres like this each day. Before such a trip, I would pull on all the layers I could, including my possum-fur hat and buff, yet still the cold would creep in. Each time we stopped to water the dogs at the house I would top up my thermos with hot tea or fresh drip coffee and Nat would have a bacon-and-egg sandwich ready. After promising to return the favour the next day, I would be off again into the dark forest completely alone with the dogs once more. If the dogs weren't listening or became tangled around a tree, I would have only a couple of minutes to fix the problem before they started chewing loose. In a worst-case scenario they could tangle the entire gangline, resulting in a huge bloody fight.

We woke one morning to a rare clear blue sky and our spirits instantly lifted. The sun had risen two weeks previously but due to the constant cloud and mountains we hadn't yet seen it. As Nat and I were feeding the dogs a hot breakfast of meat soup, the sun that had been gone for three months suddenly rose above the snowy hills on the southeastern horizon. We dropped what we were doing and stared in disbelief, feeling the soft rays of light on our chilled faces. The winter had been an extra-hard one for everyone in northern Norway and for us there had been a few really dark weeks of rain with no work, no snow, no tourists and no motivation to get out of bed and do something. But in that moment we shared together, with the sun lighting up the soft, puffy snowdrifts with a warm orange glow, and the sound of the huskies slurping their breakfast, all of the tough times seemed to fade into the background of that desolate snowy plateau. And over the next few weeks the world around us came back to life.

Usually the dogs are transferred to Tromsø for sledding when the snow arrives in late October or early November. However, that winter it wasn't until February that we left the house in Nordreisa. Finally, we could open for normal sled tours and we received a steady trickle of Norwegians who, due to Covid, were now travelling widely within their own country. The sledding I had done during lockdown and the training in Nordreisa had been a crash course in high-consequence dog mushing. For the rest of the winter, I was often leading the sled tours around the Kvaløya wilderness and now I knew every dog in the yard, including most of their personalities, strengths, weaknesses and possibly even their favourite couch in my room to sleep on.

In early May my visa for Norway ran out and with no way to extend it I was left with few options to continue my stay. If I remained in Europe, I would be constantly affected by border closures and sporadic lockdowns, and although there were a few countries that would let me in, there was no guarantee the border would stay open once I booked flights. So, after 20 months away, I made the decision to return to New Zealand. It was not an easy one to make, because although it would be great to see family and spend time at Gorge River, it meant going straight into another winter and I still had mild depression after the three months of darkness I had just been through.

I spent one last week with my group of close friends, many of whom I had worked with through dark days and rough storms, and Agnes organised an amazing going-away party in Grøtfjord, with a sauna next to the ocean. Jenny bought my car, I gave my beer-brewing kit and craft gear to Sussi, my fishing lures went to German and my avalanche probe to Stina. The rest of my ski gear was packed away for the long flight and there was one thing left to do.

Saying goodbye to Is, my beloved husky, was the toughest farewell of all. Because I couldn't take her with me to New Zealand I found her a forever home with a friend in Alta. I was delighted that she would have her own couch, her own human, and a full retirement of sleep ahead of her. However, saying goodbye to her on the ferry dock in Lyngen was absolutely heartbreaking and the whole experience of leaving Norway was the hardest thing I have been through since leaving Gorge River when I was 17. As my plane lifted off from Tromsø on a cold, snowy spring day, that world of jagged mountain peaks, deep fiords and husky dogs that I had called home for 18 months slid behind a cloud and was gone.

Epilogue

My story to date finishes here. After returning from Norway and spending two weeks alone in isolation 17 floors above downtown Auckland, I hiked home to Gorge River from the Cascade Road end. I completed the hike that used to take me five days in under seven hours, crossing the Cascade River by torchlight, charging through mud puddles and leaping from boulder to boulder as comfortably as running through the paved streets of a city. Mum picked me up by boat on the north side of the Gorge River and I settled into home life for a few weeks to spend time with my parents, using the energy of the wilderness and electricity from the sun to help finish this collection of experiences to share with you.

In some ways it has been strange writing an autobiography, because at the age of 29 I feel my life of crazy adventures and unique experiences in the wilderness of New Zealand, extreme polar regions and the rest of the globe is only just beginning. However, I never could have believed when starting that I could write so much about my life, and feel I have only scraped the surface. The largest challenge has been deciding which stories to tell and which to leave out.

It has been really emotional reliving each of these moments again through the process of writing and it has been incredibly rewarding. Segments such as leaving home, Lochie disappearing at sea and saying goodbye to Is were edited with tears streaming down my face, and each time I returned for another edit the emotions would return. My main goal in writing is to share my experiences for the enjoyment of others, and I hope everyone reading this book has taken something from the values I learned from my parents, the wilderness and my adventures across the globe.

Looking back, I can see that it was around 2009 when things changed the most for us. It wasn't just that I left home, but also that people's attitudes towards remote living, self-sufficiency and off-the-grid lifestyles suddenly changed. As much of the world's attention turned to limiting climate change and becoming more sustainable, our life at Gorge River rose to prominence as an example of how some people were already doing this and had been for decades. Around the time I was at school in Wānaka and polytech in Dunedin, I was surprised to hear people talking about me as 'one of the lucky kids who grew up in the wilderness', or saying, 'what an incredible lifestyle your parents have' or 'how happy they must be and how stressless their life is'. Living sustainably can be just as stressful and hard work, but they didn't know that and it was really interesting to see people's ideas change so fast. I was pleased, because now people would ask in a more curious and positive way what it was like to grow up so isolated, rather than with the negativity we had usually experienced before.

Mum and Dad, of course, continued to be unfazed by people's opinions one way or the other. The biggest changes in their life occurred when I left home, and then Robin three years later. Around this time, they both wrote their own autobiographies, which went to the top of the bestseller lists and raised our profile a lot. More people began hiking to Gorge River to visit 'New Zealand's remotest family', while others would fly down in their private helicopter or plane and land on our airstrip. Greenstone Helicopters in Haast even started selling flights to visit 'Beansprout and New Zealand's remotest art gallery'.

When Robin and I were kids, people worried that we were missing out on things, so, looking back now, was there anything that I couldn't make up for later in life? The short answer is no. I've talked about the social challenges I faced throughout the transition, but when it came to things like learning how to use a phone or computer or how to drive a car, there was nothing I couldn't pick up quickly. In fact, I think within two or three years I had acquired 99 per cent of the skills that I had missed out on previously. Conversely, the skills I had learned at Gorge River are not so easily picked up. It can take years to truly understand the way river and ocean currents flow, when to plant vegetables and how to fertilise a garden. I am so lucky to have gained all those skills as a kid, when it's easiest to learn. And by extending my own comfort zones and testing my limitations through extreme adventure sports and new experiences, I have continued to grow those skills exponentially.

Alongside that, I developed a love for cities, and while in Wānaka and Dunedin I learned to live comfortably around people. I took that to the next level by spending time in the world's largest cities, like Bangkok, Hong Kong, London and Shanghai. Now with all this experience, I am as comfortable navigating with my local friends through the sights, sounds and smells of a city of 20 million people in a developing country as I am leading a small group of Western scientists to one of the most isolated parts of Antarctica.

How come I ended up on this road of exploring the world and constantly seeking new adventures? I think it had a lot to do with growing up in such a wild place. After living at Gorge River, every obstacle seems surmountable, and once I left to attend school in Wānaka I had already overcome the largest challenge in my life to date. Taking the next step to the Antarctic, Arctic or the other side of the world seemed relatively easy and painless.

There is so much to discover in the world and in every place I explore there are new things to be learned from the wilderness, the people and the culture. It's fun to share what I see and learn with others through social media, and I think it's important for people to know what's happening outside their own personal bubbles.

Many people ask me what the future holds and I can never come up with a straight answer. The longer I spend on this pathway, the harder it will be for me to settle down and live in just one country or place. I love the wilderness in remote places like Gorge River, but eventually the lack of people sends me off in a different direction, in search of more social experiences. The lifestyle I lead continues to shape who I am, so I don't see any reason to change it. For now, I will stay on this pathway of constantly searching for new experiences, and I will continue to share my adventures through social media until I have enough new stories for the next volume of *The Boy from Gorge River.*

Soon I will put on my backpack, climb aboard a boat, hop on a plane or bicycle, or perhaps head off on my own two feet, and disappear over the horizon in pursuit of the next adventure. Behind me will be a set of footprints, and in front will be the whole wide world.

Acknowledgements

Now that we have come to the end, it's time to say a special thank you to everyone who has been involved in crafting *The Boy From Gorge River*. Without everyone's help, this book would certainly never have happened and my stories would not be out there for everyone to share.

I have to start by thanking my amazing parents, Robert and Catherine, for their help. Mum, thank you for reading through the entire text twice to make sure I had all my facts and grammar correct. And Dad, thank you for constantly searching through your diaries to find names, times, dates and places for the stories that kept popping into my head. Thank you to my sister, Robin, for being there at the end of the phone for motivation at challenging times throughout the writing process.

Thank you to everyone on the HarperCollins publishing team for all your patience and hard work. Special thanks to Alex Hedley for tracking me down and supporting the idea of writing the book in two separate sections. Publisher Holly Hunter, thank you for your advice towards the end of my writing, the motivating video chats during my hotel quarantine, and for completing the first major edits. Thanks to copy editor Mike Wagg for your editing and to in-house editor Scott Forbes for crafting my words into a smooth read for everyone to enjoy and putting up with my last-minute requests. Thank you Helene for the epic cover photo and to Luke Causby for the awesome cover design.

And I have to say a huge thank you in no particular order to Gaia, Nat, Lucy, Cam, Stina, Flo, Jenny, German, Bente, Sussi, Tove, Torkil, Agnes, Andreas, Katrine, Sam, Kat, Nigel, Elli, and everyone else I've been around in the last year who has supported and encouraged me to continue typing, even when the sun was shining and I wanted to be outside having fun.

And thank you to everyone who has been a part of my adventure over the years – without you there would be no story!